C000186328

A Survival Guide
for Frontline Living

Also by Sarah de Carvalho

The Street Children of Brazil

A Survival Guide for Frontline Living

Working out God's calling –
wherever he's placed you

Sarah de Carvalho

Hodder & Stoughton
LONDON SYDNEY AUCKLAND

The two extracts from 'Lifelines' by Susan Hardwick
are reproduced by permission of Kevin Mayhew Ltd

Unless otherwise indicated, Scripture quotations are taken from the
HOLY BIBLE, NEW INTERNATIONAL VERSION.
Copyright © 1973, 1978, 1984 by International Bible Society.
Used by permission. All rights reserved.

Copyright © 1999 by Sarah de Carvalho

First published in Great Britain in 1999

The right of Sarah de Carvalho to be identified as the Author of
the Work has been asserted by her in accordance with
the Copyright, Designs and Patents Act 1988.

10 9 8 7 6 5 4 3 2 1

All rights reserved. No part of this publication may be reproduced,
stored in a retrieval system, or transmitted, in any form or by any means
without the prior written permission of the publisher, nor be otherwise
circulated in any form of binding or cover other than that in which it is
published and without a similar condition being imposed on the
subsequent purchaser.

British Library Cataloguing in Publication Data
A record for this book is available from the British Library

ISBN 0 340 74545 2

Typeset by Avon Dataset Ltd, Bidford-on-Avon, Warks

Printed and bound in Great Britain by
Clays Ltd, St Ives plc

Hodder and Stoughton Ltd
A Division of Hodder Headline
338 Euston Road
London NW1 3BH

For Joao Bosco de Carvalho –
thank you for helping me do the possible,
so that God can do the impossible!

Contents

Foreword

I don't know if, like me, you read *The Street Children of Brazil* and quickly promoted Sarah de Carvalho to the level of Christian super hero. How we stand in awe of people like her who have literally given up everything to follow the call of God and push out the Kingdom of God. All she left behind, her obedience, her faith, the wonderful way God has used her to change lives and the social situation of so many children in Brazil. What a Christian. And in the back of our minds is that thought, 'I'm so pleased there are people like her doing things like that because I could never do it!'

If that's you and you want just your heroes of the faith to do the pioneering work of God in this world, put this book far away from you now. If you don't want to be challenged, then close this book. If you don't want to hear God, who might just change the course of your life and through you change the course of the life of the world around you, then go and do something else.

But if, when you read stories of people through whom God has done amazing things, you think, 'I want to do something to make a difference'; if you are not satisfied with the way the world is; if you read your Bible and believe that yes, God could and does call you, but you are not sure what to, or quite how, or why; if you want to do what God has for you to do with this one life on earth he has given you – then read on. Because after the testimony of *The Street Children of Brazil*, here is the teaching for the children of God.

Sarah is a hero of the faith precisely because she will not let us put her on a pedestal. She will not let us get away with not hearing and obeying God for ourselves. She makes it clear in this book that the God who called her and her husband Joao to do the work they do for his kingdom and being obedient to him, is for us all.

God doesn't just call super Christians – he calls normal people like Sarah and Joao and you and me. And this book is Sarah's lessons on how.

In this book, Sarah shares the lessons she has learnt, the wisdom she has picked up. She is brutally honest and deeply personal. She is disarmingly challenging and heart-warmingly encouraging. She deals with the questions we ask, the fears we all have, and the problems we face. But it is not just a practical human how-to book. It is founded and built in God's how-to. In his call and his provision. In his help and his hope. In his presence and his power.

J. John

Author's note

This book comes to you from someone who is still learning. The mistakes are all mine.

I never thought I'd write another book after writing *The Street Children of Brazil*. In fact I never thought I'd write a book full stop – I used to suffer from dyslexia – but I guess God had other plans.

Despite my unworthiness, the Lord asked me in 1990 to give up my career in television, my comfortable apartment in London, my family and friends, to go to Brazil to rescue children who are living on the filthy streets because they have nowhere else to go. During the last nine years I have faced many personal challenges in my practical daily working life. I believe that, to a point, there is little a seminary or theological college can do to prepare us for these challenges. Having also witnessed and stood alongside many other Christian workers around the world passing through similar experiences, I felt the impulse to write about some of the main issues people on the frontline face.

Together with testimonies (mine and other people's), advice and guidance that I have received from men and women of God, and key biblical references, the aim of this book is to help and encourage others to follow and persevere in their calling, whatever and wherever that ministry might be. It could be like me, working among those most in need, or it could be fulfilling some ministry in your own community, or your place of work. Perhaps God has called you to devote your life to witnessing to one person, or to travel overseas to preach to many.

This book is also written to serve as an eye-opener and encourager for all of you who are committed to faithfully supporting God's workers through prayer, love, and financial and administrative support. We couldn't do it without you!

When God calls you, the vital step is the first step. Walking with God on the frontline is an adventure: we never really know the details of the future until we turn the next corner, which we can only do when we are walking in the right direction by faith. The exciting thing is to be where he wants us to be – for that is where we find his blessing and his favour.

I want to take this opportunity to thank those of you who have responded to *The Street Children of Brazil*. We have been overwhelmed by the letters of encouragement. Also, we are so happy when we hear the news that many have been motivated as a result to reach out to the lost, the sick and the broken around the world both by physically going out and by prayer and giving. However, what fills us most with joy is when we hear that people's lives have been changed through reading of how real our heavenly Father is, and as a result have given their lives to Jesus and been saved.

I would also like to thank my 'reading committee' for this book, in particular Julie Jarman (my unofficial editor) and David Moloney (my official editor).

Introduction

If you are feeling useless, then you are not serving! I struggled with this when first I stepped out into full-time ministry. It had not been easy getting to that point. In the eyes of the world – as I explained earlier – I was about to embark on something 'crazy'. At twenty-nine years of age I was ready to get married, to have a family. I enjoyed getting dressed up and going to nice restaurants. My flat in London was decorated the way I liked it, and I earned enough to travel wherever I liked. My family lived forty minutes' drive from me. I had been fortunate enough to work on major films with stars such as Christopher Lambert and Sean Connery, and with producers such as David Puttnam (*Chariots of Fire*, *The Killing Fields*, *The Mission*). I had worked with BBC television on major entertainment shows and at the time God called me to Brazil – two years after becoming a Christian – I was earning £1000 a week producing five hours of television programmes Mondays to Fridays for Sky TV. I loved my church; it was my haven, my security. Jesus Christ had come into my life there, his Holy Spirit had poured

1

supernatural rivers of forgiveness, acceptance, peace and love into my heart there. It was where I'd discovered the meaning and purpose of life.

It was tough to let it all go, to go somewhere I didn't know.

What I did know at that point was that God had chosen me, not because I was qualified, but because it was his will. He made it so clear. My newly discovered inner peace left me every time I considered staying in London and continuing in television instead. God started to bring people across my path who encouraged me to go. Also, it seemed that every time I turned on the radio, TV or opened the newspaper or a magazine there was another programme or article about Rio de Janeiro!

God asked me to go to Brazil on a winter's evening one Sunday in January 1990. Sitting in church I'd asked God what he wanted me to do for him. Suddenly, I'd heard his voice speaking within my spirit with a quiet authority: 'I want you to go to Brazil.' I was stunned at the time. Was that me or was that God? Brazil? I'd never planned to go to Brazil ... my mind became full of questions ... What goes on there? Why Brazil? Surely God wants me to stay working in London? God, I don't want to go there! But unknown to me, Loren Cunningham, founder and chairman of Youth With A Mission, was the guest speaker that night. At the end of his challenging talk on the mission field he asked all those in the congregation who wanted 'to go' for Christ to stand up so that he could pray for them. All at once I felt as though a spotlight was shining over me; a warm current of supernatural power seemed to permeate my whole body, and I stood up and offered my life to God, wherever he wanted me to be.

A few months later, I went on a Christian teaching week where I met a young missionary from Peru. One night, during that week, she prayed with me until the early hours of the morning. All at once a vivid picture of the 'Pied Piper' flashed through my mind. In the picture there were many children, all dirty with no shoes on their feet and torn clothes on their bodies, running along behind the 'Pied Piper' who was playing a flute. Into my mind came the words, 'You are a Pied Piper, Sarah, and you are dancing these children out of danger.' I remember thinking I can't work with children, I don't play a musical instrument, I don't know any stories and when I sing the dogs howl! But at that precise moment I heard that still small voice say, 'Sarah, it's my love that will draw the children to you, not a musical instrument.'

Amnesty International had still not released their report with its revelations of the horrendous killings of street children at the hands of extermination squads. There had been no major publicity in the media. However during that same week I met Lynne Green, the former director and current executive chairman of Youth With A Mission, who by 'divine' coincidence had just returned from Brazil. I remember asking him, 'Do you know if there are children living on the streets who are in danger?'

'Danger?' he repeated with concern in his voice. 'There are millions of children forced to live on the streets because of terrible home situations, and hundreds of them are being murdered.'

When I heard that, what could I do? What was my choice? If God could save even one of these children through my life, who was I to say I don't want to go? This had not come in response to my prayers, or even my desires. The whole revelation had its source solely in the sovereign will of God. If I were to reject God's will so clearly revealed, how could I expect his blessing on my future?

God doesn't select people because they have a diploma, a title, riches or beauty. But he needs us to say, 'Here I am!' When we do God prepares his chosen. In my situation, with a full-time missionary calling, I had to come to terms with the fact that I couldn't just jump on an aeroplane with a suitcase, arrive at Rio's international airport, run onto the dangerous streets where these kids hang out in gangs and say in English, 'Hi, I'm Sarah, follow me to freedom and safety'! No, that wasn't the way God was going to do things.

During the weeks that followed I found myself clearly guided to apply to Youth With A Mission to do a five-month Discipleship Training School in Lausanne, Switzerland, starting in October. Three months' theory was to be followed by two months' practical experience in Chile. Chile was to be an important stepping stone to Brazil. As I wrote in *The Street Children of Brazil*, during that period God was humbling me and I had to come face to face with my ugly pride. One of my chores when doing the course was cleaning the public toilets and bathrooms on the base! Suddenly I was no longer Sarah Jarman the TV producer. Instead I was quite simply Sarah Jarman the equal of everyone else on that course. Paul wrote in his letter to the Galatians: 'Am I now trying to win the approval of men, or of God? Or am I trying to please men? If I were still trying to please men, I would not be a servant of Christ' (1:10). This verse spoke to me so clearly. The only comparison I can think of to describe how I felt was of a ripe banana being peeled of its skin, a piece at a time, until left bare with its flesh only. All the old protection, the old fronts, the supports, the titles, were being stripped away from me until I was left feeling quite vulnerable, a nobody. Eventually, desperate, I said, 'Lord,

I am so weak, I am nothing before you, make me into the woman you always wanted me to be. I want your glory to shine through me, not mine.'

Now, no one can say that God hasn't got a sense of humour! He took me out of my comfortable surroundings in England, through a time of humbling self-discovery, and after two months in Chile followed by three months in Belo Horizonte where I did another course on working with street children with Johan and Jeanette Lukasse, I went to live where I'd told God I could never go! A *favela* (slum). It seems to me that when something is God's will and you are seeking him, he will make what you thought you'd never do the *only* thing that you want to do! I needed to experience life in this place of utter deprivation because otherwise how else would I have related to the children on the streets and discovered where they'd come from in the first place?

During this whole time I never imagined in my wildest dreams that I would marry a Brazilian and co-found, with him, a ministry that would rescue many destitute children and their families. What I did discover was that the more I sought to hear God's voice the more effective I became in my own calling. I discovered that prayer life was key.

1
What's my role?
I want to be useful

Once upon a time there was a small village built at the edge of a very wide and fast flowing river. One day a young boy fell into that river and he started to cry out for help. Everyone in the village ran to the river to see if it was their son who had fallen in. There was panic as the small boy kept disappearing under the rapids. Suddenly a teenage boy, renowned for his swimming prowess, found a long thick cord and tying one end around his waist he threw the other end into the crowd. 'Grab hold of the cord!' he cried out as he dived bravely into the river after the drowning child. The crowd ran along the bank with bated breadth. Eventually the teenager reached the boy and locking him in his arms he called out exhausted, 'Pull the cord!'

On the riverbank there was chaos as everyone looked at everyone else, repeating the desperate cry of the teenager, 'Pull the cord, pull the cord!' Then the appalling truth dawned. No one had grabbed hold of the other end of the cord. Each one had thought that someone else was holding it. And the two boys drowned.

This story is a parable about mission. The people who are in 'the dangerous waters' are those sent into long- and short-term ministry to reach the lost, and help the sick and the broken at home and around the world. The people 'on the riverbank' are those committed to support the workers in the river through prayer, financial and administrative support, love and encouragement. It is a vital partnership in which we all have a part to play.

When I looked up the word 'calling' in a concordance, I discovered that we all have a calling. Our calling is to imitate Jesus, who humbled himself, becoming powerless and vulnerable in the community around him, deliberately associating himself with the poorest and the most marginalised. Most of us are not called to imitate the poor in their destitution – although to live with the poor is to live with Jesus. But we are all called to identify very closely with the excluded in our society. If only we have ears to hear, the earth is ringing with the cry of despair of the starving, of the suffering, of the parched, and above all Jesus's cry, 'I am thirsty.' Working with the poor has taught me how to live the gospel. These very street children and their desperate families have broken down the barriers in me of wealth, of power, of ability and of pride. They have revealed Jesus Christ. And in myself I can now see my own poverty and vulnerability.

The Bible makes it clear that all God's people are called to minister. In 1 Corinthians 12 Paul spells out the way in which, by his Holy Spirit, God prepares each member of his Church to play a special role: 'There are different kinds of service, but the same Lord. There are different kinds of working but the same God works all of them in all men' (vv. 5–6). Later in the passage we read this: 'You are the body of Christ, and each one of you is part of it' (v. 27). No part of the 'body' can do without all the other parts. In fact, Paul affirms: 'those parts of the body that seem to be weaker are *indispensable*' (v. 22 – my emphasis).

Maybe you are a banker, accountant, lawyer or an insurance broker; perhaps you work in politics, or you are a journalist for a magazine or newspaper; maybe you are a designer, or a professional sportsman/woman; perhaps you work in a factory, or you work in a shop; maybe you are a full-time mum, or a student, or a secretary, perhaps you are a computer programmer, or a doctor or a nurse. Maybe you are highly successful in your career but deep inside you don't feel you are doing enough. You long to be part of the bigger picture. You long to help those who are suffering, who are in prison, or on the streets, or sick in hospital, or to reach people living in countries who have never heard that Jesus died for them, but you don't have the time. Well, I have news for you, you can be involved.

Maybe you have complete peace about your role in whatever world you are in, whether it be in business, medicine, the media, education, the arts, and so on. We will not all give up our jobs to go into full-time or part-time ministry or missionary work, but we are all still called to his Church and we are all still called to his cause. God will use you wherever you are, because if Jesus is your Lord and Saviour you are on your own 'frontline' for him. God wants you to trust in him one hundred per cent, to live by faith. He wants to use you to reach out to those around you. Someone once said to me, 'The first Bible anyone reads is our own lives!' – the way we live, our morals and principles, our priorities, our attitudes and concern for others.

However, where do you stand on that 'riverbank'? It is essential that you seek God and ask him to show you whose 'line' he wants you to hold. Maybe you can support a missionary, or a ministry in your home church? Or maybe a missionary or a ministry abroad? Don't miss out on the joy of partnering his work and his workers around the world, of being in that body of Christ, whose many parts form one unit. Then you will be an instrument of God's wider vision.

During the Second World War an army unit had to march out of step when crossing a bridge, because if they marched in step the bridge might fall down! This is a brilliant illustration of the power of unity: 'The body is a unit, though it is made up of many parts; and though all its parts are many, they form one body. So it is with Christ' (1 Cor. 12:12). We need one another. Working together in unity is a necessity if God's Kingdom is going to move forward. Jesus never worked alone.

So, perhaps you have been considering doing voluntary work in your community, or in your local church a few hours a week? Or maybe you plan to do short-term missionary work for a couple of months during your holidays abroad? Then please read on because this book will help you to meet the challenges you will face. On the other hand you may already have responded to God's call to go and serve him full-time. He may want you and your family to move to the other side of the world and it will require giving up your rights to your status quo. Don't worry. He knows about your needs. He's the living God. He's with you. God will not ask you to do anything in your own strength.

Therefore, although not all of us are called into those 'dangerous waters' full-time, all of us have a role to play: to love, support, intercede for and support our neighbour, and to tell others of the good news.

The harvest is big – over two billion people around the globe do not know the way to salvation.

> How, then, can they call on the one they have not believed in? And how can they believe in the one of whom they have not heard? And how can they hear without someone preaching to them? And how can they preach unless they are sent? As it is written: 'How beautiful are the feet of those who bring good news!' (Rom. 10:14–15)

Have a look at your feet (on second thoughts, maybe not!). Are they beautiful? There are some people who have been Christians for ten years, yet have never told anyone about Jesus, or reached out to the needy in their own community, or given to God's work and workers around the world. We are part of a 'body', a worldwide family, and we need to sow into God's Kingdom. When God's people stop saying, 'Here I am, Lord!' then his work stops being extended.

With his own mouth Jesus gave you and me this command, 'Go and make disciples of all nations, baptising them in the name of the Father and of the Son and of the Holy Spirit, and teaching them to obey everything I have commanded you. And surely I am with you always, to the very end of the age' (Matt. 28:19–20). He also said:

> For I was hungry and you gave me something to eat, I was thirsty and you gave me something to drink, I was a stranger and you invited me in, I needed clothes and you clothed me, I was sick and you looked after me, I was in prison and you came to visit me ... I tell you

the truth, whatever you did for one of the least of these brothers of mine, you did for me. (Matt. 25:35–6, 40)

When Jesus picked those fishermen to be his disciples, he said to them, 'I will make you fishers of men.' We know that the last thing Saul of Tarsus ever imagined he'd be was a 'light to the Gentiles' – a missionary! So what did Jesus do with these people? First he put a weight, a burden, a strong feeling in their hearts, a true love for 'a people' who often lived far away. I naturally love people who live near to me, my family, old friends, people from my home church. How are you going to love people you have never even seen? Such a love only comes from God. I will never forget the first time I saw a street boy when I arrived in Rio de Janeiro nearly nine years ago – it was as though my heart leapt into my mouth. I wept. The love I have for these children is not mine. Put me in a room of children from 'healthy' homes and they'll completely ignore me, and I them. Put me in a room full of street children and teenagers and it's as if we're a bunch of little magnets. This is God's burden for 'a people' I didn't know. 'Just as the Father sent me I am sending you' (John 20:21). This is what Jesus said to his disciples whom he specifically chose to be sent.

In his tape 'Get It, Got It' J. John, the well-known evangelist, relates the following tale with his usual humour:

There was a big double-decker bus and on the side of the bus there was a big poster, *'Eggs and Bacon – The Great British Breakfast'*! The bus went past a field and in the field there was a chicken and a pig. The chicken turned to the pig and said: 'Hey, look we're famous, *Eggs and Bacon – The Great British Breakfast*', just think, wherever the bus goes they're talking about us!' And the pig turned round to the chicken and said, 'It's all right for you, you only have to make a contribution, for me it cost me my life!'

God is looking for people who will make a vital contribution; but he is also calling to people who will be prepared to say, 'Here I am, I give you my life!'

HOW DO I DISCOVER MY ROLE?

Bible faith starts with hearing God – hearing what God has to say through his written Word. As I started to seek God with all my heart and was filled with his Holy Spirit I started to discover what he wanted me to do. It was, however, during a moment of total surrender that I found his purpose for my life.

I had got to a point where I had been so filled with Jesus's love that I just knew I couldn't keep it all to myself, I had to give it away. I would weep whenever I remembered what Jesus had done for me. Surely the least I could do was to give my life back to him? I just wanted to get as close as possible to my Lord.

When I was about ten years old my dad made a barbecue for our family in the garden. It was a hot summer's day and my two younger sisters and I played outside in the garden all afternoon. I remember hearing what sounded like a cat's cry on and off during the day. However there were a lot of cats around our neighbourhood and we were all used to their mating wail! But to our horror we later found out that the weak cry had come from our elderly neighbour, old Miss Smallbone, who had gone out of her little bungalow to feed the fish in her pond and slipped over and broken her leg. Miss Smallbone was bedridden for a long time after that. I was shocked that we hadn't recognised the cry was from her and gone to help her. It mortified me thinking of this little old lady in pain lying on the cement paving by her pond, immobile and helpless. She lived alone in her bungalow which was always very closed up and she appeared to have few friends. In fact people were slightly wary of her in the neighbourhood. However a friend and I decided that we would go round to her house to visit her and read her stories. I remember feeling a bit like Pip in Charles Dickens' *Great Expectations*! Years later after she died I found out that this had meant everything to her. We are never too young to reach out to our neighbour in love.

Amanda Williams worked for eight years in the oil industry. Then in 1986 she took voluntary redundancy. Shocked by the sudden news reports at the time of the spread of AIDS, Amanda eventually volunteered to help on a ward of eighteen people dying of AIDS at St Stephen's hospital in London. For several years she pushed a tea trolley around. Amidst the suffering that she witnessed during those months, Jesus started to become real to her. A verse she'd learned at Sunday school came back into her mind, 'Whatever you do to the least of these brothers of mine you do unto me.'

A Christian working on the ward, Sue, and another volunteer asked people at their church to pray for Amanda and they prayed her into the Kingdom. Two years later, filled with Jesus's compassion for those affected by AIDS, she went on a trip to America to visit a house where children dying of the disease were cared for. Whilst playing with them on the floor she felt Jesus say to her, 'I want my people to minister to families affected by HIV.' When she returned to England she started on her own by helping a two-year-old boy who had only a few weeks to live.

14

His mother had already died of AIDS. Finally in early 1990 Amanda founded 'Grandmas'. Since then over 320 families have been reached by her ever increasing team of ten full-time and eighty volunteer workers, who visit a family affected by AIDS for three hours once a week or fortnight. Today God is sending 'Grandmas' to countries around the world including Ireland and India.

'You start with a call of God,' explains Amanda, 'which doesn't appear to exist naturally. He introduces you to one child. He then shows you what is happening in a city and provides workers for that. Then when you're sitting thinking "This is enough for a lifetime, Lord", he enlarges that. In each step of obedience, he'll take you a step further.'

Acts 1:8 says, 'But you will receive power when the Holy Spirit comes on you; and you will be my witnesses in Jerusalem, and in [the Greek text says, 'as well as'] all Judea and Samaria, and to the ends of the earth.'

Once he's shown us what he wants us to do, our relationship with God will only grow when we have taken that first step. Once we take that step of obedience, we can trust God to do his part. If he has put a burden on your heart to support a work or worker in the mission field, don't wait. If he is sending you, don't miss out – *go*. Whether it be as a pastor, church planter, part of a worship team, evangelist, a missionary and so on, he is calling.

Paulo Mazoni, the main pastor of Baptist Central Church, my church here in Belo Horizonte, combined his work with a full-time job as manager of a department for the largest mining engineering company in the world. God spoke to him ten times asking him to give up his job and go into full-time service. Just imagine, the Lord spoke to him directly and through prophecies on no less than ten different occasions! The final two confirmations came in late 1998 during a three-day conference in our church with Pastor Hector Ferreyra from Argentina. During the weekend there was a tremendous move of the Holy Spirit with many miraculous healings, deliverance and prophecies. Paulo told me what happened to him: 'I stayed on late into Saturday night praying for people. Eventually there was only me and a man who introduced himself and asked for prayer. He had come from another church for the conference and was passing through some personal difficulties. As I started to pray for him he suddenly jerked up straight and spoke with a gentle authority that I knew wasn't his own. God spoke words through his mouth in the first person, things that this man had no way of knowing. God told me that I wasn't listening to him (for three years I had been resisting the calling he'd given me!). God told me not to fear, that he would use me powerfully if I would only let go and follow him, that he wanted to bring a multitude into this church, a revival into the city. He then gave me details of my type of ministry – tremendous encouragement. God's final words filled me with awe. He said that so that I would know that it was really him talking and so that I would never fear or doubt again, God would speak to me for the final time the following day! Then, all at once, the man stopped speaking, shook my hand and thanked me profusely for my prayer for him! I hadn't managed to pray for him at all!'

Paulo continued, 'The next evening, on the Sunday, after a powerful time of worship Pastor Hector started to speak, when all at once a woman stood up over the other side of the church and came and stood in front of me and the congregation. In a loud voice full of authority God spoke through her repeating word for word what he had spoken to me through the man the previous night. Only this time it was in front of my entire church!'

Paulo's fears had been on three levels: 'First, I wasn't sure of my call. I didn't want the risk of losing my job, career and everything that I'd studied and worked for, if my life was going to turn into a failure. Second, like Moses, I did not feel capable. But slowly God started to prepare me through conferences and his Word. I started to feel the anointing and with it a revelation of my authority in him. God started to build me up. Third, and finally, I was concerned for my wife, Juliana, and my two young daughters. My decision would mean a change of lifestyle for all of us. Also at that time I was offered a job as a director of a large company in Canada that would have brought me a position, large salary and benefits that I had always dreamed of. However, against all the odds, I began to open my heart to God and his will, which is incomparable, and in turn he started to prepare Juliana. Eventually she said to me that if it was God's will then that was what she wanted too.'

God is merciful – and he won't give up until we do!

Mrs Teresia Wairimu from Nairobi, Kenya, was an ordinary woman, who was longing to serve God. In 1988 she was one of hundreds and thousands drawn to Uhuru Park where evangelist Reinhard Bonnke was delivering the sick and possessed and leading thousands to Christ. She said a prayer, 'Dear Lord, bless me! Even me! I am asking for the ability and anointing to evangelise just a few people.'

However God had other ideas. In 1993 Reinhard Bonnke prayed for her during a conference in Oslo, which she'd managed to get to through sheer determination and faith. She describes the experience in her own words, 'When the evangelist came near me, I told him that I wanted the anointing of the Holy Spirit for an effective evangelistic ministry. Brother Bonnke laid his hands upon me and the power of God struck me like lightning. For three hours I was unable to move. The power of God was mightily at work. Some people carried me to a car, and I kind of woke up in my hotel room.'

When she returned to Nairobi she started a small church in a house. By the second week there were fifty and the next week one hundred and fifty! Then came the problem – there were so many people, there was no room. All the time Jesus was saving and delivering lost people. She records, 'We hired the Nairobi City Hall, but the people jammed the place so tightly that the doors broke, and then we were blacklisted for its use – no more City Hall meetings.' But the people kept coming and coming. Finally the Mayor of Nairobi allowed Teresia to have meetings in the Uhuru Park, a national sanctuary, normally reserved for top political events only. She preaches there now every second Sunday of the month. As soon as she used this venue, the crowds multiplied. People flock there by the tens and even hundreds of thousands from all parts of Kenya. God is now using her as an evangelist in other countries around the world.

HOW CAN I HEAR GOD?

Often we can worry about whether we are hearing God's voice or not. God has given us the promise that 'the sheep hear the shepherd's voice' (see John 10:14–16). God isn't interested in a one-way conversation. He wants us to hear his gentle voice too.

He can speak to us in different ways:

- through dreams
- through prophecy

- through visions
- through words of wisdom and knowledge
- through the imagination
- into our thoughts
- through a verse quickened to us while we are prayer-fully reading His Word
- through a sermon in church
- sometimes even through an oral voice

I once met a girl from French-speaking Guyana, and when she shared her testimony I felt shivers running up my spine. 'I came from a poor and unhappy family,' she told us quietly. 'One day I was at the end of my tether and I no longer wanted to live. I went to the edge of a lake near home and walked to the end of a small pier. There was no one around. I was just about to jump in when suddenly I heard a voice, that seemed to permeate right through me, saying out loud; "*Don't jump*! Give your life to me. I love you." I can't explain, but I instinctively knew it was Jesus. The voice had a quiet authority that could come from no other source but God himself. Then and there I felt compelled to fall to my knees, I wept and wept. On the edge of the lake that was supposed to have taken my life, I gave my life to Jesus. All at once a warm current of supernatural power surged through my body lifting away all the sorrow and pain.'

During a weekend conference at which I was speaking, a young girl approached me in great distress. She told me she had recently heard a talk where the speaker had stated, 'If you think that God speaks to us as I'm speaking to you now, you'll be disappointed.' The girl said to me, 'I've always expected and hoped that God conversed with us in a dialogue. Is it true what this speaker said, that he doesn't?' I don't know whether she had understood the speaker clearly, but I answered her from my heart, 'I'm sure God wants to converse with us in a dialogue, we only have to read the Bible to see that he does. Look at how the prophets and apostles chatted with him!'

Here are some principles that I have learned over the years which help me to know if it is really God speaking. Putting them into practice has changed my prayer life completely.

1 I have found that a twelve or twenty-four hour fast tunes my spirit and makes it more sensitive to hearing God's voice.
2 Any impressions can come from only four sources: your own mind, the mind of others, the mind of God, and the mind of Satan. So I take authority against any thought or activity from Satan by simply silencing him in Jesus's name (cf. Jas. 4:7) and forbidding him from stopping the will of God through my life for that day both directly or indirectly.
3 I then submit my own thoughts, imagination, and emotions to the lordship of Jesus Christ. Then I can have peace to believe that what I receive from that point on is from God.

Generally I put on an anointed worship tape and sing along with it until I feel I am in God's presence. When I have inner peace that all my desires and worries are also handed over to the Lord, I am then free to hear his voice. However, if I have no peace I ask God to show me if I have offended him or others, or whether I am guarding an offence. If there is something that I need to settle or clear up with my husband, a family member, someone within the ministry or a friend, I do that first. If, for some reason, I can't contact the person, I acknowledge before God that I will settle the issue at the very next opportunity. One thing is for sure, God doesn't let me forget! If I am guarding an offence, my prayer time is hindered if I do not release forgiveness. This is not always easy. Nevertheless from my experience, God enables me to do this super-naturally if I ask for his intervention, which is only possible once I have changed my attitude towards that person concerned (see Mark 11:25).

God usually speaks to me in my innermost thoughts by bringing into my mind pictures and verses from the Word. Over the years I have come to recognise that gentle voice. Whilst on a trip to England I was once praying with two others in an upstairs room of a house where I was due to give a talk. Downstairs people were arriving and as we prayed we could hear the muffled sounds of their voices. Suddenly in the midst of all those voices I could clearly distinguish my own mother's voice. The others with me in that room could not, but I could, because over the years of living with her, my mother's voice has become a major part of my life. It is the same with our living Lord.

Very rarely does God speak to me through dreams. In fact I could count the occasions on one hand! The few supernatural dreams I have had have occurred when God was warning me of something that we faced either as a family or as a ministry which needed urgent prayer, spiritual warfare and fasting (see chapter 5, 'Undoing Satan's work. What is my part in this?').

TEST YOUR LISTENING

To be on the safe side I always ask God for confirmation through two or three of the following ways:

- from the Word
- from my husband (who is my spiritual 'covering') or, when I was single, from my minister or spiritual leader, or a wise and godly friend
- for a sign through circumstances – often God shakes our circumstances to move us into a different direction
- from other people who may know nothing of the situation

Some people find guidance by looking at the various options open to them, or by reasoning an issue through by themselves or with a spiritual leader or godly friend. When they feel a deep peace – not a thrill or pleasure, but peace – then it can be a strong sign that it is the path down which God wants them to go. When I have received guidance, I write it down in my journal and act when I have an inner prompting that the timing is 'now'!

> 'Do not ascribe to God what is not of God. Do not easily suppose dreams, voices, impressions, visions, revelations to be from God without sufficient evidence. They may be purely natural, they may be diabolical. Try all things by the written Word and let all bow down before it.' John Wesley.

In her book, *Listening to God*,[1] Joyce Huggett relates that she tests her listening by asking herself the following four questions:

- Is the result of this piece of listening in alignment with Scripture?

- Do the circumstances substantiate what I heard? Has it come true?
- Is my attitude Christlike, characterised by humility, or is it reminiscent of Satan, the rebellious one?
- Is this still, small voice prompting me or others to live in a way which honours God and obeys him, or will the suggestion bring his name and honour into question or disrepute?

Loren Cunningham, who is chairman and founder of Youth With A Mission, warns in his book *Is That Really You, God*, that we should always beware of counterfeits.[2] We have all heard of a counterfeit bill, but we have never heard of a counterfeit bag. The reason is that only things of value are worth counterfeiting. Satan has a counterfeit for everything of God that it is possible for him to copy (Acts 8:9–11; Exod. 7:22). Counterfeit guidance comes, for example, through:

- ouija boards
- seances
- fortune-telling
- astrology (Lev. 20:6; 19:26; 2 Kings 21:6)

Whereas Satan's guidance leads us away from God into bondage, the guidance of the Holy Spirit leads you and me closer to Jesus and into true freedom. One key test I apply is to ask myself whether the leading I have received follows principles of the Bible, because the Holy Spirit never contradicts the Word of God.

Sometimes the Holy Spirit guides us in ways that are dramatic and supernatural – by a vision, for example, or a prophecy. If we are not open to the supernatural, we set arbitrary limits to God's plan for our lives. At other times the Holy Spirit may work through a nudge or a whisper. I have learned that I must be open to both, and sensitive to him no matter how he guides me.

When I first lived in Brazil my home for almost a year was Borel, one of the most dangerous *favelas* (slums) in Rio de Janeiro. During my early days there this is what I wrote in my diary:

14 August 1991

The team and I had been praying from the very top of the mountain over which Borel is built, and on the way down I saw him. I felt a nudge from the Holy Spirit to go and talk to him, but I ignored it and I said nothing to the others. Then halfway down the mountain, I felt another nudge – this time I couldn't ignore it. I told Pedro and so we all turned around and climbed all the way back up to the top! He was still there sitting in the dry earth, his big brown eyes wide with enthusiasm as his kite darted to and fro high in the blue sky above us. Flavio is paralysed from the waist down. He is small for his fifteen years and his tiny shrivelled legs were crossed underneath him. My Portuguese is poor and I felt self-conscious as I spoke to him about Jesus. Flavio smiled as he looked at this foreigner struggling with her words. His smile captured my heart. I believe this is a beginning of a special friendship. I invited him to come to church the following weekend, to a special meeting for the teenagers. On the way down Pedro told me that he had never seen Flavio in church.

24 August 1991

Today was a special day because Flavio accepted Jesus into his life! He came to church, he'd insisted that his brother and mother carry him down the mountain to the service. My eyes filled with water when I saw him, his little sister of eight came with him also! I gave him a Bible and shall visit him next week. By coincidence the pastor had asked me to speak (Marcia translated) and I spoke about the father heart of God. His earthly dad has died. Thank you, Father, because I know for you it was important that Flavio heard this talk tonight. I pray that through the power of your Holy Spirit you continue to remind him of your words.

If I'd kept on ignoring the gentle nudge of the Holy Spirit that day, Flavio would not have been in church that night.

BE DISCERNING

I used to have a tendency to talk too much about my guidance from God, usually because I was so excited! Now God has taught me to wait until he has given me permission to do so. And even when he does, he usually permits me to share that guidance with only a very few people. I have learnt it is OK to be ready to say, 'I could have been mistaken!'

There is a saying here in Brazil that goes like this, 'Their feet have left the ground, they must have too many wings on their backs!' In other words we should not demand supernatural intervention when we are capable of understanding a situation for ourselves. God gave us our intellect to be used and used to the full. When the light of our own human intelligence is sufficient for the task in hand, we don't need any further spiritual guidance.

I once read a story which for me illustrates the above perfectly about a woman who sincerely wanted to listen to God about the details of her life! Each morning, having consecrated the day to the Lord as she woke, she would then ask whether she was to get up or not. She would not stir until the still, small voice told her to dress. As she put on each article she asked the Lord whether she was to put it on. Very often the Lord would tell her to put her right shoe on but to leave the other off. Sometimes she was to put on both stockings but no shoes and sometimes both shoes and no stockings. And thus, listening to God, she would deal with every article of dress in turn! Oops!

I WANT TO BE USEFUL!

Once in his work, many of us worry about how best to serve. We want to be useful. Often we worry about what our giftings are. I have found the advice of the world evangelist Reinhard Bonnke helpful. He says that when all the schemes and strategies of evangelism, which are endlessly talked about in conferences, are reduced to practical terms, it comes down to this: 'Each Christian who is filled with the Holy Spirit and faith must do what lies at hand to be done! It is not a case of already being gifted, but of God giving us whatever gifts we need, to do what is in front of us. Gifts come with work, not work with gifts.'

When working in a team everyone will find their place. They will become unique and make a vital contribution.

Some people have outstanding talents. They are writers,

artists, competent administrators. These talents can become gifts. But sometimes the individuals' personalities are so tied up in the activity that they exercise their talent chiefly for their own glory, or to prove themselves or to dominate. It is better then that these people do not exercise their talents in community (or a team), because they would find it too hard to use them truly for the good of others. What they have to discover is their deeper gifts. Jean Vanier, *Community and Growth*.[3]

It is essential always to yield our gifts to the Lord, because these gifts have come from him for his purposes and for his glory. If we claim ownership, then we have turned our eyes away from the source and the gift will dry up. There are many gifts. For example, a friend of mine has a wonderful gift of encouragement. Everyone who knows her says that when she comes in a room the light goes on!

Whatever you do for God is a consequence of your relationship with him and not the other way around. Never forget that you were first called to Jesus Christ. He loves you unconditionally because you are *you* and not because of what you are doing for him. God wants us to work with him not for him.

'For we are God's fellow-workers; you are God's field, God's building.'(1 Cor. 3:9)

27

'YOUR MINISTRY IS TO SERVE!'

A young man worked as a volunteer for three months at the late Mother Teresa's mission in Calcutta, India. At the end of those three months he went up to Mother Teresa and asked her to pray with him because he wanted to discover what his ministry was. 'Son,' replied Mother Teresa, 'your ministry is to serve.'

> 'To serve is having nothing to lose and nothing to prove.' Charles Swindoll, *Improving Your Serve*.[4]

I will go one step further and say that to serve is to submit to one another and to our leadership. The dictionary says that 'to submit' means 'to yield'. This is a reflection of our relationship with Jesus. Whilst obedience is an act, submission is an attitude (see chapter 9 'I'm struggling with my leaders and my colleagues. What should I do?').

Mark and Clare Hester married in September 1997 and six months later they came out to Brazil to work with us here at Happy Child. They completed our third bilingual training school for working with street children and their families in 1998, and have a call to go with our organisation to Mozambique, Africa, to help rescue some of the 300,000 war orphans who are trying to survive there. Mark left a good job with an industrial design company and Clare previously managed a media project, the Big Take, with Steve Chalke, which enabled thousands of young people in the UK to campaign and raise money for street children. Clare has graciously allowed me to share with you her reflections on her first month in Brazil, and I'm sure they will help those of you who are just setting out to follow your calling to work with the poor, for however long that might be. It will also help those of you who are on that 'riverbank' to have a more vivid picture of what your missionaries or workers may be going through in the early stages of taking up their call. Clare's account perfectly illustrates this (sometimes painful) process of submission before service:

Week 1

Dusty feet. Sunshine. Insects. Kids on crack. It's all so strange. It's so far from cool clean England. So far from my family and friends and a job that made sense. I can't get my head round the fact that there is so much poverty rubbing shoulders with so much wealth. Why am I here? What could I possibly do for a street kid? I can't even understand Portuguese! How can it feel so right and so odd at the same time?

Living in the girls' house is incredible. It's a place where girls, who were once living on the streets, can start their restoration. At least here I'm able to pick up on their characters, their moods and their fears by eating meals and playing around with them. Every time I look at them I struggle to imagine them sleeping, eating and living on the streets for years. From five to fourteen years old. Using tin cans to smoke crack. Having sex to earn enough to feed the habit. It's so alien to me. It's impossible even trying to imagine having to resort to that. Their environment is so far from the comfort I have taken for granted every day of my life.

The children are often treated like dirt by pedestrians or police. Maybe it's because they've stolen from people. To me stealing is wrong, but how else can they feed themselves? I suppose it's a last resort and living on the streets is their solution to a home where a parent or parents can't cope.

It amazes me to think that although we can offer them clean clothes, a bed, showers and food here at the girls' house, they sometimes still return to life on the streets, to see their friends, have fun and do whatever it is they do. At the Day Centre, on the other side of town, boys and girls shower, wash their clothes, play and sleep. But they still find it difficult to come on a regular basis and let go of the life they know. To get a place in the night shelter, or girls' house, they need to come for a few days consecutively.

Week 2

Poor Mark, he's got a stinking cold and a homesick, emotional wife! Two weeks away from home and I'm already struggling to feel chirpy every morning. I'm sure it's usual when you settle into a completely different culture. I hope it'll pass soon, as we plan to be here some time. I know tears and sleep are good for you, but I would much rather feel normal.

Nine-year-old Sadhia and her friend Luciana went back to the streets last week, after five days here at the girls' house. They were happy here, but they missed their mates. Can't understand it myself. From what I've heard, it's the 'devil's playground'. It's pathetic, but I cried when the girls jumped on the bus back into town, as if they were my own sisters and they were running away. I couldn't do a thing about it. I'm learning it always has to be their choice. Not ours. I'd just started teaching Luciana to swim and I thought she was settling in. I suddenly realised as I had a heavy heart, that God must feel that way every time I choose to do my own thing.

How does a child of six survive for five years on the streets? What happens when a girl gets her period? Where do they go to the loo? How do they stand the smell?

Week 3

Nothing could prepare me for the way I felt this week. I'm tired of all the bus rides and walking. Frustrated because the lines are down and I can't e-mail or phone home. Sad because I don't feel myself. Confused by all these strange emotions that just won't settle!

We started street work this week. From seven till ten we walk around the city in pairs, waking up the children asleep on the streets, chatting and encouraging them to go and get food and clean up at the Day Centre. That's the aim of walking the streets; introducing them to an alternative. The smell on the streets hit me first. It keeps hitting me every time I am in town. Somehow the majestic buildings and beautiful weather can't soften the impact of the smell of urine.

I just can't get my head round them sleeping on a dirty pavement in an old T-shirt and shorts on cardboard. That's all they have. It seems so desperately wrong. Some of the kids wake up when you move close and whisper 'Hi!' in their ears. It must be a rude awakening finding strangers looking over you when you open your eyes. Wonder what they think of us!

Seeing Sadhia yesterday caught me by surprise. Asleep on a piece of cardboard, sandwiched between a boy and a girl. She looked so young and so comfortable, fast asleep. It was hard not to pick her up and take her home.

How could I have prepared for the reality of a young child being abandoned to life on the street?

Week 4

I feel like a deep-sea diver who has at last come up for air. Four weeks in, and countless emotions later, I am beginning to see beautiful landscapes with different eyes. I find myself looking at desperate poverty in the *favelas* and see character rather than the dirt and the smell. I'm able to walk home from town without jumping at every shadow. I can peel myself away from the children, to get my head together, rather than feel desperate about responding to their every whim … it's amazing to feel so normal again! The girls haven't come back. But I know they'll be OK. Eventually they'll come round when they're ready.

I've realised how much my security was tied up in my job, flat and clothes. Coming out here where none of that counts for anything, has really brought me down to earth. It's scary to discover that years of doing my own thing has distorted my perception of love, trust, humility and pride. I've never wanted to admit weaknesses, to fail or to give somebody the chance to hurt me. Up until now, I've believed God was there and loved him, but I've found it very difficult to admit that 'I needed him'. It feels good to acknowledge it.

It feels very odd to be waking up each day and knowing that my aim here is to help restore the lives of abandoned children. No great salary to achieve, no promotion to aim for. No flat to furnish or clothes to acquire. My greatest challenge is to be satisfied with whatever comes my way and not to be so busy planning tomorrow that I miss out on the experiences of today.

WHY SHOULD I PERSEVERE?

I have discovered that working on the frontline is often painful: God will work in us as well as through us. Just as Jesus broke the bread and gave it to his disciples before his body was broken for us on the cross, so we too will be taken through times and situations of brokenness where God will reveal to us what is in our own hearts. He is refining us for his glory. These times will never be easy but we must persevere, so that we do not miss out on maturity and strengthening of character. I tell my story in chapter 10, 'The refiner's fire, those desert places. Do I have to go there, Lord?' In order to be able to get through these difficult times, it is so important to receive encouraging letters from those of you who are on the 'riverbank'.

I recently read a chapter from T. D. Jakes' book *Woman, Thou Art Loosed* on the subject of birthing coming through sorrow (Gen. 3:16). If you are going to bring forth – and I'm not merely talking about babies, I'm talking about birthing vision and purpose – you will do so with sorrow and pain. If you're going to bring forth anything in your career, your marriage or your life, if you're going to develop anything in your character, it's going to come through sorrow. It will come through the things you suffer. You will enter into strength through sorrow. Sorrow is not the object; it's simply the canal through which the object comes. Don't let the devil give you sorrow without seed. Any time you have sorrow, it is a sign that God is trying to get something through you and to you. For every struggle in your life, God accomplished something in your character and in your spirit. After all, in childbirth the pain is forgotten when the baby is born. I am learning that when difficulties come I have to make the best of every opportunity. I have to interpret the situation rather than moan and complain, because out of it I will become someone new.

> 'The greater the work in you the greater the work through you. The deeper the work in you the deeper the work through you.' Dr Dan Duke, founder of A Call To The Nations.

If you are going into full-time or part-time ministry or missionary work at home or abroad, don't go expecting a position of leadership. Go to serve. God raises up his leaders in a completely different way to that which we see and know in the secular world. The paths of God often mean sacrifice and difficulties, but they lead to freedom and life. We must pay a price in prayer, intercession, obedience, perseverance, faithfulness, submission and loyalty. These are the traits that his saints have. 'My grace is sufficient for you, for my power is made perfect in weakness' (2 Cor. 12:9).

Wherever you are, if you are on the frontline, if you are a witness for Jesus Christ, you will pay a price. If you're not, then you won't!

It's a privilege to be a 'warrior' for Christ, to be on that edge between darkness and light, to help pull street children, prisoners, tramps, prostitutes, the dying, those with leprosy, AIDS victims and their families – people that are old before they are old, dead before they are dead – out of hell, away from death and bring them into the living light. I met a small boy at our day-care centre called Jefferson; he looked eight years old but he was actually eleven. He had been found on the streets by the team the day before. Jefferson had only been on the streets for a few days and in these cases the ministry has to act quickly before the child joins a gang and 'gets the habit'.

Cida, the co-ordinator of the centre, told me what happened: 'He cried when we started to ask him about his parents. He was terrified. I eventually discovered that his older sister of twelve years old, Ana Luiza, was on the streets with him. That afternoon he took me to see where they'd both been living.' Cida drew breath before continuing, 'Sarah, they had been sleeping with six tramps in the public toilets in the west of the city. As I entered these toilets, the stench was unbearable, inside the filth made me retch. We found his sister there with these men. I took her immediately to the girls' house where Dora (co-ordinator of the house at that time) and her team have taken her in. Jefferson is now living at the Night Shelter.' Accounts like this make me rejoice!

Nevertheless, every victory will prepare you for a great test. When you think you don't have enough strength to keep going, you can remember that last victory and then you want to walk forward because you know you will get through. When you burst through to the other side the blessings will come. However, there *will* be another test. Why? Because you are making a difference, you are helping to bring the rejected, the starving, the lost, the hated, the filthy, the smelly, the broken into the Kingdom of God. And through it all your relationship with God grows as he refines you, taking away all that doesn't glorify his name so that Jesus can shine through.

THE TOP TEN KEY POINTS

❑ If Jesus is your Lord and Saviour, wherever he has placed you, you are on the 'frontline'; your calling is to imitate him.

35

❑ Whose 'line' are you holding? Don't miss out on the joy of partnering his work and his workers at home and abroad.

❑ When Jesus picked those fishermen to be his disciples, he said to them, 'I will make you fishers of men.'

❑ We are all called to his Church and we are all called to his cause.

❑ Develop a secret prayer life. God wants to speak to you: 'the sheep hear the shepherd's voice' (see John 10:14–16).

❑ Once God has shown you what to do, your relationship with him will only grow once you take that first step in obedience.

❑ Each Christian who is filled with the Holy Spirit and faith must do what lies at hand to be done.

❑ Gifts come with work, not work with gifts. God wants fellow-workers (1Cor. 3:9), people who work with him, not for him.

❑ To serve is having nothing to lose and nothing to prove.

❑ The greater the work in you the greater the work through you. Every victory will prepare you for a great test, and every test for a greater victory!

2

How do I follow my calling?

Nearly four thousand years ago God said to Abraham, 'I will make you into a great nation and I will bless you; I will make your name great and you will be a blessing. I will bless those who bless you, and whoever curses you I will curse; and all peoples on earth will be blessed through you' (Gen. 12:2–3). God blessed Abraham so that he could bless others. Many of us and, therefore, many of our churches have missed this crucial point. He didn't bless Abraham so that Abraham would grow old, fat and happy wallowing in his own good fortune! It wasn't a selfish blessing. Throughout the Bible we read examples of people who were blessed and then became a blessing: Joseph was blessed and he blessed Egypt; Elijah was blessed and he blessed Elisha; Daniel was blessed and he blessed Nebuchadnezzar in Babylon; Esther was blessed and she blessed Persia; Moses was blessed and he blessed Israel. God blesses us but afterwards he puts on us the obligation that we should be a blessing for the future generation.

Mission is central throughout the Bible. Even after four

thousand years Abraham can still be a blessing to the
nations today if the words of Jesus are fulfilled: 'Go and
make disciples of all nations, baptising them in the name
of the Father and of the Son and of the Holy Spirit, and
teaching them to obey everything I have commanded you.
And surely I am with you always, to the very end of the
age' (Matt. 28:19–20).

God sends people out from the Church because there
is a debt to pay: there is an obligation. The Apostle Paul
felt obligated to the entire world to spread the good news
of salvation through faith in Jesus Christ. 'When I preach
the gospel I cannot boast, for I am compelled to preach.
Woe to me if I do not preach the gospel' (1 Cor. 9:16).
However apart from the debt that we owe our heavenly
Father for having sent his only Son to die in our place, I
can think of another kind of debt. Jackie Pullinger-To,
who has worked among drug addicts in Hong Kong and
China for nearly thirty years, once said in a talk she gave
in London in 1996:

> It was my country, Britain, that took opium to China
> out of greed years ago. For business and for trade we
> addicted the Chinese. On behalf of my country I am
> sorry that we were so greedy in the name of 'empire'. I
> have said sorry to the Chinese people. Those who I
> met forgave me and forgave us. Many of those who
> were once enslaved because of what our ancestors did
> have now become the rescuers, the releasers, and are
> being sent out to help others who are captives around
> the world.

Two years ago I was addressing a women's group at my
home church, Holy Trinity Brompton in London, and I
explained that God was speaking to us about Happy

Child expanding one day from Brazil to England and Africa. After the meeting a woman came up to me and said, 'Do you understand why God is asking you to start Happy Child in Brazil, England and Mozambique, Africa?'

I answered her honestly, 'No!'

She continued, 'Funnily enough I was only talking about this very subject earlier today. In the seventeenth century England had a monopoly on the slave trade, selling African slaves to South America. God has raised you up to reverse that circle and break bondages that were installed years ago by our ancestors.' I was blown away. It's all just a little bit curious, isn't it?

It is very clear from the Word of God that you and I need power to follow our calling. If Jesus Christ, the Son of God needed to be anointed by the Holy Spirit how much more do we need to be? Without power we cannot do anything for our Lord. When Jesus appeared to his disciples for the first time after his crucifixion the Bible says that 'He opened their minds so they could understand the Scriptures' and then he told them,

> This is what is written: The Christ will suffer and rise from the dead on the third day, and repentance and forgiveness of sins will be preached in his name to all nations, beginning at Jerusalem. You are witnesses of these things. I am going to send you what my Father has promised; but stay in the city until *you have been clothed with power from on high*. (Luke 24:46–9, my emphasis)

Imagine sending out a missionary or a worker who doesn't have the power of the Holy Spirit in her or his life! I recently heard of a true story of two girls, who in 1957 went to evangelise a tribe in South Mexico. They arrived to discover that the tribe was under a very strong demonic oppression. Those two American missionaries thought those demons weren't a problem – 'We are with Jesus,' they said! Suddenly one night a voice said, 'This region is ours, you're not going to stay here!' No one could explain the missionaries' hasty departure. Sending people out without the power of the Holy Spirit is like sending sheep to wolves.

THE ANOINTING

Dr Dan Duke (who has a Master's degree in theology) and his wife, Marti, have a powerful ministry in the Holy Spirit. Since 1983 they have worked in over forty nations, including Brazil and Mozambique. Dan told Joao and me that in Mozambique they had witnessed greater healing miracles than anywhere else. Ten years ago they founded 'A Call To The Nations' with a vision to see revival spread by ushering individuals into the manifest presence of God and leaving them there long enough to be transformed. Their teaching and team worship is inspirational and I would like to share with you some of what I have learned through their lives.

> 'People need to experience God, not merely learn about him or hear preachers talk about him.' Dan Duke.

My eyes were first opened to the anointing of God when I studied its history in the Old Testament:

40

Then the Lord said to Moses; 'Take the following fine spices: 500 shekels of liquid myrrh, half as much (that is, 250 shekels) of fragrant cinnamon, 250 shekels of fragrant cane, 500 shekels of cassia – all according to the sanctuary shekel – and a hin of olive oil. Make these into a sacred anointing oil, a fragrant blend, the work of a perfumer. It will be the sacred anointing oil. Then use it to anoint the Tent of Meeting, the ark of the Testimony, the table and all its articles, the lampstand and its accessories, the altar of incense, the altar of burnt offering and all its utensils, and the basin with its stand. You shall consecrate them so they will be most holy, and whatever touches them will be holy.

'Anoint Aaron and his sons and consecrate them so they may serve me as priests. Say to the Israelites, "This is to be my sacred anointing oil for the generations to come. Do not pour it on men's bodies and do not make any oil with the same formula. It is sacred, and you are to consider it sacred. Whoever makes perfume like it and whoever puts it on anyone other than a priest must be cut off from his people." ' (Exod. 30:22–33)

Everything that was used in the service of God had to be anointed with this holy oil: there were no exceptions! Notice that God was very specific in his instructions for the ingredients of the anointing oil – this is his divine order. We read that the oil is holy: 'make these into a sacred anointing oil' (v. 25). Everything used in the tabernacle had to be anointed with it: the tent, the ark, the table and its utensils, the basin and its stand (vv. 26,27,28). We read also that the priest had to be anointed with this same holy oil, and that this was a permanent ordinance (vv. 30,31).

It is the same in the New Testament times:

Now to each one the manifestation of the Spirit is given for the common good. To one there is given through the Spirit the message of wisdom, to another the message of knowledge by means of the same Spirit, to another faith by the same Spirit, to another gifts of healing by that one Spirit, to another miraculous powers, to another prophecy, to another distinguishing between spirits, to another speaking in different kinds of tongues, and to still another the interpretations of tongues. All these are the work of one and the same Spirit, and he gives them to each one, just as he determines. (1 Cor. 12:7–11)

Nothing has changed today. Everything or everyone used in the service of God must be anointed by his Holy Spirit. Like the oil used by Moses, this Holy Spirit is sacred and cannot be imitated. Being anointed by him will free you to move in the spirit and not in the flesh.

When God anoints you and appoints you to a specific task, then the Spirit of the Lord comes upon you to accomplish it – that is the anointing. In other words, in my case, God called me to Brazil to rescue children living on the streets. When I stepped out and said 'I'm going', then the Spirit of the Lord came upon me, and is continually released through me to accomplish that task. The same can be applied to you in your own calling.

Jesus too was anointed according to the Old Testament pattern.

'Many believe that Jesus had the miracles because he was the Son of God. But that was not the situation. Jesus did not become the Son of God when he was thirty years old. Jesus was the Son of God the moment he was born. Yet we have no records of any miracles before he was thirty years old. It was when the Holy Spirit and the anointing of God came upon him that he began his ministry.' Dan Duke

In Acts 10:38 the Apostle Peter speaks of 'how God anointed Jesus of Nazareth with the Holy Spirit and power, and how he went around doing good and healing all who were under the power of the devil, because God was with him'. It is important that we understand our particular gifts and calling for this reason: the anointing is increased in us by discovering what God has consecrated us to do, and then doing it!

In my own experience God anoints me at specific times for a specific purpose, usually when I am speaking and ministering to a group of people (children or adults), however large or small. On a recent mission trip to Recife in the north-east of Brazil, I spoke and ministered for a week in various churches and ministries who work with the poor. The anointing that came upon me for that particular time was powerful; Jesus worked prophecies, healings and deliverance wherever we went. However, as soon as I caught the plane home, the anointing went back to him. That's the way God loves to work. It's teamwork with him in the driving seat.

LAYING ON OF HANDS

Have you ever asked yourself, 'What really happens when people lay hands on other people in prayer?' As I learnt more about the laying on of hands I discovered that it is more than symbolism. The anointing comes by the transferring or impartation of the Holy Spirit through the laying on of hands of the Holy Spirit. Biblically the laying on of hands is one of the six foundational principles upon which the Church is built: 'Therefore let us leave the elementary teachings about Christ and go on to maturity, not laying again the foundation of repentance from acts that lead to death, and of faith in God, instruction about baptisms, the laying on of hands, the resurrection of the dead, and eternal judgment' (Heb. 6:1–2). However, Paul warns us, 'Do not be hasty in the laying on of hands, and do not share in the sins of others. Keep yourself pure' (1 Tim. 5:22). I am learning to be wise about who lays hands on me – we need to be responsible and choose mature men and women of God.

Warning   Paul told the young Timothy, 'Do not neglect your gift, which was given you through a prophetic message when the body of elders laid their hands on you' (1 Tim. 4:14). There are two ways that you and I can neglect this gift: first, we can neglect to ever discover it; second, we can be aware of it but not do anything about it.

WALKING IN THE ANOINTING

When the anointing is present we will see results and others around us will see the fruit through our life and work.

Have you ever seen anyone throw a stone at a fruit tree

that didn't have any fruit on it? I can easily visualise the boys on our farm in Brazil around Christmas time throwing stone after stone at the numerous huge mango trees we have there. The boys' intention, of course, is to hit a delicious ripe mango so that it will fall to the ground ready to be eaten! But, of course, the boys wouldn't waste their time throwing stones at the mango trees if they weren't producing any fruit.

If you are producing fruit in your ministry or work for God, then I can guarantee that you will also be on the receiving end of those stones! However, I have discovered that God will use those stones to refine me and the work I'm doing for him, so that I can produce even more fruit (see chapter 10, 'The refiner's fire, those desert places. Do I have to go there, Lord?').

At any fruit market we will find many fruits that are already rotten, old or over ripe, having lasted only a day, or perhaps in some cases a week. Once they turn rotten we throw them away or feed them to animals. Those of us who are working with God will, however, produce 'eternal fruit'.

> Jesus said, 'I am the true vine, and my Father is the gardener. He cuts off every branch in me that bears no fruit, while every branch that does bear fruit he prunes so that it will be even more fruitful ...
>
> 'I am the vine; you are the branches. If a man remains in me and I in him, he will bear much fruit; apart from me you can do nothing. If anyone does not remain in me, he is like a branch that is thrown away and withers; such branches are picked up, thrown into the fire and burned. If you remain in me and my words remain in you, ask whatever you wish, and it will be given you. This is to my Father's glory; that you bear much fruit,

showing yourselves to be my disciples.' (John15:1–2, 5–8)

I used to think that producing 'spiritual fruit' in my life depended on God. But as I started to study the Word I discovered that producing fruit also depends on me. You know, the only thing I can really say is mine is my own will – not even God will take that from us.

There are six biblical conditions which help us to produce eternal fruit in our life.

(a) Repentance

Jesus said, 'Produce fruit in keeping with repentance' (Matt. 3:8). This is the first challenge on how to start producing eternal fruit – through repentance. Repentance is change – a change of mind.

I used to think that repentance applied only to the things I had done wrong, but it is also very necessary for things that I have failed to do. Not only that but we have to bear in mind too the context in which we are living. We are part of a society, and often in addition to our personal sin we have to repent of the sins of our society. Daniel and Nehemiah took upon themselves the sins of others in intercession. They recognised that as human beings who belonged to a society they were responsible for their society's sins before God and therefore they needed to repent. They prayed, 'I have sinned.' Whenever Happy Child comes together as a ministry to pray for Mozambique, we are led to stand in the gap and ask for forgiveness on behalf of that country. However, our prayers are, 'Forgive us, Lord', not 'Forgive them': these prayers are more powerful but they are very humbling.

We are all fallen before God. It is only by his grace and mercy that we are able to come to the cross. There is a great danger in becoming self-righteous. For example, people curse the darkness, and I hear many people complaining about the street children – but this does nothing to help. We have to turn on the light!

(b) The revelation that God chose you

Jesus said, 'You did not choose me, but I chose you to go and bear fruit – fruit that will last. Then the Father will give you whatever you ask in my name' (John 15:16). We love to choose the best! When I go out shopping to a fruit and vegetable shop I choose the best fruit. If we are looking for someone to help us, we tend to choose the most capable person. It's interesting, isn't it?

Nevertheless, if you were God, do you think that you would have chosen you?

Often people are chosen because of their performance. We are living in a time when there are contests for the most beautiful, the strongest, the most intelligent, the most competent, the youngest … it's our world culture if you like. You never hear of a contest for the ugliest, the weakest, and so on! But God's choice is totally different. Jesus said with his own lips, 'I chose you, you did not choose me.' He chose us not because of our merits or our virtues but because of his grace.

For instance look at the type of men the Messiah, the Son of God, chose to be his very own disciples, to carry on his work after he departed. The Bible says they were 'unschooled, ordinary men' (Acts 4:13). It was because of this very reason that the rulers, elders and teachers of the law were astonished by their wisdom, courage and the miracles they performed. And as a result Jesus was glorified.

(c) Give the glory to God in all you do

I'm not a great gardener but I do know that it is possible to graft lemon and orange trees together. If you can cut the branch of a lemon tree and graft into it a branch from an orange tree, it produces a different tasting fruit. This visual picture shows us what happens when we ask Jesus into our lives. Jesus grafts his life into us. We are 'filled with the fruit of righteousness that comes through Jesus Christ – to the glory and praise of God' (Phil. 1:11).

It is very important for us to grasp that when we gave our life to God he began to live through us. Our faith is not a religion, but a relationship with him. This relationship with him produces the life of Jesus in us.

The word 'Christian' means 'Christlike'. It doesn't necessarily mean that we belong to a religion called 'Christianity'! There are many religions that believe that salvation comes by good works and deeds, but we don't practise good works to be saved, we practise good works *because* we are saved. The Bible talks about 'bad' or 'dead' works, works that do not glorify the Lord in any way. They are the fruit of our own flesh, which does not bring glory to God. It is good works that glorify the Lord.

A beautiful young girl was applying first aid to a horrendous wound on the leg of a sick old man. A youth came up beside her to watch. Eventually he said, 'I wouldn't do what you are doing for a million pounds!' The beautiful girl turned around and, looking up at him with a gentle smile, replied, 'Neither would I!'

(d) A pure heart

The fruit can only grow where there is good soil and that soil is our heart. 'Still other seed fell on good soil, where it produced a crop – a hundred, sixty or thirty times what was sown' (Matt. 13:8).

If seed doesn't fall on good ground it won't produce fruit. 'As he was scattering the seed, some fell along the path, and the birds came and ate it up' (Matt. 13:4). There will be some people who go into ministry full of enthusiasm. Occasionally we have people coming to Happy Child full of promises, 'Count on me, Sarah and Joao. I'll teach the children how to play football, do silk screen, and carpentry. I'll visit their families at weekends!' For the first few days and weeks everything is swinging and hunky-dory. But then after a while everything stops. Why? The seed fell, but the person concerned didn't understand the vision.

'Other seed fell among thorns which grew up and choked the plants' (Matt. 13:7). The thorns are the worries of the world, things, clothes, food, money, *my life*! And the thorns suffocate us.

On our farm there are many different kinds of fruit tree. Each one of them has to be of a certain age before it starts to bear fruit. There are avocados, lemons, limes, passion fruit, mango, oranges, tangerines, mulberries, bananas. Eventually some trees stop producing fruit when they get old. Yet in Jerusalem, in the Garden of Gethsemane there are still olive trees from the time of Jesus. They are over two thousand years old, and are still producing olives.

When we are old we can still produce fruit. Some older people are full of energy; my 61-year-old mother has more energy than I do! There is no retirement in the spiritual world! God has promised, 'Fruit trees of all kinds will grow on both banks of the river. Their leaves will not wither, nor will their fruit fail. Every month they will bear because the water from the sanctuary flows to them. Their fruit will serve for food and their leaves for healing' (Ezek. 47:12). Ministry is for all ages. In the old days fruit had its seasons, but today with modern technology and chemicals it can be produced all year round. What God hopes for us, too, is that with the Holy Spirit we will produce fruit all year round. 'The fruit of the Spirit is love, joy, peace, patience, kindness, goodness, faithfulness, gentleness and self-control' (Gal. 5:22).

I like to visualise it like a flower: at first there is a bud and then, suddenly, at a certain time it opens, 'boom!' and produces a flower. We often find ourselves in situations when in a split second we have to decide whether we allow the fruits to manifest or not. A well-known minister in Brazil once said to me that he always judges himself by how he reacts in bad traffic. Even if he's late for an appointment he doesn't allow himself to get upset. He allows the gift of patience to manifest itself by not sounding the horn! My lack of patience is one of the reasons I refuse to have a fish stuck on the back of our car. Whenever I sound my horn in bad traffic I think of that minister!

(e) Die to self

Jesus said, 'I tell you the truth, unless a grain of wheat falls to the ground and dies, it remains only a single seed. But if it dies, it produces many seeds. The man who loves his life will lose it, while the man who hates his life in this world will keep it for eternal life' (John 12:24–5).

This life of eternal fruit starts with being willing to die! It begins when we die to ourselves, our expectations, dreams, desires and plans. I usually have to do this on a daily basis.

However, I first understood the importance of this when I went to live in the *favela* in Rio de Janeiro in 1991, away from all my comforts and security. It came home to me even more when I found myself in the middle of crossfire between two drug-trafficking gangs – I had never felt death so close before. Interestingly, before this experience I was scared and unsure about everything. I had obeyed God and gone to Brazil but I was holding onto my life. I had to be prepared to die for Jesus. Once I had proclaimed this (it took me two days and six efforts to say it finally with my heart!) the fear left me, and for the first time I had the revelation that it was Jesus who was living through me. On many occasions I find my attitude is way off what God expects, and I have to go back to him, humble myself and start all over again.

(f) Understand that you are planted by the Lord

'He is like a tree planted by streams of water, which yields its fruit in season and whose leaf does not wither. Whatever he does prospers' (Ps. 1:3). There is a difference between a tree that is planted and a tree that grows by itself in a jungle. In the Amazon in Brazil the trees are not planted by human hands but the seed is spread at random by birds and animals.

When a man plants a tree, he will first prepare the soil. When the stones, weeds and thorns have been removed, he plants the young tree in the cultivated soil, pats it down, waters it and cares for it. In the same way I began to understand that we produce eternal fruit as a result of being planted by the Lord. 'They will be called oaks of righteousness, a planting of the Lord, for the display of his splendour' (Isa. 61:3). He will gently take out the weeds, thorns and stones in our lives. He will work in our lives through the difficult times, not the good times. It is through the sorrow that I find myself, and then he uses these times to nourish others.

Any investment we make is worthwhile for we read in Psalm 1:3 that 'whatever he does prospers'. Eternal fruit is fruit that prospers.

THE GREAT PRIVILEGE

Often people say, 'I'm sure we are living in the End Times.' Although people have been saying this for the last two thousand years and particularly through the immensely traumatic times of war, through many prophecies God does seem to be saying 'The end is near.' But how near is near?

The Bible says that first the gospel must be preached to every tribe, tongue and nation and *then* Jesus will return. We only have to watch the news or read the newspaper to discover that this is still not the case.

I heard a powerful talk recently by Pastor Hector Ferreyra from Argentina whose church has 20,000 members. There is a tremendous revival taking place in his country today. When Hector Ferreyra was one year old his violent father killed his pregnant mother. After this tragedy he lived like a street boy; no one wanted him and no one loved him – he went from house to house. It was only after he asked Jesus into his life, in his late teens, that the loneliness, anger and sadness went.

During the talk he said that God had spoken deeply into his spirit in 1997 and that he had been brought to his knees weeping. 'God is sending his sword soon because he has had enough,' Hector cried out to us all. 'God has had enough of sin in this world. And his sword is coming. Never say you were not warned. He is calling his Church to holiness, He is calling his bride. He is calling for repentance through a new and powerful revival around the world. However, this revival is for holiness.'

The exciting thing is that God is looking to you and to me! Ezekiel 22:30 says, 'I looked for a man among them who would build up the wall and stand before me in the gap on behalf of the land so that I would not have to destroy it, but I found none.' We are the hands, the feet and the mouth of Jesus today. When we place ourselves in that gap we are fulfilling one of the greatest privileges we have as Christians.

THE TOP TEN KEY POINTS

☐ God blesses us so that we can bless others
☐ Mission is central throughout the Bible.
☐ To follow your calling you need power. Sending people out without the power of the Holy Spirit is like sending sheep out among wolves.
☐ God anointed you when he saved you. The anointing will teach you how to use the anointing (1 John 2:27). An anointing is to meet a need – healing, deliverance, a blessing, a prophecy, spiritual gifts.
☐ We are warned in the Bible: 'Do not neglect your gift' (1 Tim. 4:14).
☐ In the Old Testament times everything that was used in the service of God had to be anointed with a holy oil (Exod. 30:22–33). Similarly, in New Testament times (today), everything or everyone used in the service of God must be anointed by his Holy Spirit.
☐ We have no records of Jesus, the Son of God, performing any miracles before he was thirty years old. It was when the Holy Spirit and the anointing of God came upon him that he began his ministry. If Jesus needed to be anointed, how much more do we need to be anointed!
☐ If you are walking in the anointing, you will see the fruit. Jesus said; 'I am the true vine, and my Father is the gardener … If a man remains in me and I in him, he will bear much fruit' (John 15:1, 5).
☐ Producing fruit depends on me.

❑ Six biblical conditions to help you produce eternal
fruit that prospers in your own life: repentance; the
revelation that God chose you, you didn't chose him;
give the glory to God in all you do; have a pure heart
– good soil; die to self; understand that you are planted
by the Lord.

3

I need financial and prayer support. Where's my faith?

The late John Wimber once said, 'Faith is spelt R-I-S-K and Commitment is spelt M-O-N-E-Y!'

If you are going to be dependent on God for your finances, whether you are called to work abroad or in your own country, then this chapter will be helpful to you. Equally I hope this chapter will encourage those of you who are supporting the work of the Kingdom, either through prayer and intercession, a regular financial offering, or support in other ways.

I don't know everything there is to know about faith and finances but I do know that I have more faith today than I did almost nine years ago in 1990, when God, despite my unworthiness, first called me out of my comfortable surroundings to go to Brazil to rescue children living and dying on the filthy streets. Living by faith has proved to me over and over again the reality of God. However, my faith has only increased as I have exercised it.

Living a life with God is a never-ending adventure. It seems to me that he seldom asks us to do the things that naturally come easy to us: he only asks us to do the things we are perfectly fitted to do by his grace. Someone once said to me, 'If we do what comes naturally to us we will rarely do what God would do, because we are fallen!'

The key for me has been to obey. This has not always been easy since God often asks from me more than I think I can ever do, and yet time and time again, as I have had to trust in him and say, 'OK, Lord, if this is what you want, if this is what you are asking, then give me the faith and the courage to do it and the patience to see *you* move', I can honestly say he has never failed. He has always met my need in order for me to complete his will at that time, financially as well as physically and emotionally. 'For the eyes of the Lord range throughout the earth to strengthen those whose hearts are fully committed to him' (2 Chron. 16:9). It has seldom come about at the time or in the way I expected it to, but it has always come about in such a way that the glory goes to him.

One important lesson God has taught me recently is that uncomfortable situations that arise through lack of money can just as definitely be from him as the ready provision of money. At the end of 1997 Happy Child had been running for only four years, and we had grown quickly. With a team of over forty-eight full-time workers, we already had three houses in the city and a beautiful farm twenty-five kilometres outside of Belo Horizonte. Through our programme of rehabilitation we had already managed to take over 527 children and teenagers off the streets. As well as these houses we had a small team devoted to assisting the families of children in their miserable homes in the *favelas*.

However, Joao and I were bearing the brunt of the administration, decision making and problem solving, and it was taking its toll on us as a couple and on our three small children. We hadn't put any limits around us as a family. The time had come to restructure and God needed to attract our attention. The steady income enjoyed by Happy Child from a variety of sources started to dry up (see chapter 10, 'The refiner's fire'). However, six months later, once we had stopped and reorganised ourselves both as a family and as a ministry, the money started to flow in again. Looking back, it amazes me that, through the very turbulent storm that we faced and passed through, the work with the street children and their families was not affected.

During a severe famine God led Elijah to a brook where he was able to hide out for some time. No doubt, after a while he settled into a routine as the ravens faithfully brought his breakfast and dinner every day, enjoying his calm and easy surroundings. Then slowly his brook dried up. Why? God didn't want Elijah to get too comfortable trusting in the brook, even though it had been God's provision for him at the beginning. He had greater things for Elijah, and it was time to move on.

> 'When our financial brook runs dry, we are ready to listen to the Lord who wants our wilful dependence on Him. God's only aim is to teach us and to bring us closer to Himself. We so easily move into a greater degree of independence than God sees is best.' Loren Cunningham in *Daring to Live on the Edge*.[1]

WHAT IS FAITH?

- **Faith** is trusting that God's character will never change. God himself says, 'I the Lord do not change' (Mal. 3:6).
- **Faith** is believing that something will happen before it happens.
- '**Faith** is being sure of what we hope for and certain of what we do not see' (Heb. 11:1).
- All of us are given a measure of **faith**, according to Romans 12.
- **Faith** is a gift!
- A lack of obedience destroys **faith**.

> George Muller said, 'Faith and patience may be tried, but in the end, those who honour God will not be put to shame.'

Once I made the decision that I was going to follow my call, I faced my first financial challenge. God had shown me that there would be a time of 'preparation' and training first before going to Brazil and, as I have mentioned, I felt guided to do a Discipleship Training School with Youth With A Mission in Lausanne, Switzerland, which was to conclude with a three-month outreach in Chile. However, I had three weeks to find £2000! This would cover the cost of the course, lodging and food as well as the return flights to Switzerland. I had just taken three months off after completing a gruelling fourteen-month contract with Michael Hurll TV Productions, producing five hours of television programmes each week for Sky TV. By the time I'd got this big green light from God it was at the end of those three months and I'd recklessly spent all my savings! Although I part owned a flat in London, I did not feel confident to put it on the market. That was going too far, I thought to myself – a step at a time!

A Bible verse that people were regularly receiving for me at that time was Psalm 46:10: 'Be still and know that I am God.' I wept the first time someone gave me that verse during a prayer meeting. I had been a Christian for only a few months at the time and it cut through my heart like a knife through soft butter. The reality that God clearly knew me so well stunned me. I had always been such a restless person.

I remember one Sunday in church my Bible happened to fall open at the book of James and these words jumped out at me:

> Now listen, you who say, 'Today or tomorrow we will go to this or that city, spend a year there, carry on business and make money.' Why, you do not even know what will happen tomorrow. What is your life? You are a mist that appears for a little while and then vanishes. Instead, you ought to say, 'If it is the Lord's will, we will live and do this or that.' (4:13–15)

As I read these words I felt so convicted. In a nutshell I was used to being in control. I could have told you what I had planned to do a year or two in advance! It was an extraordinary concept that the same God who had created the heavens and the earth, the same God of Abraham, Isaac, Jacob, Moses, David and Paul, the same God who raised Jesus Christ from the dead was saying he had a plan for my life, for each of our lives. It still blows my mind.

Anyhow, I did what I could, and in faith filled in the application form for the course in Switzerland, submitted myself and my plans to my pastor, Nicky Gumbel, and to my parents. It wasn't easy telling Dad. He wasn't a Christian at the time and I am his eldest child. He was proud of my career. I will never forget his words, however hard it was for him to say them at the time: 'Sarah, you must do what will make you happy.'

A few weeks before the course started Granny Joy came for lunch. She asked me what my next television production was. I gathered myself together and tried once again to explain what I knew many were finding difficult to comprehend. Her mouth did drop open for a few seconds, and then out of the blue she asked, 'Well, how much do you need?' I told her. There was silence for a few seconds and then she said decisively, 'Well, I can either give it to you now or put it in my will for you to receive after I'm dead. However, it seems you need it now rather than later,' so give me your account number and I'll pay it into the bank tomorrow.' I was speechless, she'd never given me any money before. She died a year and a half later. To this day my relatives say, 'That was the best investment Granny Joy ever made with her money in her whole lifetime!'

I STRUGGLE WITH GIVING! WHERE DO I START?

One of the first things God did with me was to deal with my attitude towards money. Two months into the Discipleship Training Course in Switzerland, I felt God telling me to sell my flat. I'd met a Brazilian girl who had visited the base in Lausanne where I was for a couple of weeks. She told me of a Dutch couple, Johan and Jeanette Lukasse, who had started a work with street children in a city called Belo Horizonte with Youth With A Mission. They were running bilingual training schools for people wanting to work with street children and their next one was starting the following April, 1991. I knew then that this should be my next step after Chile.

Despite its being a bad time for selling property, my flat sold within a few weeks. After paying off the mortgage and halving the profit with the co-owner, I had made £10,000. One of the first things I did was to pay off the debt I had run up on my credit card, and for my own good I cancelled it! 'Let no debt remain outstanding, except the continuing debt to love one another ...' (Rom. 13:8).

One Monday morning during class the course leader, Paul Marsh, announced that with one week to go to the end of the course two of our classmates still did not have the money to pay for the remainder of their course fees and their return flights to Chile. They needed £1000 each in order to go and the deadline was Friday! He suggested that we all pray for them. Oh well, I thought to myself, I certainly can't help. Now I'm a missionary on my way to Brazil I'll need all the money I've got, it's my security!

Every morning the two people concerned would rush to their mailboxes to see what God had done. By Thursday the situation hadn't changed. We all prayed again. Suddenly into my thoughts came that gentle still small voice, 'Sarah, I want you to give the £2000.' *What*! Oh no, this is not from God, I thought. This can't be right. Maybe it's my emotions? I'm feeling sorry for them! 'This is more than a ten per cent tithe, Lord,' I was talking under my breath by now. 'Be reasonable, Father!' This giving business was completely foreign to me.

It was no good. However much I tried to reason with God and myself, by that afternoon I was in a terrible state. The deep inner peace had left me. I sought out Paul, the course leader, and told him.

'Are you sure?' he asked seriously.

'Yes,' I answered with conviction, 'but I don't want anyone on the course to know.'

The most incredible thing happened to me the minute I handed the cheque over. It is difficult to put into words but I just knew in my spirit that a victory had been won – not only for those two young people, but something far bigger for me and my future ministry. I felt God say, 'I will give you back something so much greater – you have opened a door for me.' Six years later God gave us at Happy Child a beautiful farm for the street children situated just outside the city of Belo Horizonte. And I just know deep down inside that it was the fruit of some of those first seeds I sowed, when in obedience I gave far more than I would have ever given in my own strength and selfishness.

> 'Once we have given ourselves to God, we understand that what we possess isn't really ours, but God's … All that we are given, all that we accumulate during our lifetime is to be dedicated not to the creation of a personal empire but to the advancing of his kingdom in this world.' Peter Maiden, International Director for Operation Mobilisation.

I recently read a true account of a Christian businessman who was travelling in Korea. While passing a field he saw a young man pulling a simple plough, helped by an old man who was holding the handles. The amused businessman took a picture of the scene. 'I suppose these people are very poor,' he said to the missionary who was showing them around. 'Yes,' was the humble reply, 'those two men happen to be Christians. When their church was being built, they were keen to give something toward it, but they didn't have any money. So they decided to sell their one and only ox and give the proceeds to the church. This spring they are pulling the plough themselves.'

The businessman was silent for a moment. Then he said, 'That must have been a real sacrifice.'

'They did not call it that,' answered the missionary. 'They thought themselves fortunate that they had an ox to sell.'

A friend of ours, who is a young and successful businessman in London, recently said to Joao and me that his greatest fear was that he wasn't giving enough. He happens to be one of the most generous people I know. He explained, 'The awful thing is that the more I give away the more I seem to make!' Malachi 3:10 says, ' "Bring the whole tithe into the storehouse, that there may be food in my house. Test me in this," says the Lord Almighty, "and see if I will not throw open the floodgates of heaven and pour out so much blessing that you will not have room enough for it." '

In his booklet *Money Talks* Tom Rees relates a conversation he had with one of New Zealand's most successful businessmen, Robert Laidlaw. Laidlaw described a notebook he had kept for many years. It had the following entries:

February 1st 1904
Aged 18 years six months, wages £1 per week. I decided to start giving one tenth to the Lord.

February 12th 1906
Before money gets a grip on my heart, by the grace of God, I enter into the following pledge with the Lord that:

I will give ten per cent of all I earn up to £......
If the Lord blesses me with £......I will give fifteen per cent of all I earn.
If the Lord blesses me with £......I will give twenty per cent of all I earn.
If the Lord blesses me with £......I will give twenty-five per cent of all I earn.
The Lord help me to keep this promise for Christ's sake; who gave all for me.

A later entry reads:

September 1910
Aged 25. I have decided to change the above graduated scale and start now giving 50 per cent of all my earnings.

Through his gift of giving and by following these principles, Robert Laidlaw made an incredible contribution to God's work around the world.

According to the Lord, having money can be dangerous. Jesus said it is hard for a rich man to enter the Kingdom of heaven, and he warned his disciples to watch out for the 'deceitfulness of riches'. In the book of Deuteronomy chapter six God warns his people, the Israelites, after he had blessed them with flourishing cities with vineyards and olive groves and houses filled with all kinds of good things, 'be careful that you do not forget the Lord'. Even if God can trust me and my character, he knows what I need – no more and no less – to fulfil his calling on my life.

'It's a bad sign when a community tries to structure itself to ensure total security for the future, when it has a lot of money in the bank. Gradually it will eliminate all possible risk. It will no longer need God's help. It will cease to be poor.' Jean Vanier, *Community and Growth*.[2]

CAN I ASK FOR SUPPORT?

My time living in the *favela* in Rio de Janeiro was a very precious time. I felt Jesus Christ's compassion as never before, his presence with me was almost tangible. I had no material goods apart from my rucksack. My Portuguese was minimal, and I knew no one when I first arrived. When the shooting started around midnight, as it did most nights, and I lay on the floor next to my bed to avoid any flying bullets, I experienced the truth of these words of Christ: 'For whoever wants to save his life will lose it, but whoever loses his life for me will find it' (Matt. 16:25). In that place I died to myself, and discovered the wonders of working with our living God, hearing his voice daily, seeing his miracles of provision and experiencing his powerful protection. But above all I discovered that the only thing I had been created to do was to be a vessel for him, so that those living in darkness could be touched by his living presence, his living love. Surely this is what Jesus did when he was here on earth? He didn't just talk, he acted. He demonstrated his compassion through healing, through sitting with the outcasts and sinners, breaking through every preconception that the 'religious' people stood for. Human 'religiosity' is everything that Jesus isn't. As his servants we must be willing to do what is foolish in the eyes of the world, so that the 'blind' might see.

During that time God told me that it was time to write to people, to communicate what I was doing. He told me that it was important, at that time, that I raise up prayer support. He would take care of my financial needs. I handwrote a newsletter, as I was nowhere near a typewriter (let alone a computer!), and together with some pictures, photocopied it and sent it to a handful of friends around the world. One day I received a letter from two people I had never met, enclosing a $100 note. Other gifts followed, and this continued during my time in the slum. At just the right time a letter would arrive with money inside, often from people I didn't know. Even when the opportunity came for me to travel to a conference in Paraguay for missionaries with YWAM in South America, God sent me just the right amount of money to buy a ticket to fly there. It was during this conference that I met my future husband, Joao Bosco de Carvalho.

Seven months after we met, Joao and I were married in England. It was 4 April 1992. After a week's honeymoon in Gustaad we travelled on to Einigen where we did a communication school for three months with Rudi and Elaine Lack. Almost a year before we met Joao had received a grant to do this course, for two people! During this communication course we both did a research project on how to rescue, rehabilitate, re-educate and reintegrate street children. Soon after the course, we left Youth With A Mission and travelled back to Belo Horizonte, where we founded Happy Child, working alongside the local church. In September 1993 we opened our first house, a day-care centre in the basement of the Baptist Central Church.

Today, six years on, we have a team of over fifty full-time workers. We all care for around seventy street boys and girls between the ages of six to fourteen years every day. A dedicated street team visits the kids in their various gangs every morning and some evenings during the week. The latest statistics from the local government say that around ninety per cent of children living on the streets are on crack (1999). They are used by the drug traffickers to deliver the drug to the client and are given crack as a form of payment. At the day-care centre, to which the boys and girls come straight from the streets, they take a shower, eat, play football, do handicrafts. The process of trying to take the street from their hearts begins. In our experience the power of the Holy Spirit has delivered many of the boys and girls from the habit of crack but there are also drug rehabilitation centres available in Belo Horizonte. From the day centre the boys that want to get off the streets go into a night shelter and the girls to a girls' house situated in the city centre. We have to separate the boys from the girls during the rehabilitation period because they are sexually active from the age of seven years on the streets. A 'family' team complete with a Christian psychologist and social assistant makes over forty-two visits a month attending to the needs of the families of the children in the *favelas* and helping them to restructure their lives. From the night shelter the boys who have been on the streets for a long time or who have come from badly abusive homes go on to our farm situated outside the city. In this God-given place the children work with the animals, play sport, help on the land and go to school. They are given back what the 'locusts have eaten'.

We minister the love of Jesus into these broken kids' lives – the rejection and betrayal they have suffered is too much for me to bear. However, Jesus can bear it and what is more he has the power to reach deep down into each of their hearts and heal the wounds, the hurts. The power of the Holy Spirit fills these beautiful children with supernatural rivers of living water, and their lives are transformed. Jesus brings meaning to living, his love is greater than life. Their testimonies continue to be powerful tools in the hands of our Lord. These children were once thrown into the gutters of the filthiest streets because there was nowhere else for them to be, because Satan is out to destroy the image of God in our lives. When they stand before you brimming with a new-found joy, it is your life that changes because it is a holy moment.

Happy Child receives monthly financial support from the local government, from Compassion International, The Samaritan Purse, the European Community, and from individuals who have a monthly covenant with us. However, this only covers forty per cent of our budget. We have to rely on faith for the remaining sixty per cent of the finances needed for the ministry to function. Up until now we have never had to close one of the houses.

Neither Joao nor I receive a salary from the ministry. We are supported by friends who feel called to do so by God. From the very beginning Joao and I received wise advice to keep our personal family money in a separate bank account to that of the ministry. This may sound obvious, but let me remind you of 1 Peter 5:8: 'Be self-controlled and alert. Your enemy the devil prowls around like a roaring lion looking for someone to devour.'

During the communication school that we did in Switzerland in April 1992, Rudi Lack gave a seminar on 'Asking for Meaningful Support'. During it he said the following: 'A ministry or mission is made up of many types of people doing many types of jobs. However, by far the largest group of people in a ministry are the financial supporters whose giving makes it possible for the team to devote their full time to that ministry. Why do these people give? Why do we sometimes feel funny about asking for support? How can we be sure that we are not just begging for money? How can we do a better job of involving our supporters in our ministry?'

Have you ever asked yourself these questions? I have. We are going to cover four key topics to help us find the answers.

(a) Money – how are we to use it?

Superficially money is merely paper and ink. However, the lust for money can destroy a marriage; it can ruin men and women's health as they sacrifice time with family and friends in its pursuit; it drives young people in cities around the world to traffic drugs, to steal and to kill; and it has been the cause of injustice, child pornography, corruption in government, and genocide.

> Money itself is not evil. 'For the love of money is a root of all kinds of evil.' 1 Timothy 6:10.

The paper with ink engravings represents the value of one person's work or product, which has been converted into a form by which it can be carried and traded for other goods and services that an individual needs. It was God himself who devised the system: 'By the sweat of your brow you will eat your food' (Gen. 3:19), and the logical extension of this is that money comes from God.

The main purpose or function of money is to provide for the needs of immediate family members. 'If anyone does not provide for his relatives, and especially for his immediate family, he has denied the faith and is worse than an unbeliever … But if we have food and clothing we will be content with that' (1 Tim. 5:8; 6:8). The purpose of extra money is to provide for the needs of others, especially Christians. 'Therefore, as we have opportunity, let us do good to all people, especially to . . . the family of believers' (Gal. 6:10).

The average family's ambition is to make as much money as it is spending! I know in my case it seemed to me that the more money I made, the more money I used to spend.

> The multimillionaire, John D. Rockefeller, was asked, 'How much money does it take a person to be really satisfied?' And he answered, 'Just a little bit more!'

Personally, I have found contentment since I have desired less, not more. The question Joao and I try to ask ourselves is: 'How much is enough for the needs of my family?' This is very much an individual matter, but it should be considered in the context of God's Word with our conscience as our guide, and we should do our best to evaluate clearly the attitudes and value systems of those around us.

As I see it there are five main ways in which we can gain money:

- work: we can earn an income through a job
- investments
- inheritance: we can inherit money
- donations from supporters
- miracles

(b) Following in the footsteps of our biblical heroes

It really helped me when I discovered that throughout history God has set apart his people to be involved in his ministry and because they were unable to involve themselves directly with earning an income, so they were supported by others. Look at these four examples from the Bible.

(i) Priest and Levites

The Lord said to Aaron, 'You will have no inheritance in their land, nor will you have any share among them;

70

I am your share and your inheritance among the Israelites. I give to the Levites all the tithes in Israel as their inheritance in return for the work that they do while serving at the Tent of Meeting.' (Num. 18:20–1)

(ii) Jesus and the disciples

After this, Jesus travelled about from one town and village to another, proclaiming the good news of the kingdom of God. The Twelve were with him, and also some women who had been cured of evil spirits and diseases: Mary (called Magdalene) from whom seven demons had come out; Joanna the wife of Chuza, the manager of Herod's household; Susanna; and many others. These women were helping to support them out of their own means. (Luke 8:1–3)

Jesus supported himself as a carpenter until he was thirty years old, and then he was supported by others.

(iii) The early church apostles, teachers and evangelists

This is my defence to those who sit in judgment on me. Don't we have the right to food and drink? Don't we have the right to take a believing wife along with us, as do the other apostles and the Lord's brothers and Cephas? Or is it only I and Barnabas who must work for a living?

Who serves as a soldier at his own expense? Who plants a vineyard and does not eat of its grapes? Who tends a flock and does not drink of the milk? Do I say this merely from a human point of view? Doesn't the Law say the same thing? For it is written in the Law of Moses: 'Do not muzzle an ox while it is treading out the grain.' Is it about oxen that God is concerned? Surely he says this for us, doesn't he? Yes, this was written for us, because when the ploughman ploughs and the thresher threshes, they ought to do so in the hope of sharing in the harvest. If we have sown spiritual seed among you, is it too much if we reap a material harvest from you? (1 Cor. 9:3–11)

(iv) Paul

Yet it was good of you to share in my troubles. Moreover, as you Philippians know, in the early days of your acquaintance with the gospel, when I set out from Macedonia, not one church shared with me in the matter of giving and receiving, except you only; for even when I was in Thessalonica you sent me aid again and again when I was in need. (Phil.4:14–16)

Just think, this tradition has been going on for two thousand years! You and I are privileged to follow in the footsteps of these great men and women of God. Have you ever thought of that before? We need to recognise that we are dependent on the Lord for our support, and not on any system. We also need to recognise that we follow a godly heritage of people who have been set apart by God and supported by his people.

(c) Giving

I think one of the saddest things today is that many Christians around the world measure God's blessing by material wealth. There is so much talk about 'prosperity'. Surely we are missing the point? Asking for personal prosperity is selfish, and selfishness does not come from God. God blessed Abraham so that he could bless others. If we receive the blessing and put it in our pocket, the blessing stops. 'Why have you stopped blessing us?' we ask God full of self-pity, thinking he's forgotten us. And God will answer us, 'Child, my blessing is not for your pocket: it is so that you can bless your brother, sister, city, country.'

Receive it and give it. Whatever blessing we have received, whether it is spiritual, material or psychological, we have received it in his name.

(i) God owns it all

'But who am I, and who are my people, that we should be able to give as generously as this? Everything comes from you, and we have given you only what comes from your hand' (1 Chron. 29:14).

When we receive a gift, how often do we take it from the outstretched hand without having even looked at the face of the giver – in all areas of our lives? God says, 'Who has a claim against me that I must pay? Everything under heaven belongs to me' (Job 41:11).

I remember during a Sunday morning service in a small village church in Surrey, the vicar announced at the end, 'While we sing the last hymn there will be a collection.' A little old lady sitting on my right promptly turned to me and whispered dryly, 'Why does God always want our money?'

'Maybe because it all belongs to him in the first place?' I suggested, trying to be helpful!

However, her comment made me think. Why? Because she was probably not the only person thinking that in the church that Sunday morning.

I know that I personally used to struggle with this issue. A scandal that had made international news headlines when I was a teenager didn't help matters much. The reports cited that a couple, who were well-known TV evangelists, had been embezzling millions of good people's money for their own interests. Greed had got the better of them. Human beings are weak and Satan is always on the prowl. Despite the fact that we all fall short of the glory of our heavenly Father, and I am only too conscious that it is only by his grace every day that I am saved and given a way out from temptations, we need to look straight to Jesus. There are so many of God's servants doing wonderful things around the world today in his name, reaching the lost, the broken and the sick. We need to seek the Lord's direction and obtain his peace before we give, and always aim to give to projects we feel confident about.

> The earth is the Lord's, and everything in it, the world, and all who live in it; for he founded it upon the seas and established it upon the waters (Ps. 24:1–2).

(ii) God wants everything used to the full

God wants us to use all that we own to its fullest potential here on earth as a contribution to the fulfilment of his purpose – that his glory and Kingdom are extended – rather than being used for our own personal gain.

'The Christian should never worry about tomorrow or give sparingly because of a possible future need. Only the present moment is ours to serve the Lord, and tomorrow may never come. Money is really worth no more than as it can be used to accomplish the Lord's work. Life is worth as much as it is spent for the Lord's service.' George Muller, the German missionary who founded many orphanages in England in the mid-nineteenth century.

Jesus told us, 'Do not store up for yourselves treasures on earth, where moth and rust destroy, and where thieves break in and steal. But store up for yourselves treasures in heaven, where moth and rust do not destroy and where thieves do not break in and steal' (Matt. 6:19–20). Let's stop loving things and using people, and start using things and loving people!

(iii) We look after it all

'The Lord God took the man and put him in the Garden of Eden to work it and take care of it' (Gen. 2:15). Along with the great privilege of looking after God's creation comes a great responsibility. It is as if we have been put in charge of a large household or estate and are encouraged to enjoy and make full use of all that is around us – but we must also ensure that we look after the property and care for it according to the owner's wishes! 'Be fruitful and increase in number; fill the earth and subdue it. Rule over the fish of the sea and the birds of the air and over every living creature that moves on the ground' (Gen. 1:28).

(iv) God is a giver by nature and he has created a giving universe

In Romans 8:32 we read: 'He who did not spare his own Son, but gave him up for us all – how will he not also, along with him, graciously give us all things?'

One of the first differences I noticed after asking Jesus into my life, was that I started to observe and appreciate nature around me as never before. It was as though my eyes had been opened. I could see God's beauty in his creation. What struck me most is the fact that everything is created to reproduce and multiply.

The world's approach is to acquire and amass. However, we should keep to God's way.

'Give to everyone who asks you, and if anyone takes what belongs to you, do not demand it back … Give, and it will be given to you. A good measure, pressed down, shaken together and running over, will be poured into your lap. For with the measure you use, it will be measured to you' (Luke 6:30, 38).

When Joao and I first moved to the farm in the early part of 1993, I was warned by a neighbour not to leave our clothes drying out on the line at night because wandering tramps were known to enter the farm and steal them. I remember thinking, 'Goodness, if they are that desperate, let them come down and take our clothes, even if some are for women!' The same person added that if we didn't put a lock on the doors to the then empty dormitories (there were no street children living on the farm at that time) these same tramps would help themselves to one of the unoccupied beds. Before I could stop myself I said, 'Well, I'm sure that won't be a problem, we've got fifty of them!'

(v) Give according to what God has, not according to what you think you have

In a film with Burt Reynolds there is a scene in which he is drowning. Burt says, 'Lord if you just get me to the shore I'll tithe ninety per cent of my income'! And the closer he gets to the shore he says, 'Eighty per cent, forty per cent, twenty per cent.' And when he almost gets there he says, 'Yes Lord, I'm going to give you one per cent!'

There are basically two types of giving: selective, logical

giving and supernatural, spirit-directed giving.

The first type of giving is based on what you can logically afford. 'I have five units, I need three units so I can give two units.' Supernatural, spirit-directed giving is based on God's specific direction to the giver, leading the individual to invest his or her resources to meet needs. This type of giving is based on some basic principles:

- God knows what we need (Matt.6:25–33)
- God will enable you to give what he leads you to give

> 'And God is able to make all grace abound to you, so that in all things at all times, having all that you need, you will abound in every good work.' 2 Corinthians 9:8.

As we read in Malachi 3:10 we cannot afford not to give!

As a family we tithe monthly to our church, to other missionaries, and/or as God directs us. A few months ago I felt God say that he wanted us to give an offering to a couple, whom we rarely saw together. The husband teaches Hebrew at a college in Belo Horizonte and earns very little. To support themselves they both teach English. I felt God say that he wanted them to use the offering on a romantic dinner for two! Not on a $5.99 pizza, but a smart restaurant with a three-course meal! I laughed with joy, because once again God was showing me his love for his people as a Father. He is more interested in our relationship with him than in what we do. So I thought to myself, 'OK, I'll give that amount to this couple but only if I meet them together.' Since they both work in different locations and it would be so unusual to see them together, that would be my confirmation. Guess what happened? That very afternoon I bumped into them both and I happened to have the exact money in my purse!

> 'If you can't take it with you when you die, send it on ahead! You invest it by giving it to the church which helps other people to get there!' J. John

As far as tithing and giving is concerned from the money we receive for Happy Child, twice God has asked us to give away all we had in the bank! Illogical? Completely! The first time was just after we had returned to Brazil from England around the end of 1992, having just got married. Joao and I had raised $12,000 towards the starting-up of the ministry we had on our hearts in Belo Horizonte. However, whilst on a trip to Rio de Janeiro – where we'd travelled to pick up several five hundred kilo boxes of second-hand clothes which had arrived by ship from England – we visited Wellington, the leader of the Youth With A Mission base where I had worked. That morning before we set off to the base Joao said to me, 'Sarah, I feel God is asking us to give away the $12,000 to YWAM Rio towards their future work with street children. At this stage of our ministry we need to sow all we've got.'

My heart sank. 'But Joao,' I tried to reason, 'we haven't even started Happy Child yet. What are we going to use if we give everything away now?'

'Don't worry, look to God,' replied Joao confidently. 'The Bible says "whoever sows generously will also reap generously" (2 Cor. 9:6). We need to sow, Sarah!'

The second time was in late 1996 when in two weeks

we would have to pay a lot of bills for the ministry. There was only the equivalent of around $300 in the ministry accounts. During a prayer meeting with all of our team members, Joao announced, 'This morning a brother informed me of a clinic in a poor village in Mozambique which is short of medications. I feel God telling us to give all we have left to them. I think it's time to sow!' Even though this did not make any sense in human terms, Joao's conviction was infectious and we all thanked the Lord in advance for what he was about to do. Sure enough, a week after we gave the offering to the clinic in Mozambique, donations started coming in again for Happy Child.

Since then we have reaped the fruit of this sowing many times over in the ministry, and not only in material ways. For me it was another living lesson, as I had to exercise my faith.

(vi) God's way of giving includes the promise of a return
Remember this: Whoever sows sparingly will also reap sparingly, and whoever sows generously will also reap generously ... Now he who supplies seed to the sower and bread for food will also increase your store of seed and will enlarge the harvest of your righteousness. You will be made rich in every way so that you can be generous on every occasion, and through us your generosity will result in thanksgiving to God. (2 Cor. 9:6,10–11)

Our friend Dan Duke, founder of A Call To The Nations, gave a talk based on the above passage that illustrated this truth so well. I'm sure that no one in that room that night will ever forget his words – they were simple but inspirational.

He said this: 'If you take a cob of corn and you eat all the corn on it you'll have nothing to show at the end of the day. However, if you eat half of the corn and plant the rest, in a few months' time each one of those tiny pieces of corn seed that you planted will produce a new plant. And on each plant you will find about four to six new cobs. Now you have a choice. You can either eat all the corn on those new cobs, or you can eat half of what you harvested, or even a third of what you harvested and plant the rest.'

He stopped for a few seconds and then, looking around at us all and laughing, he continued, 'Let me tell you something, my brothers and my sisters. If you continued with this process, in a few years' time you're going to have enough corn to feed a whole village in Mozambique for a year!'

'Honour the Lord with your wealth, with the firstfruits of all your crops; then your barns will be filled to overflowing, and your vats will brim over with new wine' (Prov. 3:9–10). Note that God rewards the giver so that he can give more. We should give so that we get, so that we can give more, so that we can get more, so that we can give more … If we stop this cycle on the get rather than the give, then God will bypass us and will look for others through whom he can pour his resources.

(vi) God wants his children to give cheerfully
'Each man should give what he has decided in his heart to give, not reluctantly or under compulsion, for God loves a cheerful giver' (2 Cor. 9:7). The Greek word which is translated as 'cheerful' in this verse is *hilaros*, from which we get the English word 'hilarious'. A hilarious giver is one who has discovered the truth of Acts 20:35: 'It is more blessed to give than to receive.'

Two major hindrances to hilarious giving are:

- Giving grudgingly
- Giving out of a sense of duty

These hindrances rob us of the realisation that giving is a natural expression of love and obedience to God.

Often people who possess only little in material terms have a wonderful gift of giving. Over the years in Brazil, we have received love and hospitality from a variety of people who have welcomed us into their homes and families. At the end of 1997 I went on a ten-day mission to Recife, a city in the north of Brazil, together with Caroline Taylor who co-ordinated teams and overseas missionaries for Happy Child from the UK. At the end of the ten days after speaking and ministering in five local churches and three ministries working with the poor, we were absolutely exhausted. Needless to say I was also pining for my husband and children! On our last evening we were invited to have dinner at a friend's house.

The invitation went like this: 'We are poor and live in very humble surroundings but we want to bless you with all that we have,' said Risalva. She had been working with us in Belo Horizonte for over a year and was visiting her elderly parents in Recife. From the moment we stepped into this family's home Caroline and I felt blessed to the depths of our boots! Risalva's mother had been preparing food since the previous night and the table in the kitchen was groaning with every kind of cake, pie, pastry, sandwich, flan and meat that you could think of. When we sat down they even produced a bottle of white wine! 'We know that in England you all enjoy a glass of wine with your dinner,' said her mother with a twinkle in her eye. 'I want you to know,' she continued, tears welling up in her eyes, 'how grateful we are for all that you are doing for these little lost ones. Thank you for coming here to Recife and speaking in our churches. We have no large offerings that we can give you but what we can give you is before you tonight and it comes from his heart as well as ours.'

(d) Trusting God to provide

Since working on the frontline, God has shown me that he can use a variety of ways to provide for his full-time workers.

It is important not to try to dictate to the Lord the means by which you will be supported. Some people are unable to bear the sacrifice of their own pride and rely on the gifts of others so they decide they will only minister if they can pay their own way. Others fall into the trap of spiritual pride, believing that the only way to do God's work is to have him tell people to give to them, without making their needs known. Still others rely too much on people – they look more to their contacts than to God. If he were to lead them to do otherwise, they would have trouble trusting him.

I believe there are times in our ministry and walk with God when he wants to remind us just who is in control and who is the provider. In these times he performs miracles: the exact money required is provided at just the right time without us communicating that particular need. On other occasions he asks us to communicate to others, because he wants people around the world to hear about the work and have the opportunity to participate. It is an opportunity for one nation to bless another. Here on earth we are Jesus's mouth as well as his hands and feet, and testimonies of what he is doing amongst prostitutes, the homeless, the lost and the sick in South America, North America, Canada, Asia, Africa, Europe, Russia,

China, and so on, transform other people's lives. In this way people are led to Christ. However, the glory must always go to our Lord, and it is key that we seek his will to decide whether we should act or not!

> 'Keep flexible and open to His guidance … He may lead you to make an investment. Or sell something you own. Obey Him. He may even bring a business opportunity your way. Something you produce in ministry may bring financial returns. Beware of any opportunities which divert you from your full-time calling. But don't rule out creative alternatives either, or try to force the Lord to provide for you in a certain way.' Loren Cunningham.

When Jesus and Peter needed money for taxes, he sent Peter fishing, telling him he would find a coin in a fish's mouth! (Matt. 17:27)

In late 1989 Joao was a missionary with Youth With A Mission. Together with his leader he spent two and a half months organising a big evangelistic campaign for New Year's Eve on Copacabana beach. During that time they contacted around eighty local churches, spoke on radio, in seminars, and made publicity brochures. Needless to say, when he returned to Belo Horizonte at the end of it, he was exhausted. His heart's desire was a holiday! Joao started to pray. Unexpectedly, he received a letter from friends in Switzerland, where he had a little while before taken a six-month TV and video production course. The letter was an invitation for him to go to Switzerland to stay with them for a month's holiday. And what's more, the invitation included an air ticket! For Joao this was a present direct from heaven above. Little time was wasted in accepting the kind invitation, and a few weeks later Joao climbed onto a bus at the main bus station in Belo and headed back to Rio, from where his flight to Switzerland was due to leave. He had no money in his pocket. It was an overnight journey and he arrived in Rio seven hours later at 6.00 a.m. With a few hours to kill, as his flight was departing that afternoon, he decided to go for a stroll around the city.

Joao eventually found himself window shopping in a glamorous part of Copacabana beach. The shops were full of all kinds of gifts made out of stunning semi-precious stones and giant turquoise butterflies, typical of Brazil. All at once a strong desire filled his heart. 'Lord,' he cried out in his spirit, 'I have nothing to take my kind friends in Switzerland. How I would love to bless them with some of these beautiful gifts, to show my gratitude for their love and hospitality towards me.' Immediately Joao heard that familiar gentle voice say in his thoughts, 'Joao, make a list of everything you want to buy.' In faith, and with nothing to lose, he spent a thoroughly enjoyable forty minutes visiting a handful of shops making a fine list with the aid of some very attentive shop assistants, all of whom he told he'd be back soon! Stepping out of the last shop he said in his thoughts, 'Now what, Lord?' Again he felt that gentle voice say 'Turn right and keep walking.' He did what he was told and reached a corner. Then, 'Turn right again and keep walking.' He followed the instructions. 'Now cross the road and go into the phone box straight ahead.' He did and was now one block from the beach. Once in the phone box Joao began to feel extremely silly and self-conscious. 'What am I doing?' he questioned himself in his thoughts. 'Is this me or is this really God?' He grabbed the phone and pretended to make a phone call.

Suddenly, he felt something growing under his right foot. His immediate reaction was declared out loud, 'Oh no, I've trodden in some dog mess!' Copacabana beach is a place where people walk their dogs and one does have to be on the alert. He lifted up his foot to have a look, and dropped the phone. There, before his eyes, was a pile of money, every large note was neatly stacked one on top of the other. There was no wallet. 'Oh my God,' Joao managed to say, 'what have you done?' He put the phone back on the receiver and waited. He pinched himself – what was really happening? Joao's heart started to beat faster. He waited to see if anyone came to claim the money. But no one did.

Without counting the money but with a grin that never left his face, Joao went back to each shop. After buying everything that he had noted on his list Joao had exactly enough money to buy some lunch and catch a bus to the airport, carrying a very bulging bag!

A few years later, after we were married, Joao took me to visit his friends, Daniel, Francoise and Muriel, while we were doing the communication school in Switzerland. During lunch together Daniel, a pastor, said movingly to us, 'Whenever I am having a bad day and my faith is affected I look at the beautiful book holders you gave me made out of semi-precious stones, and I remember the miracle, Joao.' Daniel's voice became full of emotion as he continued, 'It reminds me of his faithfulness and that he is real. My faith immediately grows and I feel encouraged.' Daniel had given up a good job and salary as vice-director of a large college in Switzerland to follow his calling.

Don't ever think, 'I can't do it! I can't afford it!' The issue is, 'What is the will of God?' – not what you have and what you don't have.

Sarah Thaine was working at a pharmacy in London. In 1995 she heard Amanda Williams speak about her work with families affected by HIV and AIDS in London and she decided to volunteer one afternoon a week. Soon after, she was having lunch with a doctor friend who out of the blue asked this question, 'If you won the lottery, would you give up your job at the pharmacy?' Without another thought Sarah answered, 'If I gave up my job I'd go and work for Grandmas!' She shocked herself with her answer because she didn't know this was in her heart. Later that day she heard that Grandmas was looking for a full-time worker; she decided that this wasn't a coincidence and she applied for the job. It meant a reduction in salary and she thought she was doing quite well just considering it! A couple of months later she discovered that she didn't get the post. By that time she had psyched herself out of her other job at the pharmacy and she gave in her notice. Then followed nine weeks out of work. During that time God gave Sarah a heart and a passion to work with Grandmas she had never had before. Finally one morning as she was lying in bed she felt God say, 'I want you to do the job without a salary.'

'My savings were running out by that time,' relates Sarah, 'and I needed to know fairly quickly if this was the right thing to do. So I said to God on a Monday morning, "Well, if this is what you want me to do give me ten confirmations." It was all very matter-of-fact but I stipulated that one of the confirmations had to be a gift of £100!' By the Friday she had received nine confirmations. But the £100 hadn't come in. 'I was praying with a friend,' continues Sarah, 'and I showed her one of the verses that God had given me that week. It was talking about the Israelites and how they tested and tried God and it made him angry. At that point I realised that the £100 had been my stipulation and that God had been very generous in allowing so many confirmations. I couldn't put my conditions on it. So I threw my arms up in the air and said, "Well let's go for it." I phoned Grandmas and started as a full-time worker.' Sarah has not looked back since.

There is no question that when God speaks to us he will always take into consideration what we already have in our possession. Before Jesus performed a miracle and fed five thousand people, the little boy had voluntarily to give over his lunch of two fishes and five loaves of bread. When we started Happy Child in September 1993 we had the basement of the Baptist Central Church as a location for the day-care centre, and a handful of workers. However, we did not have money to function. After prayer we decided to take a step of faith and announced that we would open the doors the following Monday. God had five days to act! The very next day, the director of Compassion International Brazil, Dercy Goncalves, drove down our drive on the farm and offered us $2,250 a month to start.

When Elijah was hungry, God told him to go to one woman, who was also desperately in need, to ask her directly for help (see 1 Kings 17:7–24).

Mother Teresa said, 'I have not begged from the time we started the work. But we go to the people – the Hindus, the Mohammedans, and the Christians – and I tell them: "I have come to give you a chance to do something beautiful for God." And the people, they want to do something beautiful for God, and they come forward.' David Aikman, *Great Souls.*[3]

Joao and I lived on the farm owned by Happy Child for almost four years with our two small sons. Then as the ministry started to grow and with it our responsibilities, we were counselled by our pastors to leave the farm and live in the city in an apartment where we would have more privacy and therefore a place to rest and 'switch off'. It would also provide us with a clearer perspective on all future developments within the ministry – living on the farm made it difficult to supervise the whole set up. Whilst living on the farm our personal financial needs were minimal. We didn't have to pay rent, taxes, electricity and water bills. We spent very little on food because we generally ate the food on the farm with the boys and the team. As soon as we made the decision to move we knew that our personal needs would soar. However, we were convinced that this was God's will for us, both as leaders of Happy Child and as a family. During prayer I felt God say three things. First, he impressed on me that I should take over the responsibility of administrating our family finance and the payment of personal bills as Joao had enough on his plate with the ministry's needs. Second, he asked me to make a budget and, third, I felt I was to communicate our move to the city as a family and our new family budget for the coming year only to certain friends and people who had demonstrated a burden for us as a family over the previous years. This I did in obedience and in faith.

I started to look for apartments while Joao was on his first trip to Mozambique. The day after he returned we both went into the city to look at two. We never got as far as the second apartment, and a month later we had moved to the city. However, we still did not have enough money coming in every month to pay for the rent. I kept praying, and the more I prayed the more peace I felt. One evening the phone rang with news that a couple, whom we had never met personally, wanted to pay for the rent of the apartment; however they wanted to remain anonymous! Joao and I were so happy, it was such confirmation that we had made the right move. We really felt God's love and care for us as a family.

THE TOP TEN KEY POINTS

☐ The key is to obey. A lack of obedience destroys faith.

☐ Uncomfortable situations that arrive through lack of money can just as definitely be from God as the ready provision of money.

☐ Faith is trusting that God's character will never change. It is believing that something will happen before it happens.

☐ Once we have given ourselves to God, we understand that what we possess isn't really ours, but God's (1 Chron. 29:14).

☐ ' "Bring the whole tithe into the storehouse, that there may be food in my house. Test me in this," says the Lord Almighty, "and see if I will not throw open the floodgates of heaven and pour out so much blessing that you will not have room enough for it" ' (Mal. 3:10).

☐ Money itself is not evil. 'For the love of money is a root of all kinds of evil' (1 Tim. 6:10).

☐ There are five main ways in which we can gain an income – through an income-generating job; investments; inheritance; donations from supporters; miracles. Jesus supported himself as a carpenter until he was thirty years old, and then he was supported by others.

☐ Don't try to dictate to the Lord the means by which you will be supported. Some of us are unable to bear the sacrifice of their pride and rely on the gifts of others. Others fall into the trap of spiritual pride, believing that the only way to do God's work is to have him tell people to give to them, without making their needs known. Others rely too much on people – they look more to their contacts than to God.

❑ Don't ever think: 'I can't do it!' or 'I can't afford it!' The issue is: 'What is the will of God?' – not what you have and what you don't have.

❑ Remember God pays for what he wants, not for what you want.

4

I'm standing 'on the riverbank'. How can *I* help?

Every three or four months we send out a newsletter that goes to around three hundred and fifty people all around the world. In it we share news of what is happening in Happy Child, as well as a family update. Many of the people who receive this newsletter are committed to praying for the ministry and have formed prayer groups to pray regularly for us. These people are our partners. They are 'on the riverbank' for us, and they are a very important part of what we are doing. The work we do here is spiritual. As we take these children out from the gutters where they are being destroyed by Satan and give them a new beginning in Jesus, you can visualise the battle that goes on in the middle. Jesus said, 'The thief [Satan] comes only to steal and kill and destroy; I have come that they may have life, and have it to the full' (John 10:10).

Ezekiel describes God's longing, 'I looked for a man among them who would build up the wall and stand before me in the gap on behalf of the land so that I would not have to destroy it, but I found none' (Ezek. 22:30). Our prayer 'warriors' are called by God to stand in the gap for Happy Child and for us as a family. They really are our lifelines in times of trouble, as Joao and I experienced when we went through the 'deepest darkest valley' yet of our ministry (described in chapter 10 – 'The refiner's fire'). In the thick of the storm they respond to our cries for help, and get on their knees and pray. They reach out to the supernatural world in the name of Jesus pushing back the powers of darkness, and releasing God's perfect will at that time. Then we see the results in the natural.

Maybe you are an intercessor for your church leaders, or for a missionary or ministry in your own country or abroad. I have had the pleasure of attending the meetings of many groups of intercessors, both as a participant and as a speaker, and people have told me so often how much blessed they are as a result. Very close friendships form through the bond of prayer.

I have asked three of our many loyal intercessors to share with you their experiences on the 'riverbank':

CAROL SALTER

For the past four years, it has been my privilege and joy to meet monthly with four other women to pray for Happy Child. Each time we meet, we are updated with the latest prayer needs which Sarah and Joao fax to us. Month by month, we have been thrilled to learn of prayers answered. In fact, *The Street Children of Brazil* itself could be our prayer diary.

We have known God's presence with us; the Holy Spirit has inspired us, given us zeal for Happy Child, and verses and pictures. God has worked through us, using first one, then another, to pray for his purposes. It's dynamic!

As if this were not enough, however, God has wonderfully knit us together so that we can share anything on our hearts and pray for each other and our families. In fact, most of our prayer times have started with an unburdening of our hearts and prayer for immediate concerns. This has in no way detracted from our prayer for Happy Child but rather the reverse.

I vividly recall our meeting on 3 February 1997. We were praying for the safe delivery of Sarah's third child when – lo and behold! – the phone rang. It was Sarah to announce the birth of Jessica Joy! Another time, when Sarah was with us, my daughter was ten days overdue for the birth of her baby; if the baby didn't arrive within the next few days, she faced an induced birth. Sarah prayed that the baby would come of its own accord – and so she did, praise God!

Just this morning two of us arrived with burdens. One lady had just heard that her father in Zimbabwe was very sick. She had to decide whether to go there to see him, and needed to hear from the Lord. We prayed together and believe that she will know what to do. I, too, was concerned because our son and daughter-in-law had not returned from a skiing holiday in the Alps (there had been a series of avalanches reported in the news, and we had heard nothing). My husband and I had been praying for them, and the Lord had given us perfect peace. As I walked into the prayer meeting, my eye caught sight of the verses from Philippians 4, 'do not be anxious about anything' (which were hanging on the wall). God's peace is truly 'beyond understanding', otherwise how could I be so calm? Later in the morning, my husband called to say that they had arrived back safely.

Our times of prayer for Happy Child are to me the

very best, the most exciting and encouraging. When we agreed to pray, our paramount concern was (and is) for Happy Child, but little did we know how very blessed we would be. God has blessed us abundantly, and given us immeasurably more than we could ask for or imagine.

DIANA BEDDING

Four years ago I spent six months working with Happy Child in Brazil. It was at this time that I came to understand fully the importance of prayer as I recognised a need to rely on God in every situation. This developed a practice of prayer, which surpassed any experience of relying on God I had had in my own culture. On returning to England I knew that God had placed a calling within me which I can only describe as a strong link inside me between myself and Happy Child which has not altered with time. It has taken time to know how to respond to what God has placed in me as there is often an immediate assumption that prayer is everyone's responsibility and that a 'real' role when supporting a ministry is a practical one. Over time I have understood this not to be the case and now appreciate that though everyone is called to pray, not everyone will carry a consistent burden. My heart is for the workers who lead the children to Christ both through prayer and their practical daily example of his love.

The insight gained through working in Brazil, in relation to the day to day grass root struggles, has been invaluable in helping me to pray for the ministry and those working within it. This experience has left me absolutely assured of the power, potential and necessity of prayer within individual lives and the life of the ministry. Prayer has not only stretched my faith, allowing me to see God's glory, but it has also left me in no doubt as to the spiritual battle which surrounds any work of God.

During the development of my prayer life, God has taught me that the fundamental base of effective prayer is a vulnerable and honest relationship with him, which is based on his Word. It is essential to recognise the enemy's attempts to draw you into self-recrimination, pride, guilt, hopelessness or self-pity in order to hear God effectively and not to give up.

Praying for the ministry, and those involved in it, has been affected through regular corporate prayer meetings and individual contact with those working out there. Through this I have been privileged to witness wonderful answers to prayer, which have increased my personal faith. Seeing God act in the minute and the magnificent serves to fuel my worship, my hope in him, and my knowledge of his authority over all things.

FENELLA BRISCOE

We can't all go but we can all pray. To support those on the mission field in prayer gives us a much wider vision of God at work today. Being involved in praying for frontline mission is so exciting because we see direct answers to our prayers in such wonderful ways. It's a real privilege and I would encourage every Christian to get involved in mission prayer.

ADMINISTRATION SUPPORT – OUR PARTNERS

Since we have been working in Brazil several people, notably Caroline Taylor, Fiona Saunderson, William and Flora Saxby and Julie Jarman, have faithfully applied themselves to serving God by meeting our administration needs in the UK. This involves a wide range of functions:

- Preparing our newsletter, which goes out three or four times a year to approximately 350 people (privately funded).
- Updating and reviewing our database.
- Answering letters and enquiries from people interested in knowing more about Happy Child or perhaps interested in working with us, and sending out brochures/leaflets; putting people on the mailing list.
- Mailing forms and reference forms to people wanting to work both short term and long term with us; interviewing and selecting.
- Mailing forms and reference forms as well as further information to people wanting to do our yearly three-month training course for workers (April–June); interviewing and selecting.
- Generating and communicating awareness of the ministry in churches, schools, home groups and so on.

As you can see this type of support from home is invaluable.

I invited William and Flora to share with you their experiences from the 'riverbank':

'In 1995 we spent six months in Brazil working for Happy Child. When we returned to "ordinary life", we soon came to realise – and in fact believe it even more strongly now – that the support provided (from the back line so to speak) is critical to the success of the frontline work.

'The analogy of war is a useful one to illustrate missionary work overseas, and how we see our role. History is littered with examples of armies that were defeated because they could not effectively resource their troops at the front. Their supply lines had become over-extended – munitions, food, money, reinforcements, medical and other supplies could not reach the soldiers – ultimately the army was defeated. Similarly a missionary effort cannot last long without effective supply lines and actually apart from munitions (which could be prayer) the resources required are the same as those for an army – money, food, expertise, medicines.

'We have come to realise that our contribution (small though it is) is to support the missionary workers out in Brazil. Specifically we pray for and give financially to the work. We have also been able to visit the project and encourage friends who work there. We are also involved in the day-to-day administration of the UK charity side of the mission. There are many other people involved in the back up and one of the great privileges for us has been to see how key men and women (in this case the trustees of the charity) can provide strategic vision and advice for the leaders out in Brazil. It sometimes feels more humdrum compared to the frontline work, but the spiritual battle is no less real and we need to be mindful to pray just as we would if we were about to go onto the streets. We also see that gifts that we take for granted – financial acumen, administration and so on – are truly God-given talents that we can (and he does) use for the benefit of the Kingdom.

'The main tension is that in reality the division between a back line and a frontline is not so clear.

Working with street kids in Brazil you fight poverty and oppression and the evil is stark. In the West one fights materialism, unbelief, apathy and the constant pressure of time that threaten to choke the life of Christ within you. God's ways get squeezed out – there are too many other important things to do! We have found that being able to keep in touch with our friends in Brazil (e-mail has been a real blessing to us) and get them to pray for us or give their perspective on life has been a real help. In this way, we help carry each other's loads and hold the rope for each other.'

HOW DO I FIND THESE PARTNERS?

If you are looking for people to support you personally, both in prayer and financially, ask God to show you whom he is calling into partnership in your ministry. Remember they are not donors. You are offering them the privilege of partnering you in God's ministry, and they will be able to sow into the Kingdom of God and see something grow. It is God's desire to restore relationships, first between us and him, and then between us and each other. When we rely on others for financial and prayer support in order to do God's work a strong link is forged between the giver and the receiver. The giver may never even visit the ministry or country where the missionary is working, but their hearts will be linked. He or she will grow closer to what God is doing around the world, and relationships will be strengthened.

People often ask me whether it's OK to receive money from unbelievers. Here are a selection of opinions I respect:

> • 'When considering whom to contact, don't automatically rule out people who are not born again Christians. Of course, you should be especially sensitive in how you present yourself and your work, and pray carefully for the Lord to help you. But if it is true that when someone gives his treasure, his heart gradually goes with his treasure, then an unbeliever can be brought closer to the Kingdom of God as he gives to God's work.' Loren Cunningham, *Daring to Live on the Edge.*[1]
>
> • 'We will not ask unbelievers for money although we will accept their contributions if they offer them of their own accord. (See Acts 28:2–10.)' George Muller in his autobiography.
>
> • 'Money is amoral. However, it is important to know the source of the money first, i.e. whether it is from prostitution, gambling, or stolen, and so on, before accepting it.' Pastor Marcio Valadao from the largest church in Belo Horizonte with over 10,000 members.

Have you ever felt confused as to whether you are asking or begging? If you have had the go ahead from God to communicate your needs, here are three reasons which might explain why you are still feeling uncomfortable asking:

- a poor self-image, you do not feel worthy
- you're not sure where you are going
- asking is beyond your comfort zone; you feel more comfortable giving than receiving – this is pride.

Ricardo was one of our first team members when we founded Happy Child in 1993. He had worked with Youth With A Mission for many years before joining us, and had a calling to go to Russia to work with street children there. After a year and a half with Happy Child he met and married Rachel, who is English, and after a time of preparation they both left to go to St Petersburg. (I tell more of Ricardo's and Rachel's story in chapter 7, pp. 166–9).

However, before leaving for Russia, Ricardo set out to raise the support they would both need there. After making his list of needs with a budget, he worked out that the two of them would need over $1,000 a month to live on; this included renting an apartment, food, lessons in the Russian language, transport, health insurance and so on. He decided to set himself the challenge of finding thirty people (as many people as there are days in a month) who could commit themselves to giving the equivalent of $35 a month. After six months of speaking in churches and thereafter to individuals in those churches who came forward showing an interest in supporting them, as well as to friends and family, Ricardo achieved his challenge. Once in Russia, Ricardo and Rachel sent a newsletter every two months to each of those thirty partners as well as others. Without fail his hand-written and Xeroxed letters arrived in our homes keeping us in touch with all that was going on in St Petersburg and in their ministry. When they returned to Brazil less than two years later they both diligently went to visit each of those partners in their homes with photos and presents for everyone. They had dinner with Joao and me at the end of their visit and needless to say they were exhausted, but it had been a great encouragement for them.

Ricardo told us, 'Some of our friends want to increase their giving. We are already tithing to a couple of missionaries who work with us in Russia, however there are others in our team who receive very little and this means that we can bless them too.' Thirty people who might never get to St Petersburg, Russia, are involved with what God is doing there with the street children through the lives of Ricardo and Rachel.

The checklist for a winning newsletter:

- Is it easy to read? Does the opening sentence grab the reader's interest? Is the letter too long or too short?
- Does it make the reader feel important as a partner and not as a donor?
- Have you acknowledged your partners, involved them and educated them with what has been happening? Does it offer solutions, hope and change?
- Have you written with enthusiasm? Have you talked about your activities and your involvement with the ministry?
- If you have been going through a difficult time and want to share that, then make sure you are focusing on what God has been doing in your life. Steer clear of the 'self-pity' zone, otherwise the reader will go down with you!
- Remind yourself, 'My ministry is valid.'
- Give statistics, i.e. if you are working with children in Mozambique, Africa, communicate that there are around 300,000 war orphans living on the streets.
- Are your prayer requests clear? Have you told them about the answer to their prayers from the previous letter? Share about the victories following the tests.
- Share about the miracles.
- Are the future projects for the ministry explained? Are your future plans clear?

- Is what you say credible and true in the letter?
- If God has said 'ask', have you actually clearly asked for a contribution? Does the reader know exactly how much money you need? Is the need personal or for the ministry? If there is an urgency, does the reader understand that he/she must move quickly? Have you suggested that they pray and ask for direction and peace from God first, before giving?
- A picture is a thousand words, a bad picture is a thousand bad words!
- Have you ministered to their lives?
- Always remember to put your contact address and if necessary your bank details.

WHY DO OTHERS RECEIVE AND I DON'T?

If you ever find yourself asking this question, then here is another important checklist for you:

- Do I have the right motivation? (see Matt. 6:19 and 1 Tim. 6:10); holiness – is my life right before God? (see 1 Pet. 1:13–25); humility (see Jas. 4:10); purity of heart? (see 1 John 1:7)
- Am I seeking God and his Kingdom? Am I walking in his will for my life? (Look at Jer. 9:23–4; Matt. 6:33; John 17:3; Ps. 37:3–5.)
- What about my attitude to those who have authority in my life? Am I submissive and respectful? Am I being critical and speaking badly about them? Do I always pray for them and always bless them? (See Jas. 4:11,12; Heb. 10:19–25; Rom. 13:1–7.) Do I have a wrong attitude towards my parents? (See Eph. 6:1–3.)
- Am I generous and faithful – a sower? Am I tithing

and giving offerings to God with joy? (Mal. 3:10,11) Do I owe anyone money? (Rom. 13:7)

- Am I sowing in good soil? (Acts 20:35) Cain's offering was rejected by God because his attitude was wrong!
- Have I claimed the promises of God? Have I made a list and a budget? Am I sharing my needs with others? (Jas. 4:2,3; Rom. 12:13)
- Have I taken authority, in the name of Jesus Christ, against the enemy? (Jas. 4:7)

Remember, God pays for what he wants, not for what you want!

A word of warning Don't judge others, their house, apartment, furniture, car, clothes and so on. They may have had to go through many fiery tests to get where they are. Be careful not to judge God's anointed. God has to break us in order to work through us. 'The greater the work in us, the greater the work through us.' In the same way that we break the bread to remember what Jesus did for us, this is what he will do with us. In those refining times we must try and interpret what he is doing and not become negative and critical of situations or others around us. Otherwise we will miss the point completely and he will only have to take us through it again in some other way. Why does God refine us? Because he loves us and he needs to show us what is in our hearts.

Whatever happens, God will always take care of us. If we are his workers on the frontline he will always provide for us at the right time. As I have already mentioned, when I first came to Brazil in 1991, I shared a room with eight other girls at YWAM in Belo Horizonte. My only piece of furniture was a bunk bed. It was a time in my life when I needed to be broken, and I was thirty years old! Then I moved to Rio de Janeiro where I lived in the middle of a *favela* – God put me there so that I could let go of all my comforts and identify with the people he'd called me to reach. Then after Joao and I returned to Brazil, after our wedding at the end of 1992, to set up Happy Child, we both lived in a borrowed run-down out-house on a friend's property. After six months we moved to our farm outside Belo Horizonte. When we eventually moved from the farm to the city as a family, I had been living for nearly six years in community and Joao had lived there for twelve years. God has his ways and his timing.

It is important to add that when we have a need God doesn't always answer by giving us the money to buy it. In the ministry we regularly receive donations in the form of food, clothing and blankets. Doctors and dentists give their time free to attend the children and their families.

Dora, who has worked with Happy Child for the last five years, tells the story of how she was once needing toiletries: shampoo, toothpaste, face cream, deodorant, sanitary towels. She asked the Lord to supply her with the money she needed to buy all these things, but her prayer was answered in a different way. 'I was working at the farm at the time,' Dora explained. 'One Saturday a few people came to visit the children for the day. There was one girl I remember because she was shy and hardly spoke a word all the time she was with us. However, two days later I received a phone call saying that that particular girl had been praying and felt God tell her to give me a gift!' Dora laughed as she continued, 'I couldn't believe my eyes when I eventually received it a few days later. I was handed a large holdall and when I opened it I found every kind of toiletry you could imagine, even things I hadn't thought of. God is our Father, he really is!'

THE TOP TEN KEY POINTS

❑ 'I looked for a man among them who would build up the wall and stand before me in the gap on behalf of the land so that I would not have to destroy it, but I found none' (Ezek. 22:30). God is looking for people to say, 'Here I am'! Don't miss out.

❑ If you are on the 'riverbank' then you are 'partners' to God's work and his workers. You are part of his wider vision.

❑ Administration support for those on the mission field are people 'at home' who assume the responsibility of: sending out newsletters; updating and reviewing the mailing list; answering letters and enquiries; interviewing and selecting people wanting to work; communicating and promoting awareness of that particular ministry on your behalf, and so on.

❑ Communication through newsletters, fax, phone or e-mail must be kept open constantly with your supporters, and vice versa.

❑ When we support God's work and his workers both at home or abroad nothing can hold back his blessings in return.

❑ If you give into God's work you will be closer to what he is doing around the world, and your relationships will be strengthened.

❑ Intercession will stretch your faith.

❑ We can't all go, but we can all pray.

❑ Ask God to show you the people who are called into 'partnership' in your ministry. When writing a news-

letter remind yourself, 'My ministry is valid'.
❏ If you have felt confused as to whether you are asking
or begging, then perhaps you're not sure where you
are going.

5

Undoing Satan's work. What is my part in this?

Please pray with me before we start this chapter:

> Sovereign Lord, Glorious Father, I declare your great-
> ness; I declare your goodness; I declare your faith-
> fulness. I declare that you are my Sovereign and that
> you are Sovereign of this occasion. I thank you for the
> total and complete victory which once and for all Jesus
> won over Satan and all his subordinates. Now, in the
> authority of the Lord Jesus, I forbid any presence or
> activity of the enemy of any sort, direct or indirect,
> and indeed of anything that would get in the way of
> what you want to achieve. Come, Holy Spirit, take
> control of me. Direct this study, illumine my mind, so
> that this time may contribute to your Kingdom and
> your glory. Thank you in Jesus's name. Amen.

The children we rescue through Happy Child have only
ever known trauma. With a few exceptions, their whole

life has been one bad scene. They have many problems, often ones which are demonically produced. As a ministry we come against these demonically produced problems over the children/teenagers' lives, as well as those of their broken family members' lives, in the name of Jesus. This is a spiritual ministry. We can give the children a home, food, schooling, training, friendship and so on, but there is a powerful spiritual dimension that needs to be dealt with if they are going to be free to have a new chance in life and become whole as human beings. From what I have seen with my own eyes over the last nine years, it is only Jesus Christ who can do this. He gives us and the team the calling, the love and the strength to achieve it physically and emotionally, but he also gives us the authority to set them free. It is Jesus who breaks the lies, rejection, hatred, anger, and abuse in these desperate but precious lives, and then fills them with his Holy Spirit of love, joy, peace and wholeness. It's powerful. It's beautiful. It's victorious. This is God's glory.

THE SPIRITUAL BATTLE

In order to walk in the victory that is ours, we need to understand our place in Christ.

Dr Wilbur Pickering has a Master's degree in theology and a PhD in linguistics. He served with Wycliffe Bible Translators for thirty-eight years and later founded and ran the Advanced School of Missions in Brasilia. He, his wife and two daughters lived with a tribe in the Amazon jungle for almost ten years. He wrote an alphabet for their language so that he could start to translate the New Testament for them.

Dr Pickering says that, in his four years of theological study, not once was the important issue raised of the need to bind Satan. 'During our first two years in the Amazon while I learned their language and culture we were clobbered,' recounts Wilbur. 'We made an excellent floor rag! We were attacked in our bodies and our minds. The Indians were being attacked, they were being kicked around. I did not know how to show that Jesus was stronger than the demons. Before telling them, I should have been showing them. I failed.'

Wilbur continued, 'The Indians practise a form of spiritism. They all have to make peace with the demons to pacify them, through rituals and so on. The cold hard fact is that the Indians are persecuted by the evil spirits. What they do is purely logical: if you are being kicked around by a bully, what do you do? You try and be nice to the bully, to keep him happy, especially if you don't have a "big brother" around to protect you. They do not know of any greater benevolent power to help them. They did not have a concept of a superior being, a creator, and even if they did they had no idea of how to make contact with him to get help. They don't like the bully. Brazil is riddled with spiritism. This is not mere superstition. They are just waiting for someone to arrive and tell them there is a big brother.'

We often assume that the plan of redemption was the reason why Jesus came to this earth. Well, that was part of it, but only part of it. The full picture is revealed in Hebrews 2:14: 'since the children [that's us] have flesh and blood, he too shared in their humanity so that by his death he might destroy him who holds [or in the Greek *had*] the power of death – that is the devil.' Jesus had to conquer Satan (and destroy him) in order to make the plan of redemption possible.

The big problem lay back in the Garden, where the first man, Adam, had been commissioned by the creator to administer this earth. When Adam decided to act on the basis of Satan's word instead of on the basis of God's word, he turned the administration of this world over to Satan. Whether or not he understood the consequences of what he did, that's what happened. Humanity fell. This is to say we lost our innocence, we became rebels against God, and as a consequence we have to live with a world controlled by the enemy.

This mistake of Adam's could not simply be put right by future generations. The sinful nature that became part of his very being has been passed on to each of us: it is like a genetic inheritance. In the same way that we inherit the physical characteristics or personality of our parents, so too the sinful nature in the seed of Adam has been passed on to every one of his natural descendants. It has given Satan a hold over our lives and there is nothing, in our own strength, that we have been able to do about it.

That's why the virgin birth was a necessity. Jesus could not have a human father, because the seed of the man was already bad from the beginning. He was born perfect, he was born free of the seed of Adam – without sin.

The first Adam was born into a perfect world, only he blew it. Jesus ('the last Adam' – see 1 Cor. 15:45) came into a bad world, a world that was already controlled by the enemy. These were the circumstances in which he had to win through. Jesus was certainly God but he didn't live as God on this earth, he lived as a human being subject to the Holy Spirit. Although he was God it was as a human being that he won over Satan. It is a mystery to us that Jesus could be God and man all at the same time. It is one of the mysteries of the Christian faith, which we can't explain. That is what the sacred text says and either we accept it or we don't. I do.

God the Son, the creator, came to recover what the first Adam lost. In order to do that he had to win over

Satan on Satan's own turf, his own pitch, so to speak. If the Lord Jesus had committed any sin before he got to the cross, we would all be lost without a hope. The wages of sin is death. If Jesus had sinned on his own account he would have had to pay for his own sin and therefore he would not have been able to pay for ours. By living in Satan's world and going to the cross a sinless human being, he recovered all that the first Adam had lost.

Ephesians 2:6 declares: 'And God raised us up with Christ and seated us with him in the heavenly realms in Christ Jesus.' This is talking about *us*. If we are in Christ we are also seated at the Father's right hand, far above all principality, power and might, **which is why we can undo Satan's work.** We have that power!

WHY DO WE STILL HAVE TO FIGHT?

Jesus said, 'As the Father has sent me, I am sending you' (John 20:21). The Father sent the Son to destroy Satan and undo his works. Jesus is now sending us, and here we come to the crux of the issue. Although Satan has been well and truly defeated and a lake of fire has been prepared as a resting place for him and his angels, for his own reasons for his own sovereign purposes, which he has not chosen to explain, the Creator still allows Satan and his angels to operate in this world. We know where they are going, they know where they are going – we just don't know when they are going to get there (they may know more about that than we do).

So the victory is assured. Yet for his own reasons God still allows Satan and his angels to operate in this world. It seems clear that they are only permitted to work within certain limits. If Satan could do anything and everything he jolly well pleases he would certainly have killed me when I was living in the *favela* of Borel in Rio de Janeiro eight years ago (Phil. 1:21–6), and I'm still here. The problem is that the Bible does not tell us where those limits are and therefore we cannot presume upon them. We have to do just what it says in 1 Peter 5:8 and be eternally vigilant because our enemy like a lion is just pacing around us waiting to gobble us up.

So it is not our job to defeat Satan. That has already been done. What we have to do – and this is what I have been building up to – **is undo the work of Satan in this world.** Jesus said, 'As the Father sent me, I am sending you.'

In our societies we are totally surrounded by Satan's works. In Brazil the social situation is truly desperate: crime is rampant and getting worse. Corruption is widespread and getting worse – Brazil does not have to take lessons from anybody anywhere on the subject of corruption. Moral corruption is also prevalent, dominating the television, magazines – the media. The soap operas are even beginning to feature incest. If there happens to be a virgin somewhere in the plot she apologises to everyone for being a virgin.

We are surrounded by the works of Satan in our society, not to mention our own homes and our own lives. We are obliged to live in the middle of this society, our children are obliged to grow up in the middle of this society, and so are our grandchildren, and it's not nice.

So we need to ask whose fault this is, because it would be great to change it. I say the fault lies with the Church: it's *our* fault. For centuries the Church has lost its understanding of why we are here. We are here to undo Satan's works, 'to proclaim freedom for the captives and release from darkness for the prisoners'. But instead, we have allowed Satan to take control of society from the outside in. Satan is at work in the schools, the Government, the media, the streets, the public squares, everywhere.

I am sure that is why God is anointing the interdenominational 'Alpha Course' with such power across the world. The Alpha Course is a fifteen-session practical introduction to the Christian faith designed primarily for non-churchgoers and new Christians. It has been created to serve all denominations, traditions and backgrounds. Devised and developed by Sandy Millar, Nicky Gumbel and their team at Holy Trinity Brompton in London, this competent and popular course is now being run in over 5,500 churches throughout the United Kingdom, in over 135 penal institutions and in more than 96 countries. It has been used to lead hundreds and thousands of people around the world to Jesus. Why is it so popular? It's not the message that has changed but the way the message is presented and packaged, giving it an appeal to those who have been put off church through tradition and religiosity over the years. It has been brilliantly reproduced into books and videos that make the course ideal for others to emulate and run in their own churches and house groups. I did the Alpha course in 1989 and it changed my life forever.

THE SINGLE MOST IMPORTANT THING WE CAN DO TO UNDO SATAN'S WORK

In Acts 26 Paul is defending himself before King Agrippa. Paul tells the King of how Jesus appeared to him from heaven to give him his missionary commission.

Then I asked, 'Who are you, Lord?'
'I am Jesus, whom you are persecuting,' the Lord replied. 'Now get up and stand on your feet. I have appeared to you to appoint you as a servant and as a witness of what you have seen of me and what I will

show you. I will rescue you from your own people and from the Gentiles. I am sending you to them to open their eyes and turn them from darkness to light, and from the power of Satan to God, *so that* they may receive forgiveness of sins and a place among those who are sanctified by faith in me.' (Acts 26:15–18, my emphasis)

Jesus's words make it clear that before someone can be saved someone else has to do something about the power of Satan over their life. 'So that' indicates a consequence, and so there must be a prior condition. The Lord Jesus is saying that Paul has to start by opening people's eyes which must mean that, up until that point, they have been blind.

Down through the ages we have been sending out missionaries to take the light of the gospel to 'blind' people. Now what good does light do to someone who is blind? A blind person can't see the light. The fact that the Lord came back from heaven to say this to Paul probably shows that it is significant! We have been sending out missionaries carrying light but many have not known how to open eyes. This is a problem. When you do that you don't get very many results.

Now the Lord Jesus said the same thing, though not in so many words, when he was still on earth. In Mark 3:27 we see Jesus casting out demons and this was not something the Jews, the scribes and the leaders were accustomed to. They did not wish to acknowledge him as the Messiah, and therefore they had to come up with an explanation about how it was happening. So they said that he was casting out the demons by the power of Beelzebub, the prince of demons. Now in his answer the Lord Jesus doesn't waste time with 'Beelzebub' – he calls him Satan, which is the enemy's proper name as well we know. He asks how can Satan cast out Satan? In verse 27 Jesus says, 'no one can enter a [Greek text says 'the'] strong man's house and carry off his possessions unless he first ties up the strong man [or binds him]. *Then* he can rob his house.' This is exactly the same truth that Jesus came back from heaven to tell Paul.

The 'strong man' is Satan (Jesus has just been talking about him in this context), so Jesus is saying you can't plunder Satan's house without first binding him. What are Satan's goods? What are we going to steal out of his house? Now I take it that this refers to human beings who are under Satan's control. As a matter of fact there are really only two houses in this world: either God's house or Satan's house. There is no neutral ground. Jesus said, 'He who is not with me is against me, and he who does not gather with me, scatters' (Luke 11:23). That makes it fairly clear!

So I judge that we have to take people out of Satan's house. But Jesus says that in order to swipe Satan's goods you have to bind him first!

HOW DO WE BIND SATAN?

Jesus does not tell us specifically how to 'tie up the strong man'. James commands us, 'Resist the devil' (Jas. 4:7) but does not tell us how. We are told by Paul that 'the weapons we fight with ... have divine power to demolish strongholds' (2 Cor. 10:4) but we are not told in detail how to use them. Our challenge is to find out by holding onto Scripture, by doing, by trying. In this way we are more dependent on God.

To bind Satan is to stop him from doing something before he does it. It is an offensive procedure as opposed to a defensive one. We stop the enemy before he acts. It is a more superior way of going about it. The best defence is a good offence! If you can keep the enemy dodging he can't stop and organise himself for a counter attack.

'Spiritual warfare is learning to recognise the strategies of the devil, refusing to co-operate with him and cutting him off in the name of Jesus Christ. What would I do to me if I were the devil? Recognise the strategies by knowing the nature of the devil, "the devil comes to kill, steal and destroy" (John 10:10).' Dean Sherman, author of *Spiritual Warfare for Every Christian*.[1]

My own strategy is (out loud or in my spirit) to affirm my place in Christ at the Father's right hand, and therefore far above all principality, power and might. That's my power base, that is where I am coming from. Ephesians 1:20–1 says that Jesus is at the Father's right hand and Ephesians 2:6 says that we are there too. Then I forbid the enemy to attack a given person or situation (as I prayed at the beginning of this chapter). We can isolate an area and declare it off limits. We don't know how long our prayers will continue to be effective for – I guess that's why we need to pray constantly! What I do understand is that we have to be specific. After every time of intercession, for instance, in a group or on my own, I always forbid any retaliation from the enemy against me, my husband, my marriage, my children, our health, our finances, our ministry, our families, our relationships and the will of God through our lives. I am always specific.

If you are going to get onto the frontline and try to advance the frontiers of the Kingdom you will inevitably find yourself vulnerable to attack. This is why you need to understand fully your place of victory in Christ. But as Nicky Gumbel points out in his book, *Questions of Life*, in the chapter on 'How to Resist Evil': 'God and Satan are *not* equal and opposite powers. God is the Creator, Satan is part of creation, but he is already fallen (Isa. 14:12–15). Next to God he is small, and when Jesus returns, Satan will be utterly wiped out.'[2]

> 'Think the thoughts of the Bible, agree with the thoughts of God. That is spiritual warfare.' Dean Sherman.

WHY DO I NEED TO PUT ON THE ARMOUR OF GOD?

God is looking for an army. He is looking for warriors. He is calling us. And we have the wonderful gift of his armour to protect us from our enemy!

> The armour of God is Jesus.

When I was living in the *favela* in Rio de Janeiro, I had my first taste of what it means to be 'light in the darkness'. During my first few days there I remember one morning I was taking a shower under the cold water pipe in our tiny bathroom when suddenly I heard God's gentle voice saying in my thoughts, 'Sarah, put on my armour.' Now I had never done this before. However, I had read Ephesians 6, and all at once, then and there, the words that are written in verses 10 to 17 came back into my mind. So out loud, haltingly, I said, in no particular order, the following prayer; 'In the name of Jesus I put the helmet of salvation on my head, submitting all my thoughts, imagination and desires under the Lordship of Jesus Christ; and I put on the breastplate of righteousness over my chest, submitting my heart and emotions at the feet of Jesus; and then (I was really getting into the swing of it by now with a new authority in my voice!) I take the sword of the Spirit in my right hand and the shield of faith in my left to ward off the fiery darts of the enemy. And I place the belt of truth firmly around my waist, and finally the shoes of the gospel on my feet, that wherever I walk I will be walking in the footsteps of Jesus. Amen.'

Thereafter, if I've forgotten to pray this prayer, even as I am walking out of my door in the morning, I feel an inner nudge: 'Sarah, put on the armour of God!'

'Dressing for success is a reality as well in the spiritual realm, and it involves putting on the whole armour of God. In fact, that's the only way to dress for success in the Lord, because the whole armour of God is a prerequisite to taking the kingdom of God by force, winning the race and withstanding the enemy in evil days. Each piece of armour is nothing more than a manifestation of the Lord Jesus Christ – and the character traits manifested by Him, which were a reflection of the character of God Himself – as our defence and our offence while we live out our lives in this world. We're talking about a way of releasing the character of Jesus Christ so that the One who is on the inside of us can be manifest on the outside of us.' Larry Lea, author of *Weapons of Your Warfare*.[3]

The Bible says that we need to be strong, because we wrestle. Strength and perseverance are needed, not just knowledge. Fighting in the spiritual realm works in the same way as fighting in a physical battle in the army: if you get hit by the enemy and retreat or back up you'll get hit again, but if you resist the enemy, you'll send him flying. Don't believe that if you get into spiritual warfare bad things will happen to you. Jesus is with you. You just simply need to forbid any retaliation from the enemy in the name of Jesus. The sacred text says, 'He who is in you is greater than he who is in the world.' Amen! When you have the power of God in your life, when you have Jesus ruling and reigning on the throne of your heart, then he who is in you *is* greater than he who is in the world. Decide today that you will seek first the Kingdom of God and that you will experience the fullness of his righteousness, peace and joy in your life. Say out loud, 'Devil, I won't be defeated. I will experience the Kingdom of God. I will resist you with all that I have and all that I am.'

Remember that God is omnipresent – everywhere at the same time – and the devil is limited in time and space. God is omnipotent – he does whatever he wants to do. But the devil is not all-powerful. He must operate under the rules set out for him by Someone who has everything under his control. The devil can only operate within the parameters that God allows him.

CONFRONTING SATAN ON THE FRONTLINE

God is raising up his army. He is waiting for us to say, 'Lord, let me be a great warrior in the army you're raising up today!' Much of the war round us may not be visible but it is no less real. It happens behind locked doors: abuse of all kinds; drunkenness; anger; hatred; deceit; perversion;

broken relationships; raped emotion. Remember that the blood of Jesus has already broken the power of the devil and is a force in this universe available to every child of God for deliverance and salvation from every situation, circumstance or sin. The devil cannot penetrate the blood of Jesus. Claim the blood of Jesus over your entire being, over your spouse and children, over your work and over your church.

Dora went out with our first team to Mozambique after completing our training course at the end of 1997. In total nine people went to help Heidi and Rolland Baker's ministry, 'Arco-Iris', which takes care of over 250 war orphans and street children near the capital of Maputo. Dora explains what happened: 'After five years of working with Happy Child in Brazil I thought I'd learned a thing or two about spiritual warfare. However, during my first week in Mozambique, I didn't sleep for one whole week. I would toss and turn, read and try to pray. An anxiety and fear came over me that I'd never experienced before. Eventually I was so exhausted that I could not participate in the team's activities during the day. I became desperate, even my prayers during those wakeful hours, seemed empty and powerless. Nevertheless, every day I would remember to put on "the armour of God".

'One morning, feeling dazed after another long night, I crawled onto the sofa in the sitting room in the house where we were staying, and sat down. The others came and joined me. Suddenly, without any explanation the air-conditioning metal box that was fixed inside the wall directly above me shot out and landed right on my head. It was about two feet by one and a half feet in size and extremely heavy. Everyone screamed and ran to my rescue, it took two of them to lift it off me.

'However, believe it or not, I felt no pain. There were

no cuts or bruises and I didn't even have a headache. All at once I just knew that something supernatural had taken place. The "helmet of salvation" that I had put on my head in the authority of Jesus Christ had protected me from what I believe was a spiritual attack and could have left me in hospital for some days. There is no other explanation.'

Nevertheless, after seven days of not sleeping Dora was beside herself with exhaustion and despair. Finally she sent an e-mail to one of our prayer groups in England with a plea for help. The group met up the following day to pray, and sent her very encouraging verses that same afternoon. For the first night since she had arrived in Mozambique, Dora slept blissfully! And the very next day she was able to participate in the team's activities with the children.

But all was not over yet. At the end of her second week a few of the team went to visit an enormous dump site, the size of a football pitch, where hundreds gather to eat the remains of the litter from the city. Pure misery and poverty at its worst. What she saw was horrendous.

Dora recalls, 'When I saw human beings brought to that level I just couldn't believe it. Hundreds of people of all ages filthy, starving, eating the litter, babies with mosquitoes feeding off their mouths. The stench made me want to retch. Then, all at once that same anxiety from my first week in Africa returned. I felt an oppression come over me as never before, an invisible evil presence. I stepped back from the others and said out loud in desperation, "Jesus, have mercy on me!" I wasn't coping with what I was seeing or feeling. It was as though God was miles away. The sense of evil fell heavy around me like a thick blanket. Satan was at my side and I felt him say, "You are in my house"!

'Inside me I started to cry out to the Lord, and all at

once I opened my mouth and started to speak in a different language in melodic tones. Suddenly I felt my spirit being lifted on this volume of supernatural worship and it was as though space opened up all around me. Suddenly, I knew deep in my innermost being that God had sent his angels – they now surrounded me. The evil left, it couldn't stay. Suddenly, I felt the Lord saying in my spirit with his gentle authority, "Confess my sacred Word." Stepping back further from the others I cried out loud: "I can do everything through him who gives me strength" (Phil. 4:13); "They overcame him by the blood of the Lamb and by the word of their testimony; they did not love their lives so much as to shrink from death" (Rev. 12:11). As I confessed these words with my mouth the presence of the Holy Spirit filled me and seemed to wash my weary spirit, lifting the fear and the anxiety. Eventually I felt led to intercede for the rest of the team who had started to hand out bread to the starving inhabitants of that miserable place.'

Iara was another member of the team which went to the litter dump that day. She too had felt a terrible oppression fall upon her. That night she started to bleed, and she bled for a straight twenty-eight days! Eventually she became bedridden, too exhausted and weak to even walk. Desperate, Iara tried on a number of occasions to e-mail her church in Sao Paulo, Brazil to ask for prayer, but curiously the e-mails kept returning to her 'undelivered'. She persisted, however, and finally she got one through. Her whole church interceded for her that same night. The very next day the bleeding stopped.

These two accounts show us how vital our prayer groups and intercessors are if God's work is going to be extended on the frontline. They give a vivid illustration of the link and partnership between those 'on the riverbank' holding the line for the people in 'the dangerous waters'.

Just to lighten things up a bit let me tell you a story from Joao's Youth With A Mission days. Apparently one after-noon a few missionaries went to make some visits in a nearby *favela*. In a humble, one-roomed hut, a young man started to pray for the family who lived there when all at once a woman fell to the floor and started wriggling and groaning. The young man started to rebuke the demon saying, 'Satan, leave this woman in the name of Jesus!' As he spoke these words he put his right arm high up above his head gesturing with his index finger. However, his finger went straight into an exposed light socket which was dangling precariously down on two wires, and he gave himself a sharp electric shock! 'Ouch,' he cried out. 'You can leave me too!' he added, laughing, and clutching his hand.

THE TRUE POWER OF PRAYER

At the end of *The Street Children of Brazil* I wrote that we were halfway towards completing the purchase of our farm from the Lagoinha Baptist Church in Belo Horizonte. We eventually agreed to pay the remaining $136,000 ($6,000 for furniture and phone line) in three instalments: $50,000 dollars in May, $40,000 in August and $46,000 in November 1996. In February 1996 we received another donation from a family in Singapore who had already given so generously towards the buying of the farm. With a note saying, 'We hope that this money will help Happy Child to buy the farm, we are praying for you', this family put another $50,000 into our bank account. This secured the first instalment due in May.

However, by the due date of the second instalment we

only had $10,000 in our bank account, money that some local churches in Belo Horizonte had donated. The Lagoinha church started to put pressure on us because they were building a new temple and had bills to pay. The whole ministry got on their knees. In the middle of all this Joao was leaving for a three-week trip to Mozambique with Mark Hester.

'What shall I do?' I asked Joao feeling desperate. 'You can't leave me here alone with all this pressure.'

'Sarah, don't worry. God is in control,' Joao answered in a matter-of-fact tone of voice.

Two days after he left for Africa I got a phone call from Marcia, Joao's assistant.

'Sarah, I had this strange dream last night and I felt I had to share it with you.'

'Go on,' I answered intrigued. Marcia wasn't one to have dreams and visions.

'Well, in the dream, all of the workers and the children were marching around the farm buildings praying and singing. Like Joshua and the city of Jericho!'

'How extraordinary,' I managed to say.

'I don't know what you think. But I believe this is all linked to the buying of the farm,' added Marcia.

Suddenly I knew without a doubt that God was indeed in this. 'Let's all do it! We've got nothing to lose. The Bible says that the ways of God are not our ways. And he got his people to do some surprising things in the Old Testament!'

So that very night we all gathered in front of the large white farmhouse. It was a clear warm night and the sky was full of millions of glittering stars that seemed to hang just above our heads. I explained about Marcia's dream and that I felt it was from God. He was going to do something powerful, supernatural. Opening the Bible at the book of Joshua chapter six, someone started reading about Jericho's walls falling down all those thousands of years ago. Well, we didn't want the buildings to fall down, that was for sure! But just maybe something was going to be released in the spiritual realm. 'I will give you the keys of the kingdom of heaven; whatever you bind on earth will be bound in heaven, and whatever you loose on earth will be loosed in heaven' (Matt. 16:19).

We decided that we would take our example from Joshua and we would march around the farm buildings seven times, alternating between praying and claiming the farm in the name of Jesus for his work with these children, and praising the Lord. The Bible says that God inhabits the praises of his people (Ps. 22:3). The angels are present too whenever praise is expressed, whenever someone cries, 'Holy, holy, holy is the Lord.' He sends them to be 'ministering servants' on our behalf. (Heb. 1:14).

Off we set, and let me tell you we really were a bunch of amateurs. Our singing was flat and our marching was not in a straight line. Most of the boys thought it was extremely funny. Well, I must say, if I'd been a fly on the wall I would have been highly perplexed and amused. We finished our seventh circuit and said good night to one another. 'Oh well,' I said to God as I walked down the hill to our little family house on the farm, 'make the best of what we did, if you can!'

Thereafter followed the most exhausting night I can remember. I had nightmares and felt a heavy oppression in my bedroom, greater than I had ever known before. I am not one to remember my dreams either – and this night I had two! One was of an evil character whom I saw inside the farmhouse. She told me that the farm was hers and that she wasn't leaving. The other was of a menacing character selling fish! (Joao's vision is one day to operate a fish farm as a way of using the land and producing a source of income for the ministry.) He also told me that the farm was his and he wasn't going.

The next morning I crawled out of bed exhausted and called for an emergency prayer meeting with all the leaders in the ministry. By 2.00 p.m. that same afternoon we were all together on the farm. I explained to them the dreams I had had that night. 'Whatever we did last night, however ridiculous it seemed to our own human eyes, has stirred things up in the spiritual realm. Let's have a time of worship together first and let's ask God to show us anything in our own hearts that we may need to set right first between one another and him – there must be unity amongst us if God is going to achieve his purpose today. We'll ask for the Holy Spirit to direct this time of inter- cession. Remember it is Jesus through us – the Bible says that he has the authority on earth and in heaven. We cannot fight this battle in our own flesh.'

What happened over the next hour and a half is some- thing which no one in that meeting will ever forget. As we began to pray I sensed we were keeping an appointment with God. The Holy Spirit fell upon us, and the atmo- sphere was permeated by an invisible presence that seemed to settle like dew. It was as though we were all at once lifted to a new level of communion with the Lord. Sud- denly, certain people in the room started to pray out loud, one after the other, with words and an authority that could come from no other source but God himself. It was spiritual warfare, and Jesus was right there with us. Through us he broke the hold and rebuked the plans that Satan had to stop the will of God taking place on that farm in the future. After an hour or so we all felt a tremendous release, as if we had come out into the light at the end of a tunnel. A sense of peace came into the room which was almost tangible. For us all it was a sign that a victory had been won. In the spiritual realm the issue was settled. After the meeting I felt God wanted us to repeat the march on two further occasions.

The first took place early the next morning at 7.00 a.m., and we decided to fast also. Many of the boys and some of the workers did not look very convinced. This time, however, we were better organised. Ingrid, who was our worship leader and taught music to the children, led the march playing her guitar with some of the boys behind her playing their recorders. Then I walked behind them with Anderson (leader of the street team) walking behind me, and so on. Dora walked at the very back. There were about forty of us in all. Before we set off, I prayed and God gave me a prophecy. I spoke it out in faith: 'I feel God is saying that after this march he is going to release some money. God is going to do something tremendous.' 'Amen,' said a few of them. Looking around I could see that many were still not convinced.

We set off, singing as we marched, the boys playing their recorders. It still wasn't the most animated of events, but we did it. *Then* something amazing happened. As we approached the front door of the farmhouse after our seventh circuit, the telephone started to ring. Someone ran in to answer it. 'Sarah, it's for you!' I went in to attend the phone call. What I heard was spine tingling. 'Hold on a minute!' I said to the person on the other end of the phone. I ran to the front door where everyone was still recovering and I shouted, '*Gente* [folk], listen up. You are not going to believe it! Someone has put $23,000 into the account!'

'Hurrah! Hurrah!' cried everyone, jumping up and down.

'Let's do it again,' said one of the boys, now fully animated.

'Yes, let's do it again,' shouted the boys with joy, their hunger forgotten.

'I think we should have a time of thanks and praise to God, this is fantastic!' said little Juarez with his gorgeous smile.

Everyone entered the house as I ran back to the phone to thank my patiently waiting caller.

What a time of celebration! It was fantastic just to see the faces of all those precious boys, overwhelmed with excitement, and yet with awe. They had been part of a miracle. They had seen God move with their own eyes. But before we'd finished celebrating the phone rang again. Two women had felt called to give $5,500 towards the farm! Well you can imagine the atmosphere when I announced this next piece of news to the exuberant crowd. It became electric – God was having a wonderful time!

These offerings made a total of $28,500. Adding the $10,000 that we already had in the account meant that we were only missing $1,500 to make the $40,000. 'O Lord,' I pleaded in my thoughts, 'please finish what you've started.'

That night as I was getting ready to go to bed the phone rang. It was Silvia. Apart from being a good friend, she is a psychologist who has been doing family therapy with the children for two years. She had no idea what had been happening that day. 'Sarah,' started Silvia, 'Luis [her husband] and I were talking tonight over dinner and we would like to give an offering of $1,500 towards the buying of the farm. It isn't much but we hope it will help.'

I burst out laughing. 'Silvia, let me tell you what happened today …'

The next day Marcia was able to call Pastor Marcio at

the Lagoinha Baptist Church with the news.

Oh by the way, we did the third march a week later. It was the most joyful and enthusiastic march imaginable. And by October, a whole month before we were due to pay the final instalment, Happy Child had already received the remaining $46,000. The farm was ours.

We have such a faithful God – that is who he is, and he can't change. In a world where we are so used to relying on what is visible and rational to our own human eyes and intellect, but is in reality so often unreliable, he is asking us to rely on what is invisible and beyond our understanding, but truly reliable because it is eternal. I am learning that it is best just to obey even if it doesn't make a whole lot of sense at the time. His ways really are not our ways.

THE TOP TEN KEY POINTS

☐ God needs 'warriors'.

☐ 'The reason the Son of God appeared was to destroy the devil's work' (1 John 3:8b).

☐ Only two perfect men have ever walked on earth: the first Adam was created perfect, placed in a perfect environment, but he blew it; the second Adam was born perfect, but lived in an imperfect world.

☐ The virgin birth wasn't just a good idea, it was a necessity! Every human being has his father's blood, never his mother's blood. The seed of man is already contaminated because of the sin factor. That's why the Holy Spirit had to furnish Jesus with the genes which the father would have normally furnished. Jesus had divine blood in him.

☐ By living in Satan's world and going to the cross a sinless human being, he recovered all that the first

Adam had lost. If Jesus had committed any sin he would have had to pay for his own sin and therefore could not pay for ours!

❑ It is no longer our job to defeat Satan; Jesus has already defeated him. What we have to do is undo Satan's work.

❑ God and Satan are not equal powers. God is the Creator, Satan is part of creation but he is already fallen (Isa. 14:12–14).

❑ 'The god of this age has blinded the minds of unbelievers, so that they cannot see the light of the gospel of the glory of Christ, who is the image of God' (2 Cor. 4:4). To bind Satan is to stop him from doing something before he does it.

❑ The 'armour' of God is Jesus.

❑ Think the thoughts of the Bible, agree with the thoughts of God – that is spiritual warfare.

6

A new culture, a whole new way of life – *help!*

A NEW LANGUAGE!

I remember that night as if it were yesterday. It was 23 April 1991, almost three weeks into my first experience of living and working in a foreign country, with the triple challenge of a new language, a new culture, and living in a community! There I was, participating in a worship meeting at the Restoration House for street boys at Youth With A Mission in Belo Horizonte, Brazil. Everyone around me was singing away. Strange words. Strange sounds. Strange people. It was all so alien. The words of each song were projected up onto the wall in front of me, but I didn't understand their meaning. How on earth was I supposed to worship God in double Dutch?

All at once a lump came into my throat and I closed my eyes, trying to fight back the tears for the third time since arriving in Brazil. 'Oh Lord,' I cried out from somewhere deep within, 'how am I supposed to worship you, how am I supposed to begin? I feel so useless, so frustrated. Help me!' Suddenly a verse jumped into my mind as if from nowhere: 'Psalm 137:4.' With nothing to lose, I turned around and picked up my small English Bible from my seat and flicked through the pages trying to find the verse. Reading it, I sank back into my chair and caught my breath. I had never previously seen this verse: 'How can we sing the songs of the Lord, while in a foreign land?' Almost immediately another verse popped into my mind: 'Psalm 21:6.' I read; 'Surely you have granted him eternal blessings and made him glad with the joy of your presence.'

Laughing and crying all at the same time, I knelt then and there, once again awed by the magnitude of God's grace. His love for me at that precise moment was beyond my dreams. Through these verses he was saying to me that he was right there with me. He knew the very pain and anguish I was feeling on the inside, he knew my very thoughts! God understood that I wanted to worship him in my own tongue, however what he was saying to me was that his presence was sufficient for me. He'd led me to Brazil and he was going to be with me every tiny step of the way – what a Father!

I confess that learning a new language at the age of thirty was a very humbling experience. At birth I was not blessed with the gift of learning languages and had struggled with French at school. However, there was no way I could fool myself and suggest that maybe God didn't want me to learn Portuguese! If he'd called me to Brazil, then the culture and the language were very much a part of that calling. I prayed and I prayed that he would give me the ability to learn without getting too frustrated with myself. Pride was my real enemy. I frequently felt as though I were two-and-a-half years old again as I floundered with the most elementary words. Then one morning I seemed to hear God speaking to me: 'Sarah, stop saying you are frustrated. This curses your efforts. Be positive and be patient.'

The minute I stopped 'cursing' myself, learning Portuguese took on a new lease of life. During the first three months, my level of understanding grew a lot better than my level of speaking. I took a few lessons during that time, bought a book on verbs and tried to discipline myself Mondays to Fridays to study for an hour daily. Every week there seemed to be a new word or verb that stood out: one of the first words that I remember learning was *pode*, pronounced 'podge', which comes from the verb *poder*, meaning 'to be able to'. Everyone seemed to be saying *pode* ('can I?' or 'you can!') to each other, alternating their tone of voice to form it as a question or a confirmation.

After three months I found myself longing to be immersed into the language, to be surrounded only by Brazilians. Having completed the 'Rescue and Restoration' course for working with street children with Youth With A Mission in Belo Horizonte, I had to admit to myself that being with other English speakers had not helped my progress with the Portuguese language. Somehow there were just too many other challenges during that time. But lo and behold, I soon found myself living in the *favela* in Rio de Janeiro, where the only person who spoke English to me was God! Like it or not I had to open my mouth and speak, making as many mistakes as I did, and bury all pride and self-esteem. The greatest challenge, however, was praying out loud in Portuguese with the rest of my small team, who were all Brazilians. This was really hard because prayers are so intimate, and in a foreign tongue, speaking very few words, I felt vulnerable and unable to express my true inner thoughts. Fortunately the Brazilians are a warm, open and sensitive people, and my inhibitions evaporated quickly.

To be honest, during my first year in Brazil the Portuguese I learned came from my little friends on the streets and in the *favela*. The children were so patient with me and somehow never made me feel foolish when I blundered. Their desire to understand me, and the love of God that they felt, seemed to override any language barriers. One of my concerns at that early stage had been, how on earth could God use me to reach street children if I couldn't speak to them? Yet as I started to go out onto the streets, under the viaducts and the not so desirable places of the cities, I learned that just by being there, holding them, smiling and praying, a powerful but un-spoken message was getting across. I discovered the beauty of relying on the Holy Spirit as never before.

After six months I found that the standard of my speaking was catching up with that of my understanding. I think it's a little like walking up a flight of steps: no sooner do you successfully master one step – feeling all chuffed and confident that you can at least hold a conver-sation or answer the telephone when it rings – than you realise there is another step beckoning you onwards with the challenge of a new set of vocabulary and a new conju-gation of verbs waiting to be conquered.

Just as I was congratulating myself on the excellence of my progress, however, I met Joao and my little balloon popped and deflated. I was feeling so pleased with myself, convinced that I was pretty fluent after only a year. Then he announced with a smile, 'Sarah, your Portuguese is the language of the streets. Did no one correct you?' I had to admit no one had. Maybe they were afraid to insult me, bless them! So after we married in England and returned to Brazil following a six months' absence, I had to start the whole painful process again. Only this time my husband was my teacher and he let little slip by, let me tell you! But the humiliation I sometimes experienced was unquestionably good for me in the long run, and made me aware of just how self-conscious I could be! These days, I find myself thinking and dreaming in my adopted language!

My friend Charlotte Richards, who now works for Horizons, experienced what I consider a miracle when she was struggling with Portuguese. She relates what happened: 'I left England in 1992 with only a short time to get ready. With some help I had begun to say "Bom Dia" (Good morning), "Boa Noite" (Goodnight) and "Meu nome e Charlotte" (My name is Charlotte) in Portuguese. The Youth With A Mission discipleship training course was in English and included homework and chores, but as we were in Brazil, I was slowly able to add simple phrases like asking for a cup of coffee, and telling the time and so on. However, after two months I was having a quiet time one morning when I thought the Lord said: "Pray that you learn Portuguese." So my little prayer group came together and prayed that for me. I did no studying, but literally two days later, Portuguese started flowing out of my mouth quite miraculously! The Brazilians around me said, "You're really speaking Portuguese!" I wasn't fluent, but suddenly I was able to say so much of what I wanted to say. A month later I became one of the translators when we split into smaller teams on outreach, and very shortly after that I was preaching in Portuguese! I still speak fluent Portuguese, and I give glory to God for this wonderful gift.'

Of course there are always the laughs that lighten the load. The word *coco* in Portuguese can be pronounced in two different ways with the help of some accents over the 'o's making a closed or open sound. One pronunciation means 'coconut' and the other means 'poo'! Jessica Davies, who worked with us for two years, tells with great humour what can happen when the wrong 'o' sound is applied!

'One really cold morning I was getting the boys up for school on the farm,' explains Jessica. 'Dona Maria, the cook, was making hot porridge with fresh coconut for breakfast and I thought I'd coax the kids out of bed with the prospect of it. So, I announced in a loud voice: "Vamos meñinos, Dona Maria fez mingau de coco para nos!" ("Hurry up, boys, Dona Maria's made porridge with poo for us!") They all shrieked and roared with laughter!'

A NEW CULTURE!

Learning to understand and respect the culture of the place in which you are called to serve is as important as learning language of a new country. We can offend people so easily without realising it, and can ourselves be offended, which is why forgiveness is vital.

Here are some cross-cultural puzzles:

- Should I give up things that are considered OK in my English Christian culture, such as drinking alcohol, but not in the culture in which I am working?
- Should I behave in a way that is appropriate to this culture, e.g. men holding hands with men walking down the street, and women holding hands with women, but not OK in my own?
- What about working in a society where the women don't wear tops? Shall I decide to do likewise, and, if I do, am I being very unhelpful to the male missionaries on my team?! (cf. 1 Cor. 9:23)

In some missions and ministries there is a rule that single men and women should not mix together, either at work or socially, unless a married couple is around. Singles can find this very trying, especially if they only want to have a relaxing evening together in a restaurant – but the problem is that otherwise the locals will think they're up to something! And what about a man and woman who might want to form a relationship? In a West African village situation that is simply impossible since in that culture all marriages are arranged.

Other difficult questions are:

- If the local culture/religion, or a certain family, doesn't want me preaching the gospel should I assume that that is the Lord closing the door, or should I persevere?
- How shall I deal with my money? It doesn't seem very much, but it would be a fortune to a local person. Should I eat local food and should I live in a mud hut, like everyone else, or should I live in a brick house that is more than most people can afford locally (yet it still lets in the creepy crawlies and retains the baking heat of the day!)? Would it be OK to live somewhere that is more comfortable, enabling me to sleep at night, so that I can give of my best during the day?
- Do I have to submit to the theology of the missionaries that have been here longer than me, who insist that women cannot be in leadership, and that I should cover my head whenever I pray?
- What about a day off? The local missionaries insist that Sunday is the Lord's Day, and although I seem to work better on Sunday than any other day, they feel that taking any other day off is inappropriate.

In some cultures the time factor is all important. Others focus on events. Brazil is event-orientated, and I come from a country that is time-orientated! With these opposing emphases, the shocks on a human level are inevitable. However with God's love, with his grace and with his calling, we can die to our own natural way of doing things. It is so easy to become critical, but adapting to the new culture requires a conscious decision. What's the point of criticising? I only end up even more frustrated. Anyway, is it Christlike to criticise? No, it is pride. I'm saying through my critical comments, even when spoken in jest, that my culture is better than theirs.

> And they sang a new song: 'You are worthy to take the scroll and to open its seals, because you were slain, and with your blood you purchased men for God from every tribe and language and people and nation.' Revelation 5:9.

God has called me to reach out with his love to a people group in another land and I must try and identify with them. I must get out of my comfortable little box, I must get off my pedestal, leave my Britishness behind, and embrace their ways as though they were mine. That is a major part of fulfilling my calling. For me living in another culture is about listening to the Spirit of God as he guides me; it means keeping my eyes and ears open to what is around me; it is about adopting another cultural identity as far as is possible, and still allowing my Christlike identity to blossom. I need to ask myself: shall I become 'like a Jew, to win the Jews'? (1 Cor. 9:20)

'The call of Jesus Christ is a call to come and die.'
Dietrich Bonhoeffer.

Is this speaking to you? Are you struggling with your new culture? Stop reading for a few minutes and pray. Ask God to forgive you for judging and criticising. Ask him to remove the barriers you have. Pray for a broken heart. Pray for God's love and acceptance for the people you are living among and their ways. As you allow Christ in, as you truly repent, he will change your perspective, he will soften your heart. Remember the Holy Spirit is so gentle that he cannot operate where there is a critical attitude.

What I quickly learned is that although the average Brazilian would not go about organising an event in the way an average Englishman/woman would, it all turns out the same in the end! So why get myself in a state in the process, if the end will turn out fine? Everyone else is going at the same pace. For instance, wedding invitations are sent out but no one is expected to reply. So the hosts simply cater for twice as many guests as they invited because, needless to say, most will bring an extra person! Joao loves to arrange barbecue parties at the farm. Usually with only a week's notice, he'll send the message out that there is going to be a barbecue and caters for over 160 people with the help of just a few people in the kitchen! I used to have a near heart attack in our early days just thinking about it, but now I take it in my stride. Why waste time worrying when no one else is?

So I stepped off my conveyor belt and I slowed down. I was too busy! By nature I love spontaneity, so for me an event-orientated culture is tailor-made. Anyway I often used to find that time routines with diaries planned months ahead made me feel claustrophobic when I was a working girl in the West.

To me, Paul is a marvellous example of a cross-cultural worker:

> When I came to you, brothers, I did not come with eloquence or superior wisdom as I proclaimed to you the testimony about God. For I resolved to know nothing while I was with you except Jesus Christ and him crucified. I came to you in weakness and fear, and with much trembling. My message and my preaching were not with wise and persuasive words, but with a demonstration of the Spirit's power, so that your faith might not rest on men's wisdom, but on God's power. (1 Cor. 2:1–5)

A cross-cultural marriage has presented a double challenge for Joao and me. It has provoked and demanded a greater effort on both our parts to understand and accept one another, and to learn about the power of forgiveness (which is a choice). I believe that Jesus is the third cord in our marriage and is one hundred per cent committed to us as a couple through thick and thin. 'A cord of three strands is not quickly broken' (Ecc. 4:12). He is the one who provides a reference point in times of trouble both through his Word and through the power of the Holy Spirit, with grace in abundance. Fortunately we both speak each other's language which I think is enormously helpful. Each one of us must make that exerted effort to comprehend the other's world. Joao always makes a joke that God had him study film and television production only to understand me, because as yet he has never used it professionally! When people ask me to give them advice on cross-cultural marriage, I am always hesitant because I think a lot depends on our individual temperaments and foibles, and our willingness and ability to 'die' to our past.

LIVING IN A COMMUNITY WITHIN A MINISTRY OR MISSION!

I was so independent. I had been nourished on individualism: the desire to win and 'go up the ladder' all my life. Aren't we all in the West? I'd experienced the possibility of assuming important and admirable responsibilities in the world. It was a physical and psychological shock making the passage into a community. I had to climb down that ladder.

(a) Boundaries and comfort

Sharing a large bedroom with eight other students from two different continents was one of my first rude awakenings into community living. My only boundary was my bunk bed with a little space to the left of it where I kept my suitcase face downwards on the hard concrete floor. It remained unpacked for the whole three months of the course in Belo Horizonte because there were no cupboards. The only light shed into that bare-walled room came through long rectangular mesh windows which ran along the top of the outside walls. I cried non-stop for the first twenty-four hours I was there. God must have made a terrible mistake, I wasn't the one he'd called! I missed my comfortable home in London, my double bed, a large cupboard with hanging space for my clothes, my sitting room with a soft comfortable sofa and walls covered with familiar pictures, my own kitchen with fitted units and a fridge full of things I'd purchased in Marks & Spencer's food department!

But what are the living conditions of the millions of

people living in the *favelas*? How do the street children live whom I'd been sent to rescue? At least I had a bed with smooth clean sheets. And I could use a bathroom that had running water and a toilet that flushed!

(b) Relationships

The eight of us in that room had different temperaments and past experiences. Our cultures, backgrounds and education varied as much as the colour of our skin. Some of us were early risers, others were night owls. We lived, washed, ate, studied and worked together twenty-four hours a day with all the daily problems, differences, mis-understandings, celebrations and laughter that went with it. However, we all had one thing in common – something so powerful, so awesome, so beyond ourselves that it knitted us together, transcending all differences, conflicts and struggles. We were all here because we loved Jesus Christ. We had all discovered in our own way God's compassion and call to the poor. We were walking in the same direction for the same person. This brought commit-ment. We were 'home' for now. It enabled acceptance and death to self. And it helped me to retreat ever so slowly, yet firmly, back down the ladder and into the place of communion. I needed to learn to respect the lines of authority that encompassed me at that time.

It was through community living that I started my journey towards wholeness. My deepest being was touched. My egoism was excised and the kernel that was the essential 'me' was able to emerge. I was reborn. It was exhilarating to be with others who had also accepted Jesus's invitation to 'follow me!' – people who were undergoing a similar experience in a new life.

(c) Identity

At the beginning I felt as though I had lost a bit of myself. I had relinquished my identity, which had been built upon my professional success, my lifestyle and my close-knit family. Nevertheless, through this vulnerability I formed close friendships within that community, rooted in prayer. I learned very painfully and vividly that my life was like that grain of wheat which had to die before new life could appear. Through the pain, I was being refined and prepared for a new and deeper intimacy with the Father. This is the ultimate goal for each one of us.

Over the years with Happy Child, I have seen how vital to strong community and team morale is the recognising and development of each person's spiritual gifts. As we share together and encourage one another in this endeavour, a strong bond of interdependency is forged. I believe that, within a team, we thus each become an indispensable link in a chain.

Here is a fun exercise which can be introduced in a team meeting to further this bond:

Pin or tape a blank piece of paper on each person's back. Then, armed with a pen, everyone writes down on this paper the gift that they consider most evident in each person's life. If there is space, a short example can be added, e.g. 'The gift of serving – you are always looking out to see whom you can help'. At the end of the exercise all participants can take it in turns to read their paper. With a team of any size, this exercise is fun, extremely encouraging and often life transforming for someone who is struggling to clarify and deepen their motivations, or to find their place in the community/team at that time.

Here is a list of gifts and talents that every ministry and community has need of: forgiveness; silence in the face of criticism; humility; holding one's tongue; listening; willingness to undertake the smaller chores and services; support of brothers and sisters; tenderness; proclamation of the Word; love; compassion; service; faith; prophecy; discernment; joy; encouragement; hospitality; teaching; wisdom; perseverance; healing; miracles.

Attitudes of envy and rivalry arise out of people's ignorance of, or lack of confidence in their own gifts. However, these can evaporate as everyone finds their own place within their team, becoming unique and necessary to the others. Nevertheless, when we take on a responsibility successfully and are admired and respected by others, we must be careful not to remove our eyes from God and become engrossed instead with our involvement in the community or ministry.

(d) Meetings

When our various teams within Happy Child are united and spiritually healthy, our work with the children and their families is one hundred per cent more effective for God. The children feel and sense this from the workers around them and respond likewise. Regular meetings are key to maintaining this level of togetherness. Communication lines must be kept open between individuals and their leaders.

There are various different types of meetings and each one needs to have an objective: to pray; to announce a vision; to share feelings and thoughts; to plan; to relax together; to solve an immediate problem, and so on. At each type of meeting the encouragement and participation of the relevant team members are vital. Don't flee from these meetings with a thousand excuses. If we are to love one another and work together, we have to meet and share.

(e) Money and budgets in the community/ministry/mission

If you are part of a community or ministry you will not feel the weight of the responsibility of finding the finances to meet its needs as personally as the leaders do. However, just being part of that particular ministry means that you are a link in that chain: you are part of the 'body'. Do you know what the needs are? Don't hesitate to participate in prayer and action (if God opens a door) that will help your leaders carry the load.

If you don't share in this way, you may never fully appreciate the material goods around you in the mission: the food, the furniture, the cars/vans, the washing machine, the telephone, the fax machine, etc., which have often been provided as a result of team and communal prayer.

In Happy Child we have an administration department that handles all the accounting, budgeting, payments and expenditure reports. The work the staff do is tremendous: not only does it give a structure and goal to the ministry, but it also releases everyone else to concentrate on their work with the street children and their families. However, this does not mean that the rest of us in Happy Child should close our eyes to what is going on in the area of financial needs. Equally we must not lose sight of the provider of all the material things around us. God is the Provider: it's his work, it's his provision. Therefore all material things must be used and looked after with a respect for him that reflects our gratitude.

On the farm we live simply and without waste. As the television reception is poor TV is rarely watched and everyone discovers a whole new way of life, at the centre of which lies a commitment to relationships. One of the great blessings is that this lifestyle allows for creativity. With a few bits of coloured paper, freshly cut bougainvillea and bamboo our refectory can be transformed with stunning effect into an exotic tropical venue for a party!

When a ministry or mission has a lot of money in the bank, or tries to structure itself to ensure total security for the future, danger-bells begin to ring in my ears. Why? The organisation, in seeking to eliminate all possible risk, will isolate itself and become completely self-reliant. It will cut itself off from all outside help because there will no longer be any needs. It may even cut itself off from the Church. In the process there will be a loss of respect for those material goods. There will be waste and even a loss of a sense of what is really essential. But above all, and probably the worst danger of all, it will no longer rely on God's provision.

(f) Problems and conflicts

By nature I don't like personal conflicts. In the early days, I would try to avoid them so much that if a conflict was brewing around me – even if I had nothing to do with it – my tendency was to wade in with the misguided intention of stifling any form of division and disagreement.

But by doing this I was getting in the way of change, of what God was doing. I came to see that conflicts can produce growth: we learn things about ourselves, learn to listen to others and to understand their point of view. I am discovering that in the tensions there is nearly always a hidden message from God for me.

I don't like facing problems either: they're stressful and can steal my joy. In our roles as leaders of Happy Child, Joao and I face a variety of problems. If it isn't a problem with a child or a teenager in one of the houses, then it could be a problem with a worker; if it isn't a problem with financial needs, then it could be a problem with finding a new location for a new project; if it isn't a problem with maintenance for the vans transporting the children to school, then it could be a problem with construction, and so on; and then of course there is the whole other question of starting the work in Mozambique and Recife – the bigger vision ... But as time goes on, the more I discover that it is not so much a question of resolving problems as of learning to live with them patiently.

(g) Those little things

There is no question that the highlights of working with God in his ministry are the big projects: the marvellous interventions, the miracles, the prophecies fulfilled when God is seen to be at work in awesome and dramatic revelation of his power. But I think that the essence of communal effort is to be found in all the little daily acts of love such as:

- forgiving an offence
- loving someone who irritates you
- remembering to forget an insult
- sharing your favourite chocolate bar!
- offering to help someone who is tired in an area that isn't your responsibility

We are all called to do the very ordinary things with the attitude of Jesus Christ; those mundane chores:

- the washing of floors
- the serving of meals to the children
- the cooking

- working in the vegetable garden
- washing and sorting the children's clothes
- arranging the flowers
- washing up the dirty dishes
- staying up all night with a sick boy
- walking the kids to school because the van is at the garage
- being patient with a girl who wets her bed every night aged fourteen
- catching three buses to visit a family in a *favela*

Living in a community within a ministry or mission is not always easy, but I have learnt an awful lot about myself and invaluable lessons about working in a team.

Wherever God has placed you, be sure of this: if your heart is right, if your ultimate aim is to imitate through your life the person of Jesus Christ, if you have submitted to God's call on your life and are walking within the centre of his will for you, then there is no challenge that God will leave you to face alone.

THE TOP TEN KEY POINTS

❑ If God has called you to a new country, he will give you the grace you need to learn a new language. Don't curse yourself. Patience is your best friend!

❑ Take language lessons, and dedicate an hour or so a day to study.

❑ Learning to understand and respect the culture is as important as the language. Don't guard offences and be prepared to say you are sorry for offending someone, even if it was done innocently: 'Bear with each other and forgive whatever grievances you may have against one another. Forgive as the Lord forgave you' (Col. 3:13).

❏ By criticising your new culture – even in jest – you are saying that your culture is better than theirs. This is pride. Ask yourself – shall I become 'like a Jew, to win the Jews?' (1 Cor. 9:20)

❏ Living in a community within a ministry or mission is all about climbing down the ladder from individualism into a place of communion.

❏ Attitudes of envy and rivalry can come from people's ignorance of, or lack of confidence in, their own gifts. This evaporates as everyone finds his or her own place.

❏ Don't flee from meetings.

❏ Learn to value the material things in your ministry and community with a fear and respect for God – this reflects your gratitude to the Provider.

❏ Conflicts produce change and growth, and teach us to listen to others and understand their point of view.

❏ The essence of community living is to be found in all the little daily acts of love. We are all called to do the very ordinary things with the attitude of Jesus Christ.

7
I am feeling lonely and disheartened. Where's my enthusiasm?

Where there was apathy,
  now there is energy.
Where there was despair,
  now there is hope.
Where I saw nothing,
  now I see everything to live for.
Thank you, Lord.
            'Lifelines', Susan Hardwick

Does the title of this chapter strike a special chord in your life today?

Take a look at the list of new scenarios I have compiled below and see if any of them relate to your own circumstances at the moment. It may help you to know that I have passed through each one of these situations and will no doubt have to face some of them again in the future as

I continue to walk forward in the centre of God's sovereign will for my life. Whatever it is you are facing, you must persevere. To leave the centre of his will now will be to choose second best or the hardest way in the long run. Remember God called you. Don't throw in the towel! I am learning that freedom is not doing what I want but doing what I ought. A ship at sea without a rudder goes nowhere!

Your heavenly Father will never keep from you what is good for you, nor will he ever leave you alone in any situation. On the contrary, what I have learned is that if I am one hundred per cent committed to him, he is one hundred per cent committed to me – through thick and thin.

But what does it mean to be one hundred per cent committed to God?

> His satisfaction is my highest ambition.

Possible situations:

- I'm feeling so disheartened. Where's my enthusiasm?
- I want to serve God to the full. How can I make the most of every opportunity?
- I don't want to be single any more. Where's my husband/wife, Lord?
- Heavenly Father, I believe you have told me what my next step is in my ministry, but I haven't felt you giving me the go-ahead. It's so hard to be patient whilst waiting for your 'green light'.
- I'm feeling tired, stressed and unwell. As a result I'm over-sensitive and/or crying easily.
- I have given my all – heart, time, prayer and energy

– to my work for you; those I was trying to help were doing so well. Suddenly everything has gone wrong and we are back to 'square one'.
- I'm struggling financially (see chapters 3–4).
- I've just had an argument/disagreement with someone close to me (see chapter 9).
- I feel so homesick for my family, friends, church, comforts and privacy I could catch the next plane home tomorrow (see chapter 6).
- I don't feel like I'm achieving anything for God in my ministry at the moment. Everything around me is falling apart. Where are you, Jesus? (See chapter 10.)

(As you can see, many of these problems are covered in another chapter. If appropriate, please refer to the one that is relevant to you today – the others will be covered in this chapter.)

You could well be facing a situation that is not included in my list. Whatever it is, don't isolate yourself and take care not to fall into the 'trap' of self-pity. Seek advice from a godly friend, your immediate leader in the ministry or the pastor of the church where you are currently living and working. Whatever your situation, the teaching that I will be sharing with you will be relevant and applicable to it.

HOW NOT TO BECOME DISHEARTENED

> The secret in every success is not quitting. Human nature says, 'If you fail three times, you quit!' God's way is not to let circumstances discourage you. Please read Romans 5.

Pastor Jaime Cisterna is a pastor from the Central Baptist Church in Belo Horizonte. When Jaime was born his parents had thirty-three children living with them! His father was a minister for forty-four years, and for thirty of those years he founded and ran an orphanage which over that period cared for more than 1,500 children. His teaching on how not to become disheartened and how to make the best out of every 'opportunity' has helped me enormously. I will weave my own experiences and those of other people into some of what I've learned from him.

Jesus said, 'I have told you these things, so that in me you may have peace. In this world you will have trouble. But take heart! *I have overcome* the world' (John 16:33, my emphasis).

We are going to break this verse up into four parts:

(i) 'I have told you these things ...'

The words of Jesus are life-changing. If we are going to walk on through life, in peace and happiness, we must meditate on the many good 'things' Jesus has said. The Bible instructs us to guard the Word in our hearts so that we do not sin. So often we forget God's promises and as a result we become despondent Christians.

In John chapters 14, 15 and 16 Jesus makes a number of wonderful promises to his disciples. Claim them for yourself today.

Do not let your heart be troubled. Jesus is saying to you today:

'_____ (put your name here), trust in me!'
You are his temple – he lives in you!
You will do even greater things than Jesus, if you can believe it!
The Holy Spirit is your guaranteed personal counsellor

– call on him!
He will never leave you.
Don't be afraid. His peace is yours!
You are connected to Jesus.
He wants you to rely on him one hundred per cent.
He chose you.
He wants to speak to you.
You plant the seed, but he will water it.
No one is going to take away your joy!
You will have trouble, but he is your peace.
Relax, your God has overcome the world!

So often I have asked myself, 'How can I do greater things than Jesus? I'm not holy like he is. I'm not God like he is. I'm not perfect like he is!' Yet in John 14 Jesus says with his own mouth that we will. 'I tell you the truth, anyone who has faith in me will do what I have been doing. He will do even greater things than these, because I am going to the Father' (v. 12).

Jesus was only one person. Today each one of us is the temple of the Holy Spirit; he lives in us. When the Holy Spirit gives us his power, we can do the things Jesus did. We have even greater opportunities because there are millions of us around the world, and many of us will live longer than the three years Jesus had to carry out his ministry. Now we have the responsibility to be available to say, 'Here I am, Lord!'

'If anyone loves me, he will obey my teaching. My Father will love him, and we will come to him and make our home with him' (14:23). God isn't saying 'maybe': he says he will! We need to receive this truth fully into our hearts and minds. He is making a promise to you and to me today and forever.

> 'Peace I leave with you; my peace I give you. I do not give to you as the world gives. Do not let your hearts be troubled and do not be afraid.' John 14:27.

The peace of God is eternal, it's complete. When I first stepped out in faith in 1991 having let go of my job and all my security, I did feel afraid. From my time in Switzerland with Youth With A Mission right up until I eventually arrived in Rio de Janeiro nearly a year later all I seemed to hear was: 'It's really dangerous in Rio. You can't go there, a single girl like you, tall and fair …'; 'I heard that someone got shot on the streets in Rio de Janeiro last week …'; 'The street children are really dangerous, they'll steal from you …' On and on went the comments from people I knew as well as those I didn't. Although I was certain in the depths of my being that God had called me, I felt fear. It was all so new; I didn't like to think that there really was a devil who was causing evil. I didn't understand my place in Christ and the victory he had won for me. I was walking into the unknown: a new culture, a new language, an unknown future. I was going out in the name of Jesus, rescuing children from death and destruction and bringing them into a new life, and without a doubt there would be spiritual implications as a result. As someone once wrote: 'Give a boy a fish and it will feed him for a day, teach him to fish and it will feed him for life. Teach him about Jesus and it will give everlasting life.' However, during that time before going out to Rio God was gently showing me my place in Christ and the power of his name. Whilst in Switzerland I wrote in my diary:

1 November 1990

The presence of the Holy Spirit fell upon us all during a time of worship this evening before class. I felt a warm current surge through my body and fell to my knees in sheer reverence of the power of God in that room. A verse came into my mind, 'Call to me and I will answer you and tell you great and unsearchable things you do not know' (Jer. 33:3). I called out to him from deep within, asking him to tell me something of my future. Immediately I heard his gentle voice speaking within my spirit with his quiet authority.

At the end he said, 'Never fear evil: even though I lead you through the valley of the shadow of death you will fear no evil for I am with you, my rod and my staff they comfort you. Even though you cross a flowing river you will not be swept away – even though you walk through fires you will never get ablaze. No bone in your body shall be broken ...' God made the world in six days – nothing is impossible for him!

I asked him to fill my mind and my heart with peace that goes beyond all understanding (as I'd read this morning in the Bible). He did, and I now feel a peace that cannot be described in human terms.

We are each connected to Jesus: 'I am the vine, and my Father is the gardener. He cuts off every branch in me that bears no fruit, while every branch that does bear fruit he prunes so that it will be even more fruitful' (John 15:1, 2).

> Without Jesus you can do nothing. This leaves you and me helpless; we have to rely on him one hundred per cent!

We are friends of Jesus. In the Old Testament Moses writes that God said, 'Shall I hide from Abraham what I am about to do?' (Gen. 18:17). In the New Testament James writes that Abraham was called 'God's friend' (Jas. 2:23). Today Jesus says the same thing about you.

'But when he, the Spirit of truth, comes, he will guide *you* into all truth' (John 16:13, my emphasis). This takes the weight off our shoulders. When we are telling a prisoner, a young man dying of AIDS or a street kid about the love of Jesus, it's not you that will convince them about a new life in Christ. That's the work of the Holy Spirit. Our job is to speak.

Don't let anyone take your joy. Hold onto this promise: 'So with you. Now is your time of grief, but I will see you again and you will rejoice, and no one will take away your joy' (John 16:22). Pastor Jaime once had to preach at the funeral of a boy aged only sixteen years, an only son. Afterwards the mother wanted to speak – she was crying a lot and no one thought she would manage it. However, through her tears she said, 'It's hurting a lot, but inside I feel a deep peace.' Such peace is illogical, inexplicable.

(ii) '... so that in me you may have peace ...'

We are all seeking for an inner peace. Many of us have tried to find it through a career, money, sex, drugs, food, alcohol, sport, and so on, yet we still feel empty inside. Jesus promised, 'I have come that they may have life and have it to the full' (John 10:10). The Greek word translated as 'abundance' implies that there is so much life it's going to pour out like water overflowing continually out of a cup. Paul writes in Philippians 4:7 of a peace that is beyond all understanding. It is a peace we could never buy.

(iii) '... *In this world you will have trouble* ...'

This is not only a prophecy: Jesus is stating the reality. We are going to suffer because we live in the midst of this world. He doesn't say, 'Come to me and you will never weep again'; he doesn't say, 'Come to me and all your dreams will come true!' But he does say, 'Come and I will give you peace – but you will have trouble.'

Paul also encourages us to make 'the most of every opportunity, because the days are evil' (Eph. 5:16). We cannot always expect goodness and kindness because these are not natural attributes of our world. In this area we can't have high expectations. But Jesus says that in the middle of all this he is going to give us peace.

(iv) '... *But take heart! I have overcome the world*'

Maybe you need money; maybe the person you love argued with you; maybe you feel lonely without real friends; maybe it isn't easy where you work. But despite all this Jesus is saying to you and me: 'Cheer up!' 'Rejoice!' 'Smile!' 'Let me look into your eyes and see a smile.' When I first read this verse I thought, I want this for me!

In Daniel 3 King Nebuchadnezzar threatens Shadrach, Meshach and Abednego by saying that he is going to throw them into the fiery furnace to burn to death, because they are refusing to bow down and worship his ninety-foot-high golden image. They calmly answer him, 'If we are thrown into the blazing furnace, the God we serve is able to save us from it, and he will rescue us from your hand, O King.' Big smiles all round!

WHERE'S MY ENTHUSIASM?

I have discovered that enthusiasm doesn't come from the outside. It doesn't come from the things I can see or measure like a hug, or a salary increase. It comes from the inside. The key is found in verse 33 of chapter 15 in the words 'in me'. Jesus could have left these two words out, but in fact 'the things' he speaks of are not enough on their own to bring us peace. It is only 'in me'. We have to be connected to Jesus. If we are not 'tuned in' to him, then we are not going to hear things clearly, and the source that brings us encouragement can easily dry up.

The original Latin and Greek words illustrate my point: the Latin word *animous* means 'the soul had something inside her' and the Latin word *animo* (literally 'cheerfulness') means 'soul'. The Greek word *enthusiasmos* (literally 'enthusiasm') means 'to have God inside the soul'. Now this could be any god: money; sex; materialism and so on.

But if it's the living God, Jesus Christ, then you have found the secret of having an enthusiastic life forever!

The reason why we are so often sad is because we depend so much on results. We need extraordinary things to happen in order to be happy. In John 15, however, we read about intimacy with Jesus. If you cut off the branches from an apple tree and put them on the ground, are they going to be able to produce anything? It is the same for us. Jesus says, 'I am the vine and you are the branches.' The fruit we bear is love, joy, peace and forgiveness.

The devil is really interested in taking away all your enthusiasm. Your enthusiasm produces cheerfulness. If he can manage to make you sad, it is as though he were spitting on the cross and saying that it had no value for you. The devil tempts you with 'things' and you are going to have to make a choice. God gave you freedom of choice. You can either choose 'things' that will make you temporarily happy, or you can choose to be with Jesus. As you go deeper in your intimacy with Jesus you will start to see things as they really are.

There is a museum in Brazil full of precious artefacts. All the diamonds and valuable paintings are behind bars and no one can reach them. However, in the centre of the museum there is a large and very beautiful stone on display with no bars around it whatsoever. In fact, anyone could easily reach out and put it in their pocket when no one is looking. Nevertheless, there is a sign next to the stone with the words, 'Please put on these glasses'. When you put them on you can clearly see infra-red rays all around the stone. You couldn't see them with your bare eyes, only with the special glasses. This is an excellent illustration of what happens spiritually when we are not in an intimate relationship with Jesus – we can't see the 'infra-red rays'! We don't see the pitfalls in the temptations that Satan offers us and when we grab them we get hurt.

When you recognise a trap of the devil you have to confront him. That's why Paul tells us that God did not give us a spirit of cowardliness but of courage (cf. 2 Tim. 1:7). Don't permit the devil to make you sad. Ask God to give you spiritual eyes.

The feature film *Beethoven* tells the story of a St Bernard dog who eventually changes the lives of every member of the family which adopts him. The little boy in the family is fed up with being picked on at school by a gang of bullies and decides to learn karate. In one scene as the boy gets off the school bus on his way home he notices the bullies waiting to pick on him. Summoning up some courage – from his karate lessons – he decides to confront them. Unseen by the boy Beethoven suddenly comes running around the corner close behind him. Taking one look at the large dog the bullies turn around and run off. The boy puts it down to his karate!

When the devil looks at you he sees the Spirit of God in you, who is bigger than you and bigger than him. So don't let the devil take your joy!

I'M FEELING LONELY, WHERE'S MY MARRIAGE PARTNER?

No one is complete as a person on their own. Everyone needs companionship. We must remember, however, that the first concept of marriage originated entirely with God – Adam had no part in it! It was God who decided that Adam needed a wife – not the other way around. He alone knew the kind of wife/mate that Adam needed. It was God who presented Eve to Adam. Adam did not have to go in search of her! If you should enter into marriage it will not be because it is your decision, but because it is God's.

As I wrote in *The Street Children of Brazil* God led me, sovereignly and supernaturally, to the mate of his choice, Joao Bosco de Carvalho. The whole revelation had its source solely in the sovereign will of God. If I had rejected God's will that he so clearly revealed to us both, how could we have expected his blessing on our future?

God can foresee just the kind of wife or husband you need. As you continue to pray and remain in the centre of his will for you, he will bring that person across your path at the right time. The waiting is not easy, but it is necessary because he is preparing you both. Be careful not to fantasise or daydream that he or she will be tall, blond and handsome or beautiful with the perfect personality, talents and godly qualities. Otherwise you may miss the very person God has chosen for you because it is too hard to distinguish between fantasy and reality. Don't worry. God is the number one matchmaker. He's not going to choose someone you couldn't even imagine kissing! Obedience to God's Word will keep you on the path that leads to the marriage he has planned for you.

Before I gave my life to Jesus I had had a few long-term relationships. I was used to always having someone. However, one of the first things God did was to distance me from any form of emotional involvement with a boyfriend for over two years – he became that person in my life, he filled that gap.

If you had sexual relations before you became a Christian it is very important to go to the Lord in prayer and bring each partner/relationship before him to break the soul ties that exist between you both in the name of Jesus. Remember: 'For this reason a man will leave his father and mother and be united to his wife, and they will become one flesh' (Gen. 2:24). The sexual act is a gift from God; it isn't just a physical experience, but rather a spiritual bonding takes place. That is why so many people are crippled emotionally by going from one partner to the next, because in each new relationship they carry with them the soul ties from previous mates. These emotional, spiritual and physical ties can be broken in your life by the power of the name of Jesus. Remember that sin allows the devil a foothold in that particular area in your life; you will find, as you break each tie – in a moment of repentance – and claim the power of the blood of Jesus over that place in the depths of your soul, that those sexual temptations you seem constantly to be fighting against will lessen considerably.

I eventually came to a point with God where I knew he wanted me to say with my heart that if he didn't want me to marry, if that wasn't his will for my life, he could take the urge and desire from me. I strongly believe that if it isn't his will for an individual to marry he does take the burning desire away. In order to come to this point, however, I had to decide that the tremendous social pressures around me to get married did not outweigh God's sovereign purpose for me. I had to believe that his all-consuming love was sufficient because 'Your love is better than life' (Ps. 63:3). In Matthew 19 Jesus says that there are some people who have chosen to be single for the sake of the Kingdom of God. Paul teaches that those who are single can give their time and attention more readily to the purposes of God (l Cor. 7). Singles are freer to travel and live abroad than married people, unless there are elderly parents who need their care. Paul warns believers that they must not be yoked together with a non-believer (2 Cor. 6:14). It is easy to marry someone who doesn't have faith with every good intention of evangelising him or her. Nevertheless, as a friend once said to me, if you imagine that you, being the Christian, are standing on a table, and your mate, who isn't, is standing on the floor next to it, it is much easier for him or her to pull you off the table than it is for you to pull him or her up onto it!

One of the keys to a fulfilled life is a willingness to give ourselves for others ... one day I shall have to account for how I used my freedom. Have I been selfishly indulgent, living to please myself, wasting my time? Have I spent my time wallowing in self-pity about my single state or about some problem that I feel is peculiarly and perhaps unfairly mine? It is possible as a single to live a fulfilled life.

Elizabeth-Ann Horsford, *Complete as One.*[1]

I eventually got so sick of living in the awful situation of constantly looking out for that man, that 'perfect' mate, everywhere I went as a single Christian woman. Indulging in flirtations or superficial relationships with the opposite sex made me feel confused, anxious and self-conscious.

> It may seem exciting to stir someone's emotions and allow your own to be stirred, but one day you may discover that your emotions have got out of your control. The result is an emotional entanglement with a person who is in no way suited to be your mate.
>
> Derek Prince, *God is a Matchmaker.*[2]

So I asked God to take over. Every morning I submitted my emotions to the Lordship of Jesus Christ, and made captive every one of my thoughts to him. I also asked God to keep every man away from me unless it was the very husband he had chosen for me.

This seemed to work very nicely for over a year until one evening, during a course with Youth With A Mission in Switzerland, a man of God whom I greatly respected on that base, came to me and said that God had told him that I was to be his wife! He even had the verses to prove it. This really took me aback, because as much as I admired him as a person the thought of marriage had never crossed my mind. He was from the Middle East, and a Christian counsellor on his way to work in America. I was embarking on my call to rescue street children in Brazil! I remember crawling back to my bedroom that night and not managing to sleep a wink. If I really was to be his wife why wasn't God telling me? I gave my heart to the Lord over and over again, asking him to give me the OK. Finally, one afternoon while I was walking and praying in the woods close to the base, I felt God telling me that he had prepared a husband for me in Brazil with whom I would start a ministry rescuing children, not only in South America but in other countries throughout the world. But before I had to face the terrible situation of trying to explain this to my dear friend, he himself came to me and confessed that he had had to recognise that it was his own heart's desire and not the plan of God. This living experience showed me just how important it is to be connected to my Lord's heart all the time, so as not to be led astray by my own flesh and will.

It's so hard to wait!

If you are one of those whom God requires to wait, be encouraged by the fact that God has required many of his choicest servants to wait long periods for the fulfilment of his promise or purpose. God uses waiting to work out various purposes in our lives. Only faith that passes the test is accepted by God as genuine! Waiting purifies our motives. You need to ask yourself, 'Why am I eager to marry? Is it because God wants it for me, or because I want it for myself?' Waiting builds your character to maturity. Someone who has learned to wait is no longer vulnerable to changing moods and emotions. He or she has found confidence, stability and an inner peace.

One man who waited with unbelievable faithfulness for God to work out his purpose for his life is our friend, Ricardo. He had married Adriana in 1988 at the age of twenty-six; but just eight days later she was fatally injured when the car in which they were passengers inexplicably ran out of control and rolled over several times. Adriana later died in hospital. When the doctors broke the news to him, Ricardo felt as if his 'body tore in two'. But at the same moment he heard amazing words of comfort from God. Despite the incredible pain of his loss, he still felt an 'indescribable inner peace'. Although he could not understand why his wife had been taken from him in such a horrific way, he somehow knew that the Lord's hand was covering the situation and that good would come of it.

Next day, at the funeral Ricardo was astonished when hundreds of people turned up: he heard later that the accident had been reported on the radio. As the coffin was lowered into the ground, Ricardo felt his heart was bursting, but he wanted to speak to the people. He stood there and preached the love of God, 'how we shouldn't love God because of the circumstances we live in but because of who he is!' In the years since, people who heard Ricardo speak that day still come up and tell him that their lives were changed as a result of that experience.

In the following months, Ricardo became convinced that God was calling him to Russia. He began enquiring about flights there, but was advised to join Youth With A Mission in Belo Horizonte, because 'God prepares his chosen'. However, in 1992, Ricardo moved away from God for a while and into all sorts of dark places. Nevertheless, the Lord had not left Ricardo, and gradually, through encounters with men and women of God, the Holy Spirit convicted him, and he returned 'in humility and remorse' to his church.

There then followed a time with Joao and me, working with Happy Child. Ricardo is a master carpenter, and the farm and the street kids who are rehabilitated there, benefited greatly from his time with us. It was now over five years since Adriana had died and Ricardo was very conscious that God still had not given him the wife and mate he needed, who would share his calling. One day he and I had a time of prayer together. I will let Ricardo continue in his own words at this point:

'One day I went to seek advice from Sarah and God used her with a prophecy saying that he was faithful and would fulfil his promise, and that by the end of the following year (1994) I would know my wife – what was more she would be a foreigner, maybe English! I trusted so much in these words that I forgot all about it!

'I met Rachel – an English missionary – for the first time when she came to visit Sarah at the farm a month later, but we just introduced ourselves and I thought no more about her. Rachel at the time was seeking solace because she had just finished a relationship after two years, also she had worked in Brazil for three years and her visa was due to run out at the end of the year.'

Rachel tells her side of the story; 'The first time I saw Ricardo at the farm, I didn't find him attractive! He was wearing his baggy blue work dungarees and funny glasses. But something clicked inside me – I now realise that it was God's prompting. However, Ricardo told me that he had a call to Russia and I thought, well that's it then because I haven't, or so I thought! We then met briefly on a bus a few months later but just said hi and bye to one another. Then for no reason at all around October 1994, nearly a year since we'd met at Sarah's house on the farm, I started to think about Ricardo. I wanted to get to know him. But I thought it would be a bit obvious if I went out to the farm, so I prayed and said to God that if it was right then he would give me an opportunity to get to know him. Exactly two weeks later there was a conference on street children at Youth With A Mission and Ricardo arrived with the team from Happy Child.'

Ricardo continues, 'I didn't want to go to the conference, but Joao insisted we all went so I gave in! I was one of the last people to enter the conference room and there were hardly any seats left. I suddenly noticed Rachel sitting at the end of a row, and immediately I felt God telling me that she was my wife. The next day I sat next to her and by the third day I was already giving her presents!'

Rachel explains, 'We spent the whole week together, and then the following week there was another conference – so in total we saw each other every day for two whole weeks! But after six weeks of hearing nothing but Russia, Russia, Russia I was feeling very confused and broke the relationship off. I had to be sure of my own calling to Russia. Ricardo came to my house one evening, and asked whether he should keep on praying or not. I found myself saying yes, keep praying, but don't contact me, because I want to hear from God about Russia. Eventually one morning God gave me a verse in Psalm 139 which jumped out at me. It said that even if I settled on the far side of the sea his hand would guide me and hold me (v. 10). For me Russia was on the other side of the world! Also I received another verse a few days later in Chronicles where David says that whatever is on your heart go and do it! I went on holiday and when I got back I called Ricardo.'

Ricardo and Rachel were married in January 1996 in England. Today they live in St Petersburg where they have founded a powerful ministry called 'New Life' rescuing the many street children living in the gutters there. Ricardo's story illustrates poignantly how God is faithful to us when we are faithful to him.

Nevertheless, marriage is not always the answer to loneliness. Sometimes we feel lonely not just among strangers but even in the midst of our own family, where, for example, we feel we are not really appreciated or understood. We often experience loneliness because we feel our essential qualities are not recognised, or because we do not feel special to anyone. People with a low-image through rejection in childhood often isolate themselves in the midst of caring people because they think they can never be loved by anybody. It would be very easy to respond with self-pity and self-absorption. The answer is to start to give yourself to others, to look to their needs and seek to help them. 'If you spend yourselves on behalf of the hungry and satisfy the needs of the oppressed, then your light will rise in the darkness, and your night will become like the noonday' (Isa. 58:10).

IT'S SO HARD TO BE PATIENT

When I was living in Rio de Janeiro the pastor of my church there used to say to me, 'Everything that happens in the Garden of God happens naturally.' In other words, when the time comes for God to move you on to another work-place, ministry, country, church and so on, that next stage will be clearly illuminated and you and your spiritual leadership will have peace about it. If there is confusion and your next step is not confirmed, don't use your current situation – which may be frustrating or unsatisfactory – as an excuse to take matters into your own hands and take action you may later regret, through knowing it to have been the wrong action.

In March 1993 Joao and I moved into the farm. For eleven whole months we did not receive the go-ahead from God to bring the street boys to live with us there. Nevertheless, during those eleven months we made a big mistake, and learned a lesson the hard way. We conceded to the pressures of people who would visit us and say, 'Where are the children? Here you are in this beautiful spacious place with kids living on the streets – bring them here, what are you waiting for?'

One weekend in November 1993, we decided to bring two boys from our day-care centre – which we had already opened in the September – to the farm. They had a great time, riding horses, swimming in the lake, running around, helping Joao in the garden. However, neither of us had peace about it, nor did Iona – our very first worker on the farm. It was as though God had left us. There was a restlessness in our hearts, and a sense that we were doing something under our own strength. None of us slept well at night. The three of us came together to pray and we felt God say, 'It isn't the time.' We each asked for forgiveness for bowing to the voice and pressure of 'man', and the children returned to the day-care centre on the Monday morning. In February 1994, during a time of prayer, I heard God say clearly, 'The doors are open, you can bring the boys to the farm', which we did two weeks later.

The ways of God are not our ways. The first year of our ministry on the farm was spent in intercession, forming a team and planning. If your work is God's then its foundation must be intercession. This is now the pattern we follow for each of our new projects; it is not always easy to wait, because we are so used to getting quick results in the world we live in these days that we can lose the ability to endure. But what I have learned is that only he knows when it is the 'right time', because the issue must be settled in the spiritual realm before it can be outworked in the natural realm.

In 1984 Joao had recently joined Youth With A Mission in their main base in Brazil near Belo Horizonte. One day before lunch he had half an hour spare and felt the nudge to go and pray. He walked to his favourite place on the top of a hill nearby and starting worshipping God. Suddenly he felt God telling him that he would take him to Switzerland to study communication – TV, radio and press. Joao was amazed. At the time he couldn't even remember where Switzerland was on the map! Joao asked the Lord that if it really was him speaking to tell him when, where and who he should contact, and when he should speak to his leaders. What's more Joao asked God to provide all the money needed for his trip through Brazilian people – this was a challenge because the churches did not have the vision for missionaries! And he had little contact with his church because Sundays were spent visiting and speaking in other churches around the city. However, he was convicted that God was God of the impossible!

For a year and a half Joao told no one, but held onto these words to himself in faith. Then one morning in 1986 whilst he was working in the vegetable garden on the Youth With A Mission base, a girl suddenly appeared from nowhere taking pictures of him! It was a missionary from Switzerland, Muriel, who was visiting the base for a few days. However, then and there God gave Joao words of knowledge about her life. She started crying and asked Joao how he knew all those things, when he didn't even know her! Muriel confirmed what Joao had said was true. At the same time he suddenly felt a nudge to share with her about God's words a year and a half earlier. He felt he had to say to her that when she was back in her own country if she should hear about any communication course to let him know.

Nine days later, Joao received a letter from Muriel saying that believe it or not there was going to be a seminar in her very church on TV, radio and press, with Alexandre Lukasik. What was more, her pastor had agreed to give Joao a grant and hospitality free. He only needed a ticket! Joao fasted and prayed, asked permission from his leader of the base Jim Stier, and in faith booked his flight. Three days later without having communicated his need Joao received contributions from a variety of people which covered the cost for his ticket.

If God speaks to you, no matter what the circumstances, he is going to provide what you need to obey him at the right time in a way that will glorify him.

One of our prayer partners in England, Carol, and her husband, needed to down-grade on their large family house. They placed the awful scenario of going to a smaller place entirely in God's hands. They prayed for months for God's guidance, as they looked at one house after another, and became anxious in spite of their faith. Which one was the right house? Where did God want them to live? Eventually, tired and feeling disheartened, they went to pray with their good friends, Robert and Eileen. Suddenly, while praying, Robert had a very strange vision. At first he thought it too silly to share, but the impression was so strong that he took the plunge and shared it anyway. It was of a tortoise! Carol took this to mean that the moving process would be a slow one.

A few weeks later they went to see a house for the second time. On the way there, they asked God for a sign: was this the right home? It didn't seem any less ordinary than anything else they'd already seen, Except for this – as they stood in the back garden a large tortoise emerged all at once from the hedge and walked slowly across the lawn in front of them!

In faith, they took this as a sign from God and bought the house. Five years later, neither of them has any doubts that this was the very house God had for them. It was worth the wait. He has used them effectively in their neighbourhood and local church, and apart from anything else they are both very happy and contented.

As we wait God is refining us and preparing us for the next stage. You may think you are ready – but he knows your heart and what's around the corner better than you do. Waiting is very much part of God's plan!

I'M FEELING TIRED, STRESSED AND LOW

We all need to rest, and we all need to eat a proper diet. If you are feeling tired or you are having difficulty sleeping ask someone to pray for you. Also stop and think about what you have eaten today: remember your body is God's temple and make sure you eat three balanced meals a day. When I first moved to Brazil it took a while to adapt to the diet of rice and beans every day – however I started to feel very well because I was eating more protein and iron daily (beans!) than ever before.

I once heard a great talk given by the rector of St Mary's Church in West Horsley, England on 'Getting a Grip on Life – Surviving your Schedule'! Rev. Peter Robinson reminded us that Proverbs says that if you want to get control of your schedule: *Line up your priorities*, 'A discerning man keeps wisdom in view, but a fool's eyes wander to the ends of the earth' (Prov. 17:24); *Lighten up your attitude*, 'A heart at peace gives life to the body' (Prov. 14:30); *Look up to God*, 'The fear of the Lord adds length to life' (Prov. 10:27).

Humour is a great stress reliever. It's life's shock absorber. It doesn't change the situation, but it changes your perspective and helps you to handle it better. I once heard about a guy who was late for his appointment. He drove around the block two or three times, but couldn't find a parking space. He pulled over on to a double yellow line and left a note saying, 'This is an absolute emergency. I promise – I guarantee – I'll be back in fifteen minutes.' He ran up the stairs, made his presentation, watching his watch the entire time and came back down in twelve minutes flat. There was a ticket on his window. At the bottom the policeman had written, 'Don't rush. Take your time. You've still got a ticket!'

We all need to lighten up because some of the biggest causes of stress are:
trying to do too much,
failing to prioritise,
taking yourself too seriously!

Stress is a warning light. When I feel stressed it usually means that I've taken my eyes off the Lord and started looking at something else. Martin Luther once said, 'I'm so busy today! I've got to pray for at least three hours!' He had his priorities right. Jesus said, 'Come to me, all you who are weary and burdened, and I will give you rest' (Matt. 11:28). That's the best deal I've ever heard of!

I HAVE GIVEN MY ALL, BUT EVERYTHING SEEMS TO HAVE GONE WRONG...

Is this you? Have you put yourself heart and soul into bringing the love of Jesus Christ to a needy person or situation, only to find, after maybe weeks and months when it seemed your efforts appeared to be bearing fruit, and you felt full of hope and enthusiasm, that with little or no warning or explanation, it has all come to nothing: your efforts, your friendship, and above all the love of Jesus you had offered, have all been rejected?

Let me tell you, all of us at Happy Child know this heartbreaking scenario. Working with these children/ teenagers can give us many disappointments but also many victories. Here are three examples.

Carlos, known to everyone as 'Penguin', had been brought up by his ailing grandmother because his mother had mental problems. His father eventually died and Carlos was sent to the streets to beg so that they could buy food and pay for medication. However, one day he never returned home – Carlos joined a street gang and started taking drugs. Our street team first met him in 1994 when he was ten years old! For two years he visited our day-care centre until finally he decided he wanted to come off the streets. Carlos came to live with us on the farm in April 1996. The first time I saw Carlos I fell in love with him: agitated, covered in scars and always asking questions, this little boy's eyes bore the expression of a child deeply hurt, a child whose childhood had been eaten by 'the locusts'. All I wanted to do was to mother him. Sometimes I would put him on my knee, and although this gesture felt awkward to him at first, he would eventually relax and slowly the tears would start to pour down his face as he spoke of his own mother, and the rejection he'd felt from her. Carlos loved my son Lucas and he would spend all his free time playing with him. For eight months this young boy lived on the farm, until eventually the lure of the streets won him back. His agitated disposition meant that he simply could not bear to sit still in a classroom for long. He didn't want to have anyone telling him what to do, he couldn't cope with a schedule – a time to get up, a time to eat, a time to go to sleep. When he left, I wept. Today he is an *aviaozinho* (a courier) for drug traffickers in a *favela* here in Belo Horizonte. But I know that a seed was planted in his heart during his time with us, he knows that Jesus loves him. I believe that God is watering that seed wherever he is.

Pamela was nine years old when she started accompanying her mother in selling drugs on the streets. Pretty, with big brown eyes and light olive skin, this little girl was full of hurts – she had seen her father being murdered. After a few months on the streets Pamela was hit by a bus while under the influence of drugs and her face was seriously wounded. She went to live in our girls' house in June 1998. Pamela asked Jesus into her life. She knew deep in her soul the price God's Son had paid for her. Her prayers were powerful, and she often received prophetic visions. Pamela loved to study at school and she loved her friends in the house. On Joao's birthday she gave him a present with a card, with these words written on it: 'Thank you for obeying Jesus and taking me off the streets.' However, one sad day in March 1999, the streets lured her back, and without warning she left. When I saw her on the streets the other night – filthy, wearing little, with no shoes and sniffing glue – my heart broke. I sat next to her on the pavement, pulled her on to my knee and held her close for what seemed like hours. She didn't resist – her beautiful eyes were clouded over from the effect of the drugs.

'Oh Pamela,' I whispered into her ear, 'come back and live with us in the girls' house.'

'I want to stay here,' she answered, slurring her words.

This is tough, really, really tough. Because her answer was completely illogical. In situations like this we must never underestimate the power of prayer.

Sometimes, however, there is a wonderful unexpected outcome to a time of utter despondency. Take, for instance, the story of little Sheila …

Sheila was three years old when her mother had to flee from her violent, drug-taking husband. They both lived on the streets until her mother eventually met another man, and they moved in with him. Two more little girls were born from this new relationship. Then in 1997 her

mother tragically died of an infection after giving birth to
a little boy. Everything at home fell apart and Sheila ran
back to live on the streets, bearing scars on her body from
her stepfather. She was only nine years old at the time. In
September 1998 our street team started to work with her
and Sheila began to visit our day-care centre in the heart
of the city. She presented herself as a solitary, self-contained
and often depressed little girl, who reacted indifferently to
the street workers. We rarely saw her smile. Eventually she
started to express interest in coming to live in the girls'
house. Two days before she was due to go to the house,
she asked Jesus into her life. However, when the weekend
came for her to go, she arrived at the day-care centre and
announced that she didn't want to move in until after the
weekend. There was nothing we could do. That very night,
on Friday 6 November, to everybody's horror, Sheila
(drugged on glue) was hit by a speeding car. Her tiny frail
body was somersaulted into the air and she came crashing
down on to the tarmac. Her head and stomach split open
and she was rushed to intensive care by ambulance.

Sheila went into a coma, with serious head and spleen
injuries. Her heart rate was high, and she was kept alive
by a life support machine. The doctors were honest and
warned that she would probably have the mental age of a
one-year-old, and could be paralysed if she survived.

The whole of the ministry fell into shock, struck again
by the forceful reality that we are rescuing these children
daily from possible death. We all knew Sheila had been so
close to coming off the streets that very same day.
Members of the ministry team set up a rota visiting her at
all hours of the day and night. She had more visitors
than anyone else on her ward! We all got on our knees to
pray for a miracle. After a week in a coma the doctor, a
Christian, warned Andy and Sally Furnival (workers in

the girls' house) that they might have to reduce the heavy sedatives or else she would never wake up. However, they could only do this once the severe swelling in her brain reduced. The following morning, on Monday 16 November, at 9.00 a.m. the doctors informed everyone that there had been no progress and she could die. Andy, with Marlene and Sandra – two workers from the girls' house – called together another emergency prayer meeting with the other girls: Fernanda (aged 10), Poliana (12), Pamela (10 – she was living in the house at the time), Patricia (6), Rosanaria (7), Josilene (10), Ana Lucia (12), Daniella (11) and Arli (13), most of whom knew Sheila from the streets. Everyone gathered in the sitting room. Marlene recalls what happened.

'We were all very upset, and I reminded the girls of how Jesus said that we would do even greater things than he did, and Jesus resurrected Lazarus after four days! I said that we would pray because God could give everything new to Sheila once again. We all started to cry out to God from the depths of our hearts placing the life of Sheila in his hands, and declaring our faith in his Word. We prayed that the hands of the doctors would be substituted for the hands of God. And that we believed that Jesus could give everything new to her. The presence of the Holy Spirit was very powerful and all at once each one of us had the conviction that God would do a miracle. Suddenly Fernanda saw a vision of Sheila walking and speaking!'

That afternoon Andy and Sally went into the hospital. Sheila was awake! Miraculously she had awoken by herself that morning, before the sedatives had been reduced! The doctors had no explanation.

After a month in hospital she came out and went to live in the girls' house where she was cared for by the team and all the girls. Just being in the presence of some of her old friends stimulated Sheila to start to walk and talk again! 'I am a walking miracle,' Sheila tells everyone today.

> All-seeing Lord – I started counting my blessings today,
> Something I've not done for far too long.
> The more I remembered,
> the more there was to recall.
> It was like a pair of scales,
> with the weights redistributed
> until both sides balanced evenly.
>   And with this new perspective
> Has come hope,
> And healing.
> Thank you for this gentle reminder
> Of so much that is so good.
> Amen.

'Lifelines', Susan Hardwick

THE TOP TEN KEY POINTS

☐ The secret in every success is not quitting.

☐ Jesus said, 'I have told you these things, so that in me you may have peace. In this world you will have trouble. But take heart! *I have overcome* the world' (John 16:33 my emphasis).

☐ God wants to speak to you.

☐ Enthusiasm doesn't come from the outside – it doesn't come from a hug, or a salary increase. It comes from the inside. The Greek word *enthusiasmos* means 'to have God inside the soul'.

☐ The reason why we are so often sad is because we depend so much on results.

☐ The devil is really interested in taking away all your

enthusiasm. If he succeeds, it is as though he were spitting on the cross and saying that it had no value for you.

❏ Don't permit the devil to make you sad. Confront him. Ask God to give you spiritual eyes.

❏ 'Be very careful, then, how you live – not as unwise but as wise, making the most of *every* opportunity, because the days are evil' (Eph. 5:15–16, my emphasis).

❏ We all need to lighten up because some of the biggest causes of stress are: trying to do too much; failing to prioritise; taking yourself too seriously.

❏ God uses waiting to work out various purposes in our lives.

8
I'm having fun.
Is there something wrong?

Have you ever been sitting in a smart restaurant with waiters serving you, having dinner with your loved one on a special night out, when suddenly you feel a horrible sense of guilt because you are a committed Christian? From nowhere the thought comes into your mind: what if someone I know comes in and finds us here having an expensive dinner? We should be eating in the cheap pizza place down the street!

During the first year of our marriage Joao used to order only soup when we went out for dinner. If someone visiting from overseas offered to take us to a nice restaurant as a treat, he used to order the cheapest dish on the menu. Joao had slipped into this mindset during his eight years as a missionary in a third world country where many churchgoing Christians have the ingrained idea that missionaries should be seen to live in abject poverty. I must quickly add, however, that this miserable notion is not limited to South Americans!

Apart from the inevitable joy that I have experienced from precious relationships formed with the boys and girls we help in Happy Child, and the deep friendships with the brothers and sisters in Christ who have chosen to walk alongside Joao and me in this ministry, I am convinced that God delights to bring his servants joy in other kinds of ways too. He wants to use the generosity of other Christians to bless us. Yet I have often found that the feeling of guilt I have just described can steal these moments of joy.

When I look around at this extraordinary universe that our heavenly Father has created, I am always struck by his attention to detail. Was God mean and stingy with his choice of beauty, colour, size and rich adornment? No! He was generous – awesomely so. In the same way, God wants to give in abundance to all his loyal children. 'No eye has seen, no ear has heard, no mind has conceived what God has prepared for those who love him' (1 Cor. 2:9).

Jesus said,

Therefore I tell you, do not worry about your life, what you will eat or drink; or about your body, what you will wear. Is not life more important than food, and the body more important than clothes? Look at the birds of the air; they do not sow or reap or store away in barns, and yet your heavenly Father feeds them. Are you not much more valuable than they? Who of you by worrying can add a single hour to his life? ... But seek first his kingdom and his righteousness, and all these things will be given to you as well. (Matt. 6:25–7, 33)

Wow! What a promise – and God always keeps his promises!

Perhaps you suffer from some of these other common missionary false guilt complexes:

- I could have spent my holidays at home instead of coming to the beach, and given the money I'm spending to the poor.
- I'm a missionary, so I should live in tiny accommodation with only the bare necessities, wear no make-up, no jewellery, tie my hair back in a bun, never have highlights and wear second-hand clothes.
- God wouldn't expect us to buy a brand new van for this ministry. We should buy a third-hand one that's old and falling apart. That way everyone will know we are poor and needy.

If you tend to think like this, then, like me, you have slipped into a 'sacrificial' mindset. But over the last nine years I have been deeply convicted that these thoughts do not come from my heavenly Father, and they certainly don't glorify or fulfil his Word which promises that a life with Jesus is one of abundance.

As a fallen human being I have the capacity to lose all perspective and balance on this delicate issue. I don't know about you, but I need to have a reference point and for me it is the words of the Apostle Paul:

> I am not saying this because I am in need, for I have learned to be content whatever the circumstances. I know what it is to be in need, and I know what it is to have plenty. I have learned the secret of being content in any and every situation, whether well fed or hungry, whether living in plenty or in want. I can do everything through him who gives me strength. (Phil. 4:11–13)

The bottom line is the condition of my heart. Frequently I have to ask myself: 'Sarah, what is going on in your heart? Is it firmly in the hands of God? Why are you desiring these things? Is this a fantasy? A dream? Or is this in line with God's plans for you. Is this provision from the hand of God?'

THE 'ATTITUDE OF LACK'

In his book, *God's Smuggler*, Brother Andrew relates how he slipped into an 'attitude of lack'![1] Growing up in a tiny village in Holland, Brother Andrew received a call from God which changed his life dramatically. Risking his life over and over again, this extraordinary man took hundreds and thousands of Bibles to Christians cut off from the Church in countries as far as Russia, Yugoslavia and Hungary. He witnessed God's intervention daily in his travels, through miraculous provision of money, visas, transport – even deliverance from death.

Yet in spite of all these experiences, Brother Andrew confesses that he and his wife Corrie, in their notions of economy, gradually slipped into a wrong mindset. They failed to 'lean back in the arms of a Father who had more than enough and to spare'. The error was revealed to him through the words of a good lady he had never met, who sent him a cheque to be used for his own personal needs. Apparently suspecting from the tone of his letter of thanks that the money would in fact go into his work, the lady immediately wrote to Brother Andrew again. Brother Andrew writes:

> She began by reminding me of the scriptural injunction that the ox grinding the corn must not be kept from enjoying the grain. Did I think God felt less about His

human workers? Hadn't I better examine myself to be sure I was not nursing a Sacrificial Spirit? Wasn't I claiming to depend upon God, but living as if my needs would be met by my own scrimping? I remember her close: 'God will send you what your family needs and what your work needs too. You are a mature Christian, Brother Andrew. Act like one.'

God really is a Father. He is as displeased with a cramped 'attitude of lack' as much as with its opposite failing of acquisitiveness or covetousness.

The devil's schemes are subtle. He is out there trying to destroy the image of Christ in us. Therefore I have to try with all my might to bring every thought and desire captive and submit it to God at all times. I need to ask myself, 'Is my greatest want and priority "to press on towards the goal to win the prize for which God has called me heavenwards in Christ Jesus"? (Phil. 3:14) Or is something else driving me?'

Ask yourself these questions:

- I want to be successful. Why? What are my motivations?
- I'd like to have more money. Why? To give and sow into God's Kingdom?
- I'd love to go and spend a long weekend in a luxury hotel. Why? Can we afford it? Is this good timing?
- I'd like to live in a large house with a large garden. Why? To keep up with my friends? Or to use it for God's purposes? Will I use it for his purposes?
- I'd love to throw all my old clothes away and buy new ones. Why? Is this a real need?

I must quickly add that there is nothing wrong with being

rich. King Solomon was one of the richest people who ever lived. God poured material blessing upon blessing into his life. However, when Solomon first took over the kingdom from his father David, the Bible gives us a glimpse into his heart. God tells Solomon he can ask him for whatever he wants. This is what he replied:

'Now, O Lord my God, you have made your servant king in place of my father David. But I am only a little child and do not know how to carry out my duties. Your servant is here among the people you have chosen, a great people, too numerous to count or number. So give your servant a discerning heart to govern your people and to distinguish between right and wrong. For who is able to govern this great people of yours?' ...

So God said to him, 'Since you have asked for this and not for long life or wealth for yourself, nor have asked for the death of your enemies but for discernment in administering justice, I will do what you have asked. I will give you a wise and discerning heart, so that there will never have been anyone like you, nor will there ever be. Moreover, I will give you what you have not asked for – both riches and honour – so that in your lifetime you will have no equal among kings. And if you walk in my ways and obey my statutes and commands as David your father did, I will give you a long life.' (1 Kings 3:7–14)

How important are money and material things to me? More important than my trust in God?

The Lord makes this point very clear. He promises, 'Delight yourself in me, and I will give you the desires of your heart' (Ps. 37:4).

As a missionary, having handed my life over to God, I

have often experienced the truth that God provides for his workers in very practical ways. What's more he loves to take care of the tiniest details. He loves it when I come to him and ask. It's that simple!

I have also lived out the promise that when I delight in my God and his will, then he really does give me the desires of my heart – often desires I never even knew I had. Before arriving in Brazil, as part of my outreach with Youth With A Mission, I spent two months in Chile. As part of the programme, we divided into smaller groups and each team of people went in the direction they felt God was guiding them. Four of us, with a heart for intercession, felt led to travel south to the islands off southern Chile to pray for the Indians who live there, many of whom we found to be sick and thirsty for the gospel. I can honestly say that I have never experienced such natural and breathtaking beauty in all my life as I did on those islands. In my diary I wrote this:

8 February 1991

The weather was hot and sunny and the sea was very calm as we arrived by launch on a beach off the Island of Tabon. A small group of local Indians met us on horseback. The scenery was quite breathtaking – volcanic snow-covered mountains towered into the sky in the far distance. The greenest land I have ever seen stretched out before us, with little farmhouses scattered here and there. Wild flowers of all colours filled the green fields, where cattle grazed. They took our ruck-sacks and put them on their horses, as we followed them in single file. A little foal stayed close to its mother. Birds of such size and beauty squawked and stretched their massive wingspan above our heads as though saying 'welcome' – I wonder what type of birds they are? As we reached the top of the hill I caught my breath: surfing in the waves to the right of the island were over fifty or sixty dolphins! Chantal and I started to laugh. I honestly thought for twenty seconds that maybe we'd died and gone to heaven!

Surrounded by such natural splendour of God's unspoilt creation, words cannot now describe the completeness of joy I experienced deep within my soul. It was one of the most special moments of my life. Because it was my heavenly Father saying, 'See, if you delight in me I will give you the desires of your heart!'

When it comes down to it, it's not about our material wealth. It's not about the money. It's finding what Paul found: that life has no meaning without Jesus Christ in the centre of it. You could be living in a mansion in Hollywood or a two-roomed hut in a *favela* in South America, but if you haven't allowed Jesus to occupy that void in you, if there is still restlessness and an emptiness in your heart, you are not in the centre of his will. You are resisting his greater plans for you – he wants you to trust and obey. Let him be your ultimate want – absolutely nothing else matters. The rest just comes as he sees fit. 'Commit your way to the Lord; trust in him and he will do this: He will make your righteousness shine like the dawn, the justice of your cause like the noonday sun' (Ps. 37:5–6). When God first gave me this verse one morning during my time in the *favela* in Rio, I remember vividly the awesome reality that he could make the work I was proposing to start with the street children 'shine like the noonday sun' – and, boy, how powerful and hot that noonday sun is in Brazil! It was so encouraging!

In his book, *Daring to Live on the Edge* Loren Cunningham says this: 'Even if God can trust me and my character, He knows what I need – no more and no less – to fulfil His calling on my life.'[2]

If your home is where your heart is, and your heart belongs to Jesus, then, wherever he is, for you it's your home!

If you are working with the poor and suffering there may well come a time when God asks you to make your home with them and live as they live twenty-four hours a day. For instance, you may find yourself in a *favela,* a refugee camp or on a poor housing estate. God may call you to work in a round-the-clock rehabilitation centre for drug addicts, AIDS victims, street children, street adults, leprosy sufferers or newly released prisoners.

As God's workers living among those to whom you are committed in his name, you will pay a price for the Kingdom – what a privilege! However, remember that what is important to your God is the condition of your heart, not your circumstances. He will take care of you; trust in him. Receive the blessings with which God will seek to reward you for being there for Jesus in that place. And when you need to rest, rest. He knows our limits.

Your heavenly Father rested on the seventh day, having made the earth and everything in it. As he rested that day, the earth kept on creating.

THOSE WONDERFUL 'SURPRISE GIFTS'

At the early stage of the ministry a visiting team from my church in England came to work on the farm over Christmas. Joao and I were exhausted, working flat out during the day and getting little sleep at night because our first-born son, Lucas, was only six months old. Then, late one afternoon Joe (a nurse) and another member of the team arrived at our small cottage on the farm with an offering from everyone 'specially for us both to go out for a romantic dinner somewhere nice!' What was more, Joe was going to baby-sit. We were really touched, and for the first time in ages went out for a dinner, just the two of us.

Joao and I continue to experience these little 'surprise gifts', often from people from far away who have no way of knowing our physical state. At the end of 1998, after a very difficult year we were at a low ebb. As a couple, we had spent little time on our own in a romantic sense. One night during the week Joao came home and insisted that I went with him to listen to a pastor from Ethiopia. I was ready for bed and feeling like going nowhere. However, I sensed a nudge from the Holy Spirit, and finding a baby-sitter to look after our three young children, we set off to the church where the pastor would speak.

To a crowd of over 3500 people, Pastor Alemu spoke of how God wants us to know him by his name – 'I am who I am!' Alemu said: 'Every blessing spiritual, material or physical is in his name. When God is in control he changes things beyond our capacities. The blessing of God is not just money. We are called to be a channel of blessing. Declare the name of God over your family, children, non-believers. The blessing breaks the curses – refuse to curse, only bless. I want to ask every married couple to stand up, face each other, and, looking into each other's eyes, take it in turns to speak words of blessing to one another!'

As Joao started to speak words of blessing to me, tears rolled down his cheeks, a lump came into my throat – when was the last time we had had simple intimacy like this? At the end Joao and I went up for prayer. No sooner had this man of God placed his hands on us than he said slowly, 'I know this may sound a little strange, but I hear God saying that you should both take a holiday.' We both laughed. He then prayed simply that our heavenly Father would provide a place and the money to do so.

The following day we got a phone call from Dercy Goncalves, the Director of Compassion International Brazil, with whom Pastor Alemu was staying, saying that the pastor wanted to meet with us again! And believe it or not, this dear man came all the way out to the farm that afternoon, looked around at our work, met the children and then quite unexpectedly asked if there was a nice place to stay close by. We told him about a country club in the mountains with swimming pools, waterfalls, restaurant and chalets. He asked us if we could kindly show it to him, which we did. No sooner had we arrived at the club when Pastor Alemu turned to Joao and asked: 'When was the last time you and Sarah were here. Just the two of you?'

Joao replied, 'A long time ago. Why?'

Alemu continued gently, 'I felt God asking me to pray for you both late last night, and as I did so he asked me quite clearly to pay for you both to have a long weekend away somewhere nice. God asked me to do this before I left.'

We were both speechless. This man must have prayed for hundreds of people that night; he had better things to do than to take the trouble to come all the way out to the farm and worry about us! I was deeply touched, first by his obedience, but more importantly by God's care and concern for us as a couple. Once again my heavenly Father was showing us that our relationship and life together was more important than the ministry.

God wants missionaries who will finish the job they

are called to, and not people who go home early because they adopted a sacrificial lifestyle that was too harsh to sustain. There may come a time when God calls you out of those particular living conditions to something more comfortable, which enables you to sleep better at night (away from the creepy crawlies!) and therefore give more of your best during the day, and for a longer period of time. From my experience he gives me what he knows I need, and not what I think I need, at just the right time. Since working on the frontline here in Brazil, God has used my living circumstances to work in my heart. He tests me to discover whether I really am committed to his service.

'CAN I USE PERFUME IF I'M A MISSIONARY? AND IF I DO, WHAT WILL OTHERS THINK?'

Some people have a very old-fashioned view of what a missionary should look like. This was brought home to me all the more vividly after a talk I gave in England when a lady came up to me and said, 'It's so nice to see a missionary wearing nice clothes, a bit of make-up and nail varnish'! Another time someone asked me earnestly, 'If I become a missionary can I still highlight my hair?'

A pastor I know from a church here in Belo Horiozonte was once given a Mont Blanc pen as a present. He later told me that he nearly stopped using it because of the amount of comments he received from other people. They used to say things like, 'Oooh, look at that – a pastor with a Mont Blanc pen!' His wife Joanna (name changed) has a wonderful gift of hospitality, and in 1998 they were able to offer hospitality to over fifty people – including missionaries from Happy Child! – who stayed at various times in their small two-bedroomed flat. Joanna's dream, she told me, was to have a house with an extra bedroom, because following the birth of her second child at the end of that year, she would no longer have the space she so desired to offer to her guests. But she worried that some of the congregation would make negative comments if they were to get a bigger house!

This is so sad! But true. We worry so much about what people think. Of course we need to be sensitive, but, if we are in the centre of God's will, he isn't going to give us anything that isn't perfect for us. If Joanna's desire to have a house with that extra bedroom is God's desire, then her fear about other people's opinions could possibly stop her asking her heavenly Father to provide it, and the very gift God has for her could remain unreleased. By the way, the fear of other people's opinions is one of the most prevalent fears in the world!

So what about those people who could make a negative comment? Are they wrong? Yes, they are. 'For out of the overflow of his heart his mouth speaks' (Luke 6:45). Maybe they are commenting out of a spirit of jealousy and judgment. I'm more and more convinced that in my walk with God, I must listen to God's voice. I pray. If the prayer request is answered because it is in line with his will, I must receive the gift with thanks and enjoy it. God loves to bless his servants – we mustn't let our fear of other people's opinions and comments rob us of our Lord's joy in giving! Nor must we deprive other people of the joy of giving. If we have difficulty receiving, our pride is blinding our hearts. In Proverbs 29:25 we are told: 'Fear of man will prove to be a snare, but whoever trusts in the Lord is kept safe.' I, for one, need to meditate on this.

During an interview with a national British newspaper in 1996 the journalist asked me to list every item in my kitchen in the cottage on the farm. By her tone of voice,

I knew what she was wanting to hear. Finally she asked, 'Have you got a microwave?' Yes, I had a microwave. A friend at our church had given it to us second-hand after the birth of our second son, Daniel. She said it would make our lives easier, as we could heat up food and baby bottles in seconds during our busy day on the farm. 'Well, well,' said the journalist triumphantly. 'How do you feel about having a mod-con that almost none of the families of the children you are helping have?' I laughed. She looked puzzled. I could have retaliated defensively and asked her what percentage of her time and money was given to helping the poor. But I didn't, because it doesn't matter. Her attitude stemmed from a twisted view of how missionaries should live, echoed sadly by many others. By the way, this part of the interview never appeared in the article!

DO YOU BELIEVE GOD'S PROMISE IS FOR YOU?

Jesus promised this, 'no one who has left home or wife or brothers or parents or children for the sake of the kingdom of God will fail to receive many times as much in this age and, in the age to come, eternal life' (Luke 18:29–30).

If you are working in a far-off city or country, then you must find a church. If you don't do this – however short-term your stay – you will miss out on this great promise, and the joy that comes with it.

I have seen missionaries from other countries and cities who have worked with us for over two years and have never ever reaped the blessings of these words Jesus spoke. They failed to receive the promise because they never did their part. They never prayed and found the church, the pastor, the family that God certainly had for them while they were here. As a result their social lives revolved solely around the ministry and the people in it. For them there was no healthy perspective, respite, or life away from the work.

Paul Williams, a missionary from England, is for me a great example of someone who did play his part, and did reap God's promise. He currently forms part of our street team, the group of loving and committed people who walk the streets every weekday at the crack of dawn and late into the dark nights befriending the children often drugged lying in the gutters and under viaducts. As a way of encouraging those of you to whom this promise applies, Paul shares some of his experience.

'I was one of a team of eight who had been sent out from my church on a short three-week visit to Joao and Sarah de Carvalho's Happy Child street children ministry. As I walked through the streets of Belo Horizonte in December 1996, I said to God, "It would have to be a strong call, Lord, to get me back out here, because I don't think I could live here!"

'The night that God confirmed his call for me to return is still very clear. Several weeks had passed since returning from Brazil. I had spent the day arranging my photographs from the trip and was relaxing listening to music. I was not thinking of anything in particular when all of a sudden I found myself sobbing deep cries and thinking of the children I had met under that viaduct. Young children. Two pregnant teenage girls and three small boys. They had made their home there. They would still be there now, but I was at home! The pain and sadness I felt was so deep that I could only reach for my Bible. As I opened it I found myself looking at the pages of Luke 18. I read through the Scripture: "Let the little children come to me, and do not hinder them, for the kingdom of God belongs to such as these" (Luke 18:16).

'Gulp! A hundred and one questions raced through my mind. "Are you really asking me to go back, Lord?" I looked around my room and my eyes fell on the clothes hanging in the wardrobe, my diary open and full of social engagements, my stereo, books, all my comforts. "I couldn't leave this, I like this stuff too much!" "You still lack one thing. Sell everything you have and give to the poor, and you will have treasure in heaven. Then come, follow me" (Luke 18:22).

'Then I saw a photograph of my brother and his wife, and my parents. "OK Lord, I could leave all this 'stuff', but could I really leave my family?" "I tell you the truth," Jesus said to them, "no one who has left home or wife or brothers or parents or children for the sake of the kingdom of God will fail to receive many times as much in this age and, in the age to come, eternal life" (Luke 18:29–30).

'In just a few minutes, God had confirmed his call. That night I lifted my hands in prayer and said "Yes Lord".

'Knowing how much I loved my family, my friends, and was enjoying my new church, God continued to remind me of this verse in the year I prepared to return to Brazil, full-time. He would be giving me a new church, new friends, and special relationships.

'Three weeks after I arrived in Brazil I was determined to make my way to a church I had passed several times on the bus as I journeyed to the farm. I knew no one there but felt sure I had to go. I went to the early Bible study, understanding nothing but the odd word. I could easily have left feeling frustrated and foolish but for some reason I stayed and there at the back of the church I was greeted by Sergio. Sergio sat beside me and translated the sermon during the main service. Amidst the garbled confused sounds coming from the pastor's mouth, it was as if God was speaking directly to me as Sergio translated the clear message in my ear: "… you are no longer foreigners and aliens, but fellow-citizens with God's people and members of God's household" (Eph. 2:19). Through these few words, God had spoken to me and confirmed that I was "at home".

'My new church soon became the source of enormous blessing and fun. When God said to me that he would be giving me new friendships I had not expected them to come so quickly. As I thanked Sergio for his translation skills, he told me that the Lord had spoken to him and asked him to "walk with me". There and then, he made himself available to serve me in whatever way he could. Since then the Lord has blessed us greatly through our friendship. The Lord has ministered to each of us through the times we have shared in prayer. His parents have "adopted" me into their family, given me a key to their home, and call me their "English son". They in turn, have become my Brazilian "Mum and Dad".

'As I attended the various church meetings so new friendships were made. After the service on Sunday mornings I often had a choice of where I could go for lunch, such was the kindness being offered by the families there. God was giving me homes and families whilst I was far from my own. Church also became a place of refuge. A retreat from the life of the ministry. At that time I was living in community on the farm and found that by the weekend I was ready for some different company and conversation. I was able to go away and stay with friends and return feeling "recharged" for the week ahead, not to mention well-fed! My new pastor had lived in the UK for two years so had an understanding of my cultural perspective. In him, I had someone who would understand the difficulties I would face adjusting to Brazilian culture, and who spoke English!

'Some months later when God called me away from the farm to work with the street team in the city, I needed to find somewhere to live. Within two weeks God placed me in a wonderful home, perfectly located, living with friends from church, and rent-free. It was hard to accept because the house was nicer than my flat in London! Where was the sacrifice in this?

'Of course, most amazing of all is the part of verse 29 that says "no one who has left home or wife …". I was not married when I set out for Brazil, so it was not possible for me to physically leave my wife, but I did give up the idea of marriage. God had never told me that I would be getting married so I never assumed I would. In truth I could no longer see much hope in finding a wife. As I saw it I would be living in Brazil with no income, no career, and no prospects. Not so! On Friday 23 July, 1999, I married Alessandra. We met … at church!

' "I tell you the truth," Jesus said to them, "no one who has left home or wife or brothers or parents or children for the sake of the kingdom of God will fail to receive many times as much in this age and, in the age to come, eternal life." During these first fourteen months living in Brazil, God has continued to "out-perform" my greatest expectations, and given me "many times as much". I went out to Brazil with the expectation of suffering and sacrifice yet continue to learn what it is to live life in abundance "in this age".'

IF I'M ENJOYING MYSELF THEN SOMETHING MUST GO WRONG TO COMPENSATE!

This cruel superstition grips us all at some time or other. We all carry guilt – a subconscious invisible guilt embedded deep in our soul that is with us from our birth. It is with us a result of what happened in the Garden of Eden when man decided to be his own god, to go it alone without his heavenly Father. However, Jesus completely destroyed the hold that this guilt has over us when he died on the cross and then rose again three days later. Jesus paid the ultimate sacrifice and for two thousand years now we have, thankfully, been able to live in the good of what he has done for us.

> That is why Paul wrote: 'Therefore, there is now no condemnation for those who are in Christ Jesus.' Romans 8:1.

So if I start spiralling into a sense of 'false' guilt, I repeat this verse in my mind and am released immediately from the lie: 'Therefore, there is now no condemnation for those who are in Christ Jesus.' Do you believe these words? They are for you too!

THE TOP TEN KEY POINTS

❑ Discern what is 'real' guilt and what is 'false' guilt.
❑ God really is a Father. He is as displeased with a cramped 'attitude of lack' as with its opposite failing of acquisitiveness
❑ What is my motivation? Is my greatest want and

priority 'to press on towards the goal to win the prize for which God has called me heavenwards in Christ Jesus?' (Phil. 3:14)

❑ God looks after his servants 'Delight yourself in the Lord, and he will give you the desires of your heart' (Ps. 37:4)

❑ 'Even if God can trust me and my character, he knows what I need – no more and no less – to fulfil his calling on my life.'

❑ When you need to rest, rest. Your heavenly Father rested on the seventh day, having made the earth and everything in it. As he rested that day, the earth kept on creating.

❑ God wants missionaries who will finish the job they are called to, and not people who go home early because they adopted a sacrificial lifestyle that was too harsh to sustain.

❑ One of the most common fears is the fear of other people's opinions. However, we are warned in the Bible that 'Fear of man will prove to be a snare' (Prov. 29:25).

❑ 'No one who has left home or wife or brothers or parents or children for the sake of the kingdom of God will fail to receive many times as much in this age and, in the age to come, eternal life' (Luke 18:29–30). If you are working in a new city and/or country away from your home then find a church. If you don't, you will miss out on this great promise.

❑ If I'm enjoying myself then something must go wrong to compensate. Wrong! The Bible says that 'there is now no condemnation for those who are in Christ Jesus' (Rom. 8:1).

9

I'm struggling with my leaders and my colleagues. What should I do?

'Why did God give me a boss like Peter? Why would God allow a person with a quick temper to stay in a position like this? I can't respect Peter at all!'

'I can't seem to please Jeff. Everything I do seems to be wrong, he always knows best. I can't work alongside him in this ministry any longer.'

'If I had been leading that meeting it would have taken half the amount of time it did to decide the issues we discussed! Christine is so slow in leadership – it's all talk and no action. She goes over and over the same point. I've had much more experience than she has in leadership, and working in a drug rehabilitation centre in the UK.'

'I can't share a room with Paul, he's so untidy and disorganised. It's driving me nuts!'

'Frank, my leader, is so hard and impatient, he hasn't

got a pastor's heart at all. I don't even think he prays enough. How on earth can he be anointed to do God's work? If I was in his place I'd do everything differently!'

'I can't work in this office any longer. My boss isn't Christian, and he is making serious mistakes.'

'Juliana has offended me so much with her arrogant tone of voice and insensitivity. I can't even cope with being in the same room as her, let alone work with her.'

'I've given up my job, career, family and country to be a missionary and save children from the gutters of the streets, not to clean my leaders' house. I'm not a maid!' said Sarah the new missionary three weeks after she arrived in Brazil! (Yes, that was me.)

Does any of this strike a chord? Working in a team, whether for a ministry, mission, church or in your work-place, is always going to be challenging. The people you are working with all have different temperaments, they all have different opinions formed from different back-grounds, cultures and education, and they are all carrying 'baggage' of one sort or another from their upbringing or other negative experiences.

OK, so you soon realise that you aren't going to 'click' with everyone – that's cool, that's just the way it is! Or so you think, until you read these words:

May the God who gives endurance and encouragement give you a spirit of unity among yourselves as you follow Christ Jesus, so that with one heart and mouth you may glorify the God and Father of our Lord Jesus Christ. Accept one another, then, just as Christ accepted you, in order to bring praise to God. (Rom. 15:5–7)

Jesus said, 'My command is this: Love each other as I have loved you.' (John 15:12)

Love your neighbour as yourself. (Mark 12:31)

Then Peter came to Jesus and asked, 'Lord, how many times shall I forgive my brother when he sins against me? Up to seven times?' Jesus answered, 'I tell you, not seven times, but seventy-seven times.' (Matt.18:21–2)

A man's wisdom gives him patience; it is to his glory to overlook an offence. (Prov. 19:11)

Set a guard over my mouth, O Lord; keep watch over the door of my lips. (Ps. 141:3)

The tongue also is a fire, a world of evil among the parts of the body. It corrupts the whole person, sets the whole course of his life on fire, and is itself set on fire by hell. (Jas. 3:6)

Obey your leaders and submit to their authority. They keep watch over you as men who must give an account. Obey them so that their work will be a joy, not a burden, for that would be of no advantage to you. (Heb. 13:17)

Submit to one another out of reverence for Christ. (Eph. 5:21)

'Impossible!' you cry. Yes, I agree with you: in my own flesh, in my own strength, these commands (for that is what they are) often seem like impossibilities. But they are written very clearly for us all to see, and therefore I take it that they are all possible, with his help. What's more, God is counting on you and me to live by them – because that way he is glorified and his will in us and through us is fulfilled. He doesn't want us to carry offences and hurts around with us.

WHY UNITY?

As a ministry we in Happy Child have learned again and again that unity is key. Without it, we as a team have discovered that our prayers are not answered, the children do not come off the streets, families are not restructured, teenagers are not healed, the children are not saved, and the ministry does not move forward: it stagnates. Satan knows that without unity the Holy Spirit cannot move. Therefore his number one strategy is to stir up and use conflicts and differences to devalue the authority of the leaders and arouse criticism and division amongst the team.

We have discovered that the following principles are key:

- Each of the teams from the seven different departments in Happy Child – the street team, day-care centre team, night shelter team, girls' house team, farm team, family team, administration department – meet together either on a daily or weekly basis to pray and intercede for the work.
- We have discovered, through experience, that our prayers are hindered when team members hold grudges and offences against each other, or when a team member is disheartened or rebelling against a decision made. Therefore a principle we have is 'lavar roupas sujas' (clean our dirty clothes). It is a time when we 'clear our hearts' of any misunderstandings, offences and negligence felt between one another. Jesus requires us to confess our weaknesses to one another and to forgive. He said, 'Forgive and you will be forgiven' (Luke 6:37). Through this we discover how much we need each other. As we obey,

God commands the blessing upon us and upon the ministry.

- Once a month the leadership from the seven departments in the ministry meet to discuss problems, solutions and future plans, and to pray. As we listen to God he gives us his heart for the children, he restores our vision, and, when we don't know, he tells us what to do. To do it God's way we have to pray and to listen.

- One afternoon each week Joao is available to spend time with anyone in the ministry who would like to speak to him personally.

- Every month or so we meet up as an entire ministry to pray and intercede. Sometimes the Holy Spirit just leads us to minister and pray for one another. In a recent meeting all the women of the ministry were led to pray for all the men. We formed a circle around them linking hands, and, as we started to pray, the Holy Spirit fell upon some of them with great power. Prophecies, words of knowledge and encouragement followed causing many to weep in reverence of his presence. Then the men prayed for all the women and the blessing was returned!

- Many of us would like to escape from meetings. We'd rather be busy in work and activity. They frighten us just because they require a commitment from us. But if unity, relationships and the vision are going to be held together and realised, we must make meetings a priority.

OFFENDED? YOUR RESPONSE DETERMINES YOUR FUTURE

In the early days of Happy Child, Joao and I made the mistake of periodically accepting onto the team workers from other ministries and churches who were carrying unresolved problems from their previous place of work. They would tell us during their interviews of the shortfalls and failings of their previous leadership, they would complain about how wrongfully they had been treated and how the ministry could have been better run if only the leadership had listened to their suggestions. Joao and I would feel incredibly sorry for each one and accept them to work for us!

However, after a little while, we would notice that the effect these people had on the team was invariably disastrous. Rebellion, criticism and division would begin to run riot. They were operating from a place of bitterness as a result of a failure to put right the wrongs of past experiences. The way they viewed their past relationships formed the springboard for their future ones. Many people go from church to church, ministry team to ministry team, trying to develop their ministry. If God puts them in a place where they are not recognised and encouraged, they are easily upset. If they don't agree with the way something is done, they are offended and depart. They then leave, blaming the leadership. They are blind to any of their own character flaws and do not realise God wanted to refine and mature them through the pressure they were under. It is not God's plan for anyone to leave with an offended or critical spirit. Such people are reacting rather than acting on his guidance. 'For you shall go out in joy, and be led out in peace' (Isa. 55:12).

Titus 3:10 gives leaders clear instructions on the course of action they should take: 'Warn a divisive person once, and then warn him a second time. After that, have nothing to do with him.' In other words be merciful. If there is someone in your team who is not producing fruit and is becoming a negative influence on the work and the team, then confront him once, even rebuke him a second time if necessary, but if the problem continues after that, then you should consider asking him to leave. What would you do if you planted a young fruit tree and after the first season it did not produce any fruit? You wouldn't throw it away immediately. You'd probably buy some fertiliser and place it carefully around the root of the young tree and water it, and give it a second chance. However, if after all that it still didn't produce any fruit you would probably throw it away.

We will be judged according to fruit, not gifting. A spiritual gift is given: fruit is cultivated.

I don't know about you but often when I'm offended I react to the situation and do things that appear right to me (and possibly a few others), even though they are not inspired by God. I am discovering that I am not called to react but to *act*. As you read at the beginning of this chapter, I was indignant that I had to clean my leaders' house and iron their clothes once a week whilst doing a three-month course on rescuing street children with Youth With A Mission in early 1991. As I was there washing their bathroom my pride was stirred: Sarah Jarman the television producer! Gave everything up to become a maid, and what's worse without choice! I was furious. Who did they think they were? Didn't they know that there were hundreds of young girls in the *favelas* without a job?

You see, whether they were right or wrong, my attitude

wasn't the attitude that Jesus displayed when he washed his disciples' feet. As I started to voice my opinion and disgust about my leaders' decision to my roommates, whose voice was I listening to? God's? I don't think so. A small matter, you might say to yourself. Maybe. But the problem was that instead of going to God and seeking him in the Word and settling the matter in my heart, I held a grudge. This grudge continued to ferment during those three months of my stay, fuelled by the slightest thing the leaders did or didn't do with which I did not agree! Eventually during a time of worship at the end of the course, the Holy Spirit convicted me. My attitude was wrong and I needed to release forgiveness. That meant I had to humble myself. I had to go and confess something to someone against whom I'd built barriers. I had to choose whether or not I would obey God. I remember asking the Holy Spirit for strength and courage at the end of that service, as I walked towards my leader to ask for forgiveness with all sincerity. Let me tell you, the release I felt afterwards was indescribable: I found that my whole attitude changed immediately. I saw them through a different filter. Today they are people I admire enormously. More importantly, if I hadn't obeyed the conviction of the Holy Spirit at that time, my ministry would have been hindered when I later moved on to Rio.

Looking back I can see that another root of my problem had also been insecurity, which had resulted in pride. I was in a new country, trying to learn a new language and to come to terms with a new culture. I had left behind my security as a successful career girl in England. I was feeling completely lost and belittled, wondering what use I would be to God and struggling with my new position. These unfamiliar feelings of insecurity had revealed my vulnerability – I needed something from my leaders at that time that they couldn't give me. My pride made me open to Satan's words and accusations.

> 'When we retain an offence in our hearts, we filter everything through it. If you stay free from offence you will stay in the will of God. If you become offended you will be taken captive by the enemy to fulfil his own purpose and his will. Stay submitted to God. We resist the devil by not becoming offended.' John Bevere, *The Bait of Satan*.[1]

HOW CAN I NOT BECOME OFFENDED?

If you and I have chosen to commit ourselves to God's care, we need to learn not to react in a worldly way, such as by taking offence. Here are some tips on how to react in God's way.

First, try to deal with the offence in your own heart. If you don't do this, you won't be able to see straight, and you won't be able to keep yourself from expressing your feelings about the person concerned. 'For out of the overflow of his heart his mouth speaks' (Luke 6:45). Go to God in prayer, and hand the situation to him immediately.

I am still learning that it is better to wait a day or so before I act. Let your emotions settle for a while. Try to analyse what the underlying problem might be. Is it spiritual warfare? If you believe it is, resist the devil and silence the thoughts or attack in Jesus's name. Take authority over the demonic powers (Jas. 4:7). Alternatively, there might be a physical explanation: are you tired, or perhaps the other person is tired and under pressure? Or perhaps you need to accept the rebuke and learn from it?

Maybe you were wrong? Perhaps there was a misunderstanding that you need to try to explain?

Take the words spoken or the particular incident that offended you and in your spirit put them into a 'coffin' and declare them dead! Break the power of the 'sting' of those words or that action that offended you in Jesus's name. Submit all your thoughts to Jesus. 'We demolish arguments and every pretension that sets itself up against the knowledge of God, and we take captive every thought to make it obedient to Christ' (2 Cor. 10:5). If need be, after a day or so, seek the counsel of your pastor or a wise godly friend about the matter.

If you need to apologise then do it soon, because if you resist, your heart will harden and you won't be free to pray and to walk forward in God's will for you. Sometimes I need to say I'm sorry just for 'guarding' an offence, even if I feel I was right. Once I felt that one of the deacons in our church here in Brazil was resistant towards the church getting more involved with Happy Child. An opportunity arose and I spoke to him about it to clear up any misunderstanding. I started the conversation by apologising for the offence I was holding against him.

Remember, sulking and feeling sorry for ourselves gets us nowhere – we distance ourselves from Jesus in the process, and become a drain on those around us. If you still feel strongly that the way you were spoken to or the way the situation was handled was wrong, then ask for the opportunity to talk to the person concerned and explain how you feel. If you don't do this quickly, your relationship with him or her will be broken and bitterness will grow. Don't kid yourself that you can bury the problem and forget it! A lack of forgiveness is a stumbling block and you will become vulnerable to Satan's works.

A believer who chooses to delight in the Word of God

in the middle of adversity will rise above feelings of offence. That person will be like a 'tree planted by streams of water, which yields its fruit in season and whose leaf does not wither. Whatever he does prospers' (Ps. 1:3).

CONFRONTATION IS HEALTHY – IT CAN BE DONE LOVINGLY

Are you in a conflict with a colleague? Or even your leader? Or are you in a position of leadership and need to confront a member of your team? Here are some tips that I have learned and am still learning that I hope will help you.

Timing is everything. Choose the right time. Be sensitive, don't jump in feet first and make the conflict worse. If you need to speak to your leader, call first to make a day and a time to talk in his or her office. If the problem involves a colleague say to him or her, 'X, can we please talk together at lunch time or after working hours this week?' Make a day and a time.

Start your conversation by suggesting you pray together first. Prayer has an interesting impact on the resolution of a conflict. It takes an issue between two people who have chosen sides, often against each other, and welcomes into the relationship a third person – Jesus. Dr Gary Rosberg, a marriage and family counsellor, says he always prays a prayer like this in front of/with the other person in the conflict with him: 'Lord, this is a tough one. I'm angry right now, and I want to demand or react. Please soften my heart and my approach to this person. Be in the centre of our discussion so that we will not sin in our anger and frustration. Help us to resolve our problem and come together in this conflict.'

Be watchful. Hold your tongue; listen first. Be teachable. Be thankful. When we are thankful to God, we humble ourselves. As we allow him access into our lives, our pride is diminished and our hearts are softened. Don't attack the person. Remember who your real enemy is. Focus on the problem that caused your difference in opinion, or on the offence. If your emotions are still at boiling point, then you have not had enough secret prayer time with your heavenly Father. Be ready to say you are sorry. Be ready to change.

God works in our lives through other people. It is like two diamonds rubbing together, smoothing the rough edges! I try and ask myself, 'What have I learned about myself through this conflict?'

Leaders: if you are co-ordinating a team in God's work, then, as I've already said, unity is power. God has taught me and continues to teach me the authority in these words,

> How good and pleasant it is
>> when brothers live together in unity!
> It is like precious oil poured on the head,
> running down on the beard,
> running down on Aaron's beard,
>> down upon the collar of his robes.
> It is as if the dew of Hermon
>> were falling on Mount Zion.
> For there the Lord bestows his blessing,
> even life for evermore. (Ps. 133)

However, to keep this unity you will need to learn to confront your team members. During the four years Joao and I lived on the farm God gave me a big heart for the team members and the area of intercession. The foundation of this ministry is intercession and we often met nearly every day during the week to pray together.

God taught us the need for clear hearts and transparency between one another. Our times of intercession would not flow until we were 'one'. It was at this early stage of the ministry that God started to make me sensitive to the Holy Spirit in a new way. I had sought as a leader to be able to discern if anything was hindering the Holy Spirit in our midst – for example, if anyone was holding a grudge against another person. Often we can get so frustrated with one another that we close our hearts and our minds and our mouths and admit nothing to the person face to face (only behind his or her back!) because we don't want to confront or to confess. However, God will show me, in my spirit, who is sad, who is unhappy, who is angry, who is holding a grudge against another person, who is far away from Jesus, who is under attack from the enemy. I learned during those early years in leadership to start every intercession time with a time of waiting on the Holy Spirit in silence, asking him to be at work in our hearts. If after a while the two people or the person that he was making me aware of did not confess or open up, then I would confront them very gently, 'I sense that you, X, are very disheartened with Y. Would you like to share with us how you feel, so that we can talk things through and settle the conflict?' Or sometimes God would show me the need to speak to Z quietly on his or her own. In this way the team learned not to bottle things up and hold grudges, as well as experiencing the living power of unity once matters were settled. For the power of God would come all at once and our prayer times would be transformed and guided in a supernatural way, with brokenness, prophecies, revelations and words of knowledge. In other words it was only when there was unity that we could really pray what was on God's heart, thereby releasing his will in the spiritual world so that it could become reality on earth.

By working in this way I learned that what God wants

is fellow-workers. It is only when we are completely sur-
rendered to him in this incredible place of prayer that an
incomparable partnership begins to operate. From that
place he teaches us that he wants us to work with him; he
warns us of the enemy's strategies; he builds us up to
understand fully that in Christ we too are seated at the
Father's right hand, far above all principality, power and
might (Eph. 2:6). He strengthens our weaknesses; he fills
us with his love; he brings us back to the cross when we
stray; he reveals his promises and plans for our lives; he
releases new gifts; he heals and restores us to him.

WATCH YOUR TONGUE!

Your words can be used very destructively by Satan. The
mouth is a very powerful instrument. James warns us:
'The tongue also is a fire, a world of evil among the parts
of the body. It corrupts the whole person, sets the whole
course of his life on fire, and is itself set on fire by hell'
(3:6). Satan wants to use our words to bring curses and
destruction instead of life, freedom, and glory to Jesus.

When you speak negatively, when you speak unbelief,
fear, division, slander, gossip and criticism you are cursing
others. If you and I are going to be God's instrument we
must do all we can to keep our mouths shut to the devil.
We must speak faith, the truth: words that build up, that
comfort, that love, that bring unity.

One of the attitudes that God does not tolerate for
long is criticism. Over the last eight years I have noticed
that people who fall into this 'hole' for any length of time
don't remain very long on the frontline. God seems to
take them out quickly. One of the reasons is that critical
attitudes are like a 'sickness' that affects and drains the
team and infects God's work. Whilst on the one hand it is

human to have highs and lows, we need to get a grip on negative attitudes quickly by recognising the root of the emotion and spending time talking it through with a godly friend in prayer and repentance at the feet of Jesus. If a worker draws his or her life's energy from the people around them (i.e. friends, family, spouse, colleagues, leaders) rather than from God, then when difficulties arise he or she will soon find themselves spiritually bankrupt.

A team member who suffers from an 'inferiority complex', which implies a low sense of worth, can be more prone to negative feelings than a worker who is confident. The tendency then is to transfer these feelings of worthlessness onto the people and circumstances around them, rather than identifying and facing the inner problem. This can be draining for everyone.

> 'Whatever forces have gone into shaping our thoughts and ideas about ourselves (and we must be careful not to hold bitterness or resentment against those who nurtured us), we who are Christians must stand before God and draw the estimate of ourselves from Him. However little worth there may be in our nature, God put worth upon us by dying for our salvation. No one is to be despised (not even by himself or herself) when they were dear enough to God that He shed His sacred blood. That is the ground of our worth, the solid, sufficient and only basis for it. And it is the same for everyone. This last statement must be allowed to soak into our minds, for it is only when we see that worth is not something that is earned but something bestowed that self-despising can be rooted out of our minds.'
> Selwyn Hughes, *Your Personal Encourager.*[2]

RETALIATION – 'I WON'T BE WRONGED!'

King David is my favourite Old Testament servant of the Lord. His love and faithfulness to his heavenly Father, his repentance and remorse before him when he failed, and his honesty and humility in leadership are a wonderful example.

In *A Tale of Three Kings* Gene Edwards tells a story based on the biblical figures of David, Saul and Absalom to illustrate brokenness, submission and authority.[3] When I read it, what struck me most was David's lack of reaction to King Saul's endless attempts to kill him. I was also intrigued by the question, why did God allow this in the first place?

When 'mad' King Saul threw spears at young David in a rage of jealousy and anger, David didn't do what I would have done. David didn't throw them back at him to show that he could stand up for himself and would not be wronged! What is so humbling to me is that, despite the awful circumstances, David never forgot it was God who had made Saul king, not men.

David's fear of God never allowed him to forget King Saul's remarkable achievements of uniting Israel and making it a kingdom, after hundreds of years of it being held together by a series of judges. In fact Saul had been mightily empowered by the Holy Spirit – he was a prophet, able to do the impossible for God. David remembered this in reverence to God, and, when eventually driven out of the city and into a dark, cold cave by the now 'mad' King Saul, he still did not open his mouth against his leader!

What impresses me most is that when David left the kingdom, he left alone. He did not divide the kingdom, and take others with him to found a new one! He didn't storm off with a rebellious spirit. In my experience people who do this, don't usually dare to leave alone. Instead, in this miserable place, in this miserable cave, David started to sing. And as a result he became one of the most remarkable hymn writers the world has ever known, sharing his thoughts with us, thoughts that comfort our broken hearts.

> 'David the sheep-herder would have grown up to become King Saul II, except that God cut away the Saul inside David's heart. The operation, by the way, took years and was a brutalising experience that almost killed the patient. And what were the scalpel and tongs God used to remove this inner Saul? God used the outer Saul.' Gene Edwards.

After his time in the cave, David's personality was altered. He was barely recognisable. As others eventually had to leave Israel because of King Saul's worsening behaviour, they made contact with David in his cave. However, he never set out to retaliate against Saul, as many of them wanted. He accepted God's sovereignty. Slowly these hundreds of fugitives started to follow David, but he never spoke about authority, or submission, or rules. And as a result they didn't fear submission or authority – the topic didn't even cross their minds. They simply followed David because he was who he was! A man who showed submission and not authority, patience and not rules. He feared no rebellion because he did not mind if he was dethroned. He knew he had hardly lifted a finger to get there in the first place. After Saul's death, King David went on to become one of the greatest leaders of all time.

'Beginning empty-handed and alone frightens the best of men. It also speaks volumes of just how sure they are that God is with them.' Gene Edwards.

I have come to realise that walking with God is full of mountain tops and deep valleys. He has to take me into these deep valleys so that he can break me and prepare me for the next mountain top. He has to break me because my heart is arrogant – I think I am broken when really I am not. My heavenly Father needs a broken vessel.

It is a frightening fact that we all have Saul in us. I can so easily condemn in King Saul what I can see that I myself am capable of. Oh how I would love to see every church, ministry, mission and business run by King David! But there wouldn't be any King Davids if there weren't any King Sauls. And come to think of it, who am I to decide which of the two a leader is? Surely only God knows whom he anoints – and he is not about to tell you and me anyway!

REBELLION – A BLESSING OR A CURSE?

'Consequently, he who rebels against the authority is rebelling against what God has instituted, and those who do so will bring judgment on themselves' (Rom.13:2). Strong, hard-hitting words! What on earth did King David do when his very own son, Absalom, rebelled against him and his kingdom? In fact, Absalom even took over, for a very short while. Surely this would have stirred David to react just a little, after all he had worked for during his reign. Wasn't this his right? And how on earth had Absalom allowed himself to think in the first place that he could do a better job of running the kingdom than his own leader and father? He was indeed so convinced that he ended up dividing the kingdom of God and stirred many up against their king.

O Lord, is there an Absalom in me too?

Absalom was young, handsome, full of vigour, ambition and ideas. His rebellion started slowly:

- showing people problems they had never noticed;
- consoling the frustrated with the answers they wanted to hear;
- suggesting that if he were leader he would be more compassionate and do away with all injustices;
- encouraging men to become restless as more and more 'unfairness' was brought to light, as they sat in their meetings and talked;
- demanding how long could they put up with their current leader? Surely, if handsome Absalom were in a position of power he'd do everything differently!

'In the spiritual realm, a man who will lead a rebellion has already proven, no matter how grandiose his words or angelic his ways, that he has a critical nature, an unprincipled character, and hidden motives in his heart. Frankly, he is a thief. He creates dissatisfaction and tension within the realm, and then either seizes power or siphons off followers. The followers he gets, he uses to found his own dominion. Such a sorry beginning, built on the foundation of insurrection. No, God never honours division in His realm.' Gene Edwards.

King David had a dilemma. Should he suddenly, after all these years, become a King Saul and try to stop Absalom? Or, for the sake of the kingdom, should he risk losing everything, by doing nothing? After all, maybe God wanted Absalom to become king. If so, who was he to interfere? The throne was God's after all. Nevertheless, his closest advisers and friends challenged him to retaliate, to stop this Absalom who spoke against him day and night!

What would I do in a similar dilemma?

King David was emphatic: 'Be gentle with the young man Absalom for my sake' (2 Sam. 18:5).

> King David desired God's will more than he desired a position of leadership.

As it turned out God delivered the kingdom back under David's leadership. However, on hearing this good news from a messenger, the king did not celebrate: his primary concern was for the welfare of Absalom! When David heard that he had been killed, the day of victory was turned into a day of mourning (2 Sam. 18 and 19).

Satan has clear goals:

- To establish anarchy, to create chaos.
- To demoralise those in authority.
- To put in our minds a false concept of submission and authority, because Satan knows the power inherent in submission to authority before God.

This is why we all need to pray for our leaders in Government, in our workplace and in our church.

SUBMISSION – 'DOES THIS MEAN SLAVERY?'

Izabel Zwahlen and her husband Roland ran an orphanage
at the main Youth With A Mission base in Belo Horizonte
for many years. Apart from their own three children, they
'parented' scores of abandoned boys and girls of all ages
and helped them through the horrors of emotional and
physical abuse in the pit of poverty and misery. Izabel is
also a gifted teacher and writer and we at Happy Child
have been profoundly affected by her wisdom. She explains, 'When we work in a team restoring these broken
children's lives, we are representing the family, their
parents. So what strategy is Satan going to do to try and
attack that team of four or five people? The same strategy
he used to destroy the family of that child in the first
place!'

I used to think that submission was something people
did if they were without 'backbone'. People centuries
ago were submissive, not today. To be submissive meant
slavery! However, since becoming a Christian and working on the frontline, Jesus has shown me that it means
the very opposite. When you know who you are in God,
you will do what Jesus did. He took off his robe, put on
a towel, knelt on the cold stone floor and washed the
feet of his disciples. Do you think Jesus did this to show
that he was a great guy, better than everybody else? No,
the very opposite. You see Jesus knew who he was; he
knew where he came from and where he was going to.
Satan could say whatever he wanted to Jesus to try
and talk him out of submitting to God's will, but he
failed every time. Why? Because Jesus knew that God's
authority was greater.

> Oswald Chambers said that the greater the spiritual maturity, the greater the need to obey and submit. Often we think it's the very opposite. We think that the more mature we are, spiritually the less we have to obey! This is not true.

Two thousand years ago, in a city called Capernaum in Israel, there lived a centurion, who was highly regarded by the Jews. They loved him, because he loved them and had even had a synagogue built for them. What's more, we later discover that this centurion had a great faith. One day as Jesus was entering the city, the centurion sent some elders of the Jews to invite him to go to his home to heal his highly valued servant who was dying. Jesus answered them by saying that not only would he accept this good man's invitation to go to his house, but that he would also heal his dying servant! However, when Jesus was nearing the house the centurion sent out more friends of his to say to Jesus:

> Lord, don't trouble yourself, for I do not deserve to have you come under my roof. That is why I did not even consider myself worthy to come to you. But say the word, and my servant will be healed. For I myself am a man under authority, with soldiers under me. I tell this one, 'Go', and he goes; and that one, 'Come', and he comes. I say to my servant, 'Do this' and he does it.

What I find extraordinary in this true story, however, is Jesus's response. Turning to the crowd that was following him, he said in amazement: 'I tell you, I have not found

224

such great faith even in Israel' (see Luke 7:1–10). Jesus was amazed because the centurion understood how the spiritual world functioned. He knew that even Jesus submitted to a higher authority. Our problem is that often we don't!

Now I can hear some of you asking right now: 'That's fine, Sarah, but how can I submit to someone when I don't agree with them? I don't respect certain characteristics of this person. Do I still have to submit?' I have been in this predicament too. The only way through is to have faith and believe that there exists a higher authority behind that person. If you don't, your life will become very difficult. We cannot allow ourselves to adopt wrong attitudes.

We have to recognise that authority is something important for God. Every authority, whether in the church, in mission, in ministry or in the secular world of finance and business, comes from God. Jesus said, 'All authority in heaven and on earth has been given to me' (Matt. 28:18). 'Everyone must submit himself to the governing authorities, for there is no authority except that which God has established. The authorities that exist have been established by God' (Rom. 13:1).

Imagine you are driving your car to work. Suddenly for no apparent reason, a policeman appears from nowhere blowing his whistle and indicating with fury that you have to stop. What do you do? No question there is a brief temptation to put your foot on the accelerator and drive right past him! But you stop, because a higher authority – the law – has given that policeman authority.

So, in answer to your question, you are going to have to look to the higher authority that is behind your leader. Remember, the Bible makes it clear that all authority, Christian or non-Christian, comes from God. In the last instance God is sovereign, and he is the one behind that person. Accept his sovereignty. If something has to be changed in your leader's life, your wrong attitude won't help God to change it. I am learning that when I stop and look at myself and the way I could change, rather than the way the other person could change, my attitude improves in leaps and bounds, and with that I draw nearer to Jesus.

If you work as a deacon or leader in one of the ministries within your church and your vicar or leader makes a change you do not agree with, it is not your place to react. Nor is it your responsibility to change that decision. If you try to do so you will be assuming an 'illegitimate authority'.

Take a husband and wife situation: imagine if the husband is not being attentive to his wife, doesn't bring her flowers or chocolates, is not affirming her in her role and is insensitive to her need to talk and share her innermost feelings. Then along comes another man who sees these mistakes and assumes the place of that husband towards the suffering woman. This other man has taken on an 'illegitimate authority'. Yes, he was right that the husband was not giving affection to his wife, but that didn't give him the right before God to assume his place!

Relax. You don't need to interfere because your leader is accountable to God for everything he or she has done. Trust the Lord's words that it is 'not by power, not by might, but by my Holy Spirit'. Do you believe that the Holy Spirit can speak better than you can? In this case it is you that will have to change. If you can't, then you will have to leave your church quietly. Don't divide the kingdom.

LOYALTY – MIRIAM AND AARON OPPOSE MOSES

'Miriam and Aaron began to talk against Moses because of his Cushite wife, for he had married a Cushite. "Has the Lord spoken only through Moses?" they asked. "Hasn't he also spoken through us?" And the Lord heard this' (Num. 12:1–2). This, for me, is a very good example in the Bible of people who failed to recognise the authority delegated to a person from God.

So here is Miriam complaining about the fact that Moses has married a Cushite woman, thereby casting doubts on his leadership abilities (see Num. 12). But look who heard them. God! What's more he acted immediately and came down in a pillar of cloud and stood at the entrance to the tent. He summoned Miriam and Aaron saying, 'Listen to my words!' The Bible says that 'the anger of the Lord burned against them' (v. 9). However, when God addressed them he never mentioned the Cushite woman. What made him angry was the fact that Miriam and Aaron were not afraid to speak against his servant Moses (v. 8). When God finished speaking he left them, the cloud lifted and Miriam was covered in leprosy!

What happens next is an example to me. Moses, the very one of whom she spoke so badly, stood in the gap and interceded for her (v. 13). And the Lord replied to Moses, 'If her father had spat in her face, would she not have been in disgrace for seven days? Confine her outside the camp for seven days; after that she can be brought back.'

Miriam suffered the consequences of her actions, but the truth of the matter is that the rest of the people suffered with her because they couldn't move on until she returned. In the same way, when there is a lack of recognition and loyalty for the people that God places in

SURVIVAL GUIDE FOR FRONTLINE LIVING

leadership, whether in the church, in a ministry, mission, workplace or marriage, then the anointing that is over them and their work doesn't move forward and goals are not reached!

OBEDIENCE – 'WHY SHOULD I SAY YES, WHEN I WANT TO SAY NO?'

Although Emmy Wilson did not have a problem with the leadership in her church, she was one day summoned to the office of her vicar, Sandy Millar, at Holy Trinity, Brompton, and asked to do something that she didn't want to do. She explains: 'I wasn't called to the prison work, I somehow got led into it. I had previously been working for the Earl's Court Project in London for five years, so I was already working with people I never dreamed of working with – people with HIV, prostitutes and alcoholics, all of whom had a totally different lifestyle to anything I had ever experienced myself. Then back in 1990 Sandy Millar asked me if I knew that he was on the board of visitors for Holloway Prison. This surprised me because I had no idea that he had this job. I wondered what he was getting at and he suddenly said, "Em, I was talking to the chaplain yesterday at a meeting and he told me that they are very short-staffed at the prison. He was wondering if I knew anybody who could get involved, and I thought of you. I wonder whether you would think about helping at Holloway Prison?"

'I looked at him and said, "Sandy, the Earl's Court project was a big enough leap for me, but prison work is not me. Why have you asked me?"

'And he said, "Oh, I just thought you'd be quite good at it!"

'I was amazed that Sandy should consider that I was

remotely suitable to be recommended to work in a prison environment. I had never dreamt when I became a Christian that I would end up working in prison!

'But he's my spiritual leader and I respected his thoughts on this, and also some months before we'd had the prophets over from Kansas City and they had actually prophesied over me. I thought at the time that the word they had spoken over me was for the Earl's Court Project, but when I went back to read it I thought perhaps that it was relevant to prisons.

'So rather out of obedience, not out of desire, I went for my interview at Holloway Prison. To my slight shock the chaplain said, "When can you start?" I was convinced after my interview that he would think that I was totally unsuitable!'

Emmy started working in Holloway Prison in 1991. Today eight years on, Jesus has used Emmy, Paul Cowley (his testimony is included in chapter 11) and their team of volunteers powerfully to reach hundreds of individuals who are hurting and lost in prisons. The Alpha Course (which I mention in chapter 5, see page 113) is now taking place in well over 135 prisons throughout the United Kingdom. Often we can think that prisoners deserve their lot and they can be left to suffer the consequences alone. However, the Word of God says something completely different: 'Remember those in prison as if you were their fellow-prisoners, and those who are ill-treated as if you yourselves were suffering' (Heb. 13:3).

Maybe one day your leader will ask you to take on a role in a ministry that you never imagined yourself doing. Perhaps it will be something that you have actually once said you would never ever do! However, remember that there is a higher authority behind your leader, and that if you open your heart to it and to God and obey, you could be embracing the very plan God had for you from the very beginning.

Emmy concluded: 'I'm *so grateful* to God because I truly am happiest when I am inside gaol sharing the gospel and praying for the inmates. Talking of which, last week we were at Dartmoor Prison doing a three-day Easter mission (1999). I've been going there for three years now, and this was the most awesome mission to date. Each day ninety to a hundred men attended the chapel, and on the last day, we baptised twenty-six men. We know of at least thirty men who committed their lives for the first time. The testimonies were so exciting.'

RESPECT

God knows what we need. He puts people over us in a variety of types of different roles to meet those needs.

Now I can still hear some of you say: 'But my leader is ready to pull the rug from under my feet!' 'That guy is destroying the ministry!' 'That pastor is a stumbling block for my ministry!' 'My leader is always correcting me, he never leaves me alone.'

However, I don't find these words in my Bible! Who was it who gave the anointing? My Bible says that God gave

> some to be apostles, some to be prophets, some to be evangelists, and some to be pastors and teachers, to prepare God's people for works of service, so that the body of Christ may be built up until we all reach unity in the faith and in the knowledge of the Son of God and become *mature*, attaining to the whole measure of *the fullness* of Christ. (Eph. 4:11–13, my emphasis)

> If you happen to be led by a person who has less experience than you, invest your experience with humility and respect in the life of that other person.

It is those who are most unsure of their gifts, abilities and capacities who are often the people who have the most difficulty in submitting to authority. We have to recognise our gifts and our abilities and, more importantly, we need to recognise and respect the gifts and abilities given to our leaders, our colleagues and friends. If you have problems with self-image and self-worth, you will find it more difficult to submit to authority than people who have a healthy self-esteem. However, as you develop a prayer life with God, you will begin to discover your identity in him and this will be key for you in being used by God.

Some of you are visionaries, like my husband Joao. You receive visions and ideas from God and speak them out, while others run with the vision. 'Write down the revelation and make it plain on tablets so that a herald may run with it. For the revelation awaits an appointed time; it speaks of the end and will not prove false. Though it linger, wait for it; it will certainly come and will not delay' (Hab. 2:2–3). Some of you are the executives of the vision. Your leader approaches you with an idea and, as he or she speaks, your mind starts to turn over and you know exactly what to do in order to reach that goal. Or maybe you are that person who will support and encourage those people who are going to execute that vision.

'Some people have a spirituality of movement and hope. They are called to travel and carry the good news to do great things for the kingdom. The spirituality of St Paul and the apostles was of this kind. The spirituality of others is to stay where they are – it is the "spirituality of the circle". They have more need of a regular rhythm than of constant movement.' Jean Vanier, *Community and Growth*.[4]

TIPS AND A WARNING FOR LEADERS IN GOD'S WORK

Everyone in the church should do a leadership course – so that they learn to be led!

Jesus said, 'The kings of the Gentiles lord it over them; and those who exercise authority over them call themselves Benefactors. But *you are not to be like that*' (Luke 22:25, my emphasis). The note to this scripture in my NIV Life Application Bible says this:

The world's system of leadership is very different from leadership in God's kingdom. Worldly leaders are often selfish and arrogant as they claw their way to the top (some kings in the ancient world gave themselves the title 'Benefactor'). But among Christians, the leader is to be the one who serves best. There are different styles of leadership – some lead through public speaking, some through administering, some through relationships – but every Christian leader needs a servant's heart. Ask the people you lead how you can serve them better.[5]

In other words kings rule through dominance but leadership in God's kingdom is different. Jesus wasn't authoritarian in his leadership, but at the same time he wasn't democratic. Imagine this scenario: Jesus is standing at the side of the lake. He wants to go across to the other side so he suggests it to his disciples. Peter looks at the weather – he's an experienced fisherman – and says, 'Nah, not today lads, looks like bad weather's on its way!' So all the disciples who agree with Peter vote. John is a good friend of Jesus so he sides with him, and they are left with a divided group. No, Jesus was the leader. He didn't need democracy. We need to lead like Jesus – with a close team of disciples around him and with the heart of a server. He led people into the purpose that God set out for them through his Word, and by his Holy Spirit.

Luke 22:25 also tells us that some kings in the ancient world gave themselves the title 'Benefactor'. When God starts to prosper the work of your hands, people will come and say to you, 'Look what an anointing you have, what beautiful work you are doing.' In this situation we have to be really careful because the glory belongs to God. There are a lot of people who like to give their leaders a pat on the back. They like to flatter. But don't let people do this to you. Flattery is a trap from Satan. Proverbs 26:28 says, '… a flattering mouth works ruin.' Take all that this flattering person is saying and in your heart or out loud put it where it belongs. (Please note that 'to encourage', 'to build up' or 'to affirm' a person in leadership is completely different to flattering them.)

GOD LOVES GOOD RELATIONSHIPS

Finally, make every effort to relate to your leaders. When was the last time you prayed for them? Or stopped to inquire whether they had any outstanding prayer needs? When was the last time you spoke a word of encouragement to them? Or sent them a note with a verse or a word of knowledge you received specifically for them? God doesn't want barriers between leaders and a team. He wants relationship. Get rid of your expectations of your leaders: be ready to bless them; and you will find that God will bless you too.

THE TOP TEN KEY POINTS

❑ Working in a team is always going to be challenging. But when serving God we are told that, 'May the God who gives endurance and encouragement give you a spirit of unity among yourselves as you follow Christ Jesus, so that with one heart and mouth you may glorify the God and Father of our Lord Jesus Christ. Accept one another, then, just as Christ accepted you, in order to bring praise to God' (Rom. 15:5–7).

❑ Unity is power. 'Submit to one another out of reverence for God' (Eph. 5:21). Without it our prayers are not answered, our work is hindered, and the Holy Spirit cannot move freely. Satan knows this and that is why his number one strategy is to bring division. We need to be alert and resist his efforts.

❑ Offended? Your response determines your future. 'A man's wisdom gives him patience, it is to his glory to overlook an offence' (Prov. 19:11).

❑ We will be judged according to fruits not gifting. A spiritual gift is given; fruit is cultivated.

❑ Confrontation is healthy and it can be done lovingly; timing is everything; pray together first; hold your tongue, listen; be thankful to God, be humble; don't attack the person; be ready to say you are sorry.

❑ Control our mouths! Cursing is using your tongue to speak over people what God would not say. Blessing breaks curses.

❑ Retaliation is rebellion. Rebellion causes division. Division is Satan's work not Jesus Christ's. Who are you serving?

❑ King David desired God's will more than he desired a position of leadership.

❑ Submission is not slavery. When you recognise that behind every leader there is a higher authority, when you know who you are in God, you will do what Jesus did. He took off his robe, put on a towel, knelt on the cold stone floor and washed the feet of his disciples.

❑ When there is a lack of recognition and loyalty for the people that God places in the front to lead, the anointing that is over them and their work doesn't move forward and goals are not reached for his Kingdom.

10
The 'refiner's fire', those desert places. Do I have to go there, Lord?

Lord, it is only you who can place the calling in my heart to serve the broken. Lord, may that calling be like a thorn in my heart. As I open up my heart through a split second of total surrender to you, may your own hands place that sharp thorn in me. I know that the piercing pain will be a process of death to self, as you lead me through your refiner's fire so that I may see what is in my heart that has to die. Thereafter, Lord, may I never do anything in your service out of my own mind or physical strength, but out of the pain of that thorn in my heart.

One of the great misconceptions we can have of the Christian faith is that from the moment we stand up and follow the vision and call that God has given us, everything will go smoothly!

We only need to read our Bibles to know this isn't true. The life of Joseph, for example, clearly illustrates that sometimes God will allow situations through which we are brought to our limits, in fact often limits that we didn't even know we had! When Joseph was thrown into prison after he had honoured God by standing firm and refusing to have sex with Potiphar's wife, he didn't drown himself in self-pity or unbelief because of his grim circumstances, but rather concerned himself with the purpose of God and with the possibilities offered by the pit. He didn't react to the situation, he interpreted it. But Joseph was human and he must have passed through times when he wondered how on earth God's vision for him would fit into it all. I mean, how many people rise from prison to a place of supreme authority? No doubt Satan would have made the most of his opportunities, yet Joseph resisted him. It was a conscious decision requiring great strength of will.

> 'No Christian has ever plunged into a pit of affliction without finding God there in the midst of it.' Roger Ellsworth, *Faithful under Fire*.[1]

When difficulties come it is easy to say to ourselves, 'God would never allow anything to go wrong – it's the devil who does that.' The Bible says that we need to be on the alert at all times because our enemy, the lion, is always on the prowl, and we must resist him. There is no question (as we covered in chapter 5 'Undoing Satan's work') that when we step out in the name of Jesus we have to be aware of the effect that this has spiritually. We must have a full understanding of our spiritual weapons. Nevertheless, we need to ask for discernment because there is no escaping the truth that, when God gives us a vision, he will take us into the 'refiner's fire'. Affliction and difficulties will come. Because the greater the work in us, the greater the work through us. The deeper the work in us, the deeper the work through us. In these pit times I have been brought to my knees and cried out to God with a cry of absolute desperation. However, it has been at these times that I have seen my own heart. And when I have come out the other side I have come out with a greater revelation. But take heart, because I'm still smiling!

Before God uses you he makes you a nobody. As long as you are a 'somebody', God says, 'I can't use you.' God took Moses to the desert to make him a nobody. Just imagine, Moses had been brought up in Pharaoh's household and was accustomed to a good lifestyle with servants running around him. However, he had been ready to defend his people the Israelites in the midst of their cruel slavery; but he had been ready in his own strength. Once in that dusty desert, far from any luxury lifestyle, Moses tended sheep! And let me tell you God was in no hurry to give him his next instructions – he waited forty years. The first instruction he gave Moses was, 'Take off your shoes'! His shoes represented his past experience and God was going to start something new in his life. Then Moses heard, 'So now, go. I am sending you to Pharaoh to bring my people the Israelites out of Egypt.' And poor Moses, like most of us, said 'How?' God's reply, in simple terms was, 'I'll go with you! When you speak, I'll speak for you. Now you are a nobody I can stay with you, we can go together!' (See Exodus 2 and 3.)

One of my favourite books is *Hinds' Feet on High Places* by Hannah Hunnard, first published in 1955.[2] It is a beautiful allegory dramatising the yearning of God's children to be led to new heights of love, joy and victory.

The story focuses on a deer called 'Much-Afraid' who has crippled feet and lives in the 'Valley of Humiliation'. Her cousins are called 'Spiteful' and 'Gloomy'! Anyhow, the Shepherd invites her to the 'high places' situated on the mountain tops above the valley.

> 'It is true,' said the Shepherd, 'that you would have to be changed before you could live on the High Places, but if you are willing to go with Me, I promise to help you develop hind's feet. Up there on the mountains, as you get near the real High Places, the air is fresh and invigorating. It strengthens the whole body and there are streams with wonderful healing properties, so that those who bathe in them find all their blemishes and disfigurements washed away. But there is another thing I must tell you. Not only would I have to make your feet like hind's feet, but you would have to receive another name, for it would be as impossible for a Much-Afraid to enter the Kingdom of Love as for any other member of the Fearing family. Are you willing to be changed completely, Much-Afraid, and to be made like the new name which you will receive if you become a citizen in the Kingdom of Love?'
>
> She nodded her head and then said very earnestly, 'Yes, I am.'

The rest of the book is about her adventures – pits, waterfalls and all!

It was God who birthed Happy Child in 1993, not man, and he constantly reminds us that he is in control. It is *his* vision. We have been through very challenging times to get to where we are today. After five years the ministry had grown very quickly: there was the rescue house and two restoration houses in the city for street girls and boys;

there was the farm for boys who had been on the streets for years; there was the family team and the street team; the accounting and finance had to be dealt with; there was a yearly training course, a full-time team of over forty-eight workers and teams going out to Mozambique. Joao and I were carrying the decision-making alone, and therefore the consequences. Joao is a visionary and a man of action, with a determination and a perseverance that reminds me of a cannon ball shooting out of a cannon! God could not do without his visionaries. Nevertheless visionaries, in general, do not enjoy administration – they don't like sitting in an office for too long!

Although I like pioneer work, I am the person who runs along behind the cannon picking up the pieces. I enjoy taking care of the people, the team: ministering, encouraging, organising, interceding. If the team is happy the children are happy. However, often in the past, I have worried too much about our workers – 'mother hen' – and have carried things I didn't need to. I don't know whether being the eldest in a family, which I am, brings out a tendency to want to protect people from problems and conflicts. Yet, God has shown me, and is still showing me, that conflicts between people can be healthy. He has also taught me that when someone is going through his or her own 'refiner's fire' the best thing I can do for them is to pray, encourage, and lead them into the Scriptures and not to step in and try to do God's work for him.

Joao and I are both strong people, and as Nicky Gumbel said to us during our marriage service, 'The greatest thing that you two strong Carvalhos ("oak trees" in English!) can learn is to forgive one another quickly!' This has been so true. From almost the moment we married we started to pioneer a new ministry, and then to run it. For four years on the farm we had practically no privacy as a family and little time for intimacy as a couple. The ministry had grown quickly, and we were on edge and tired most of the time, especially with two little baby boys of our own. I think if we'd been just running the farm we could have coped, but we were running the whole of the ministry as well as the farm and had all the responsibility of paying the bills at the end of the day. God is faithful, but we are human and the weight of that responsibility is real.

At the end of 1997 God led me to the deepest darkest valley that I have so far ever been through. When we moved to the city, following advice from our pastors, we stupidly brought our office with us. We had a lot of extra pressure with the opening of the girls' house and the construction on the farm. Joao had a new vision of building three large lakes for fish farming, a large pool, a restaurant that could double up as a church, a roller skating rink and sports courts on the farm. These could be enjoyed by the children but also rented out to the local churches on occasional weekends and bank holidays as a way of using what we had to produce a source of income for the ministry. The teenagers could help out and earn a bit of pocket money and the churches would have the chance to see our work at close hand. However, most of the team, including me, could not grasp the vision at that time with everything else that was going on.

As a couple our marriage started to suffer under the strain. There was tension, arguments and little peace at home. The office in our apartment made it impossible for Joao to switch off. Our telephone rang every three to five minutes. I had given birth to our daughter, Jessica, by then and she was a small baby. It was not a healthy atmosphere for the children, who seemed to be ill constantly.

God had to move us forward. He had to act. The finances in the ministry started to dry up! Eventually we couldn't pay the phone bills and the lines were cut; we couldn't pay for petrol and insurance for the cars and the vans, so there was no transport; and our workers started to feel the pressure in the ministry. One morning I woke up thinking, 'How did Jesus manage to do what he did without cars and telephones?' By this point Joao's emotions were on his skin. Later I wrote in my diary, 'While I was in the middle of it all I felt I was only living each day because I was breathing. It was as though my soul had no life in it any more. It was the deepest sense of loneliness I had ever felt.'

Then niggling thoughts started to come into my mind, 'Give everything up and go back to England. Your family is there. You could get a job.' This was very tempting. Yet something deep inside me told me that there really was no going back. I had been spoilt for the ordinary. There was just too much at stake. Somewhere within the depths of my soul came a grace that I had never experienced before. My lifeline was Jesus. Funny, I always used to pray lying on my bed. But it was during these days of desperation that God gently said to me one day, 'Sarah, pray on your knees.' From that moment on I only feel right praying on my knees.

One evening I was crying and I felt indignation towards God. I cried out, 'Why? Why? If everything that comes from you is good why am I suffering so much in every part of my life? You called me to Brazil, you gave me Joao as my husband, you put us together for your purposes, you birthed this ministry. Why is everything so difficult? I feel guilty when I'm spending more time with my children than with the ministry, and equally I feel guilty when I'm spending more time with the ministry than with

243

my children. Our marriage is really suffering, my children are sick. I do not think I can go on. Why, Lord, why?'

All at once into my thoughts came, 'Ephesians 2:7'. I quickly opened my Bible and read: 'in order that in the coming ages he might show the incomparable riches of his grace, expressed in his kindness to us in Christ Jesus'. It spoke to me so profoundly – my relationship with God was going deeper and I was living to the full 'the incomparable riches of his grace'.

Finally in February of 1998 I went to see my pastor. He listened to everything and then he said, 'Sarah, I advise you to leave the ministry for a while. Be a wife to Joao and a mother to your three children. Joao is looking at you as a co-worker and not as a wife!'

'That is not going to be as easy as you think,' I answered honestly. 'I supervise all the houses, take care of personnel and training. In fact our next course starts in a month's time. Also I do all the correspondence with our trustees in England. I don't know whether Joao will accept this advice.'

'Sarah, you must not co-ordinate the next course,' continued Pastor Marcio gently but firmly. 'God will raise up someone else to do that. Your situation is serious and you must act quickly. Also I strongly suggest that you move to a new apartment and that the office comes out of your home immediately. I cannot give you one example of when a working office in a residential home has worked. You must separate the ministry from your home. It is a place where you should both switch off. No one in the ministry or connected with it should have your home telephone number. Don't worry, I will speak to Joao about this,' promised Pastor Marcio.

His wise advice came straight from God. We moved to a new apartment within a month and set about putting our new limits in place. The office came out of our home and went into the Central Baptist Church where we have our day-care centre. It was very difficult for me to let go of the day-to-day things of the ministry, after all it was in my heart. Also I still felt a deep sense of sadness as a result of all that we'd been through. Then God acted powerfully.

In March we got a phone call from Compassion International Brazil – who had just cut our money for the girls' house because they considered there were not enough children in it – asking us to go out for dinner with four of their American staff who were flying into Belo Horizonte just for the night. We had never met any of them before, nor they us. Joao thought it was an opportunity to convince them to give us back the contract for the house. However, God had other plans!

In the restaurant I sat opposite a man called Vince, from Colorado. He was black, and as broad as he was tall. He had worked with street people for seven years. Joao was sitting at the end of the table and two of the other Americans sat either side of him. They too made Joao look very small. The fourth man sat opposite a friend who had come with us. Within five minutes of sitting down, Vince looked straight at me from across the table and said, 'Sarah, *don't give up!*' His words hit my heart like a bolt of lightning. From that moment on it was as though we were the only two people in that place. 'God has called you to work with these children,' he continued with authority in his voice, 'and it's not everyone who has that calling. You would not be happy anywhere else, Sarah.' I started to feel the presence of the Holy Spirit. A warm current seemed to surge right through my body. 'God is going to make you into his warrior again!' When he spoke these words something unlocked in the depths of my being. I started to weep, oblivious to my surroundings. He leapt from his chair then and there and came round to my side of the table, placed his hand on me and prayed. Now Vince didn't know me from a bar of soap: he certainly didn't know about my conversation with Pastor Marcio. Suddenly he said, 'Sarah, you have to let go. God is calling you to a new ministry, a new role – mother to your children and wife to Joao. For this next stage of the ministry Joao has to be the "priest".' My mouth fell open, this was wild. What a confirmation!' 'Sarah, I can feel that you have a very sweet spirit, but you also have a very strong spirit. That's great and was necessary at the beginning of the ministry, but now it's time to let go and encourage Joao. This is going to be crucial if the ministry is going to grow at this stage.'

'How do I let go, Vince, it's hard?' I asked through my tears.

'There is going to be a funeral tonight! Bury it and later on God will resurrect it. Stop worrying. The Word says, "Don't worry … Cast your burdens on me … Ask for whatever you want in my name …" God will raise up others to support Joao. How old are your children?'

'Lucas is five, Daniel is three and Jessica is one year old,' I answered.

'Your children are at a perfect age, I can see you sitting on the floor reading them a book and they are sitting around you. This is such an important role for you at this time.'

I looked over at Joao, he too was obviously being powerfully ministered to by the large Americans sitting at either side.

'Sarah, I feel strongly that when God brings you back to the ministry on a day-to-day basis it will be really *cool*! I do not have any doubts that we four only came to Belo Horizonte today for you. God brought us all the way from

Colorado to Brazil to speak to you tonight.'

Vince then leapt to his feet again and prayed for me. We must have been such a sight in that restaurant. I was burning and glowing like anything with the power and presence of the Holy Spirit. The sadness and despair that I had lived with for the previous five months had completely left me and was replaced with an indescribable joy at God's love for me.

Before we left they all ministered to us as a couple and a family. 'Your marriage and your children are more important than your ministry,' said one of them. 'Joao, we husbands have a much tougher job than our wives. Because the Bible says that we have to love our wives as much as Jesus loves the Church. And Jesus died for the Church!' Another said, 'Every night before you go to bed don't pray, but bless each other with words.'

On this subject, Kerry the wife of Stuart Lees, Vicar of Christchurch in London, recently said to me, 'Sarah, I am bringing up four children, and I cannot always accompany my husband to the various conferences, events and international trips as a result. But you know something: I am building my wall in Jerusalem, and that wall is my children. In ten years' time I won't remember how I felt missing that conference, but I surely will remember that wall I built in Jerusalem. I don't want to get to heaven not knowing whether my own children are going there or not.'

We all left that restaurant in the early hours of the morning, having hardly touched our food. That verse about Jesus being the 'bread of life' really came into its own that night. The waiters have never forgotten us! I left that place ten feet off the ground. In fact I saw three young prostitutes with very little clothing on standing on the curb of the pavement waiting for their next clients and I floated up to them without a second thought and told them how much Jesus loved them. They were completely bowled over.

A week after our experience with 'the four large prophets', God brought a man called James Odgers all the way from Cape Town, where he had dropped everything in order to help us set into place a new structure for this next vital stage of the ministry. James was the perfect person for this, not only because of his years of experience in administration and banking, but because of his love for Jesus and compassion for the poor. Over ten years ago he founded the Besom Foundation in London. The Besom Foundation helps people 'make a difference'. It provides a bridge between those who want to give money, time, skills, or equipment, and those who are in need, and ensures that what is given is used effectively. The service it provides is free. Since 1989 hundreds of projects have been funded, ranging from the setting up of a children's village in one of the poorest areas of South Africa on the Eastern Cape to supporting a pastor in St Petersburg, who crawls along the sewers to get to the young heroin addicts, taking them from there to a rehabilitation centre outside the city. 'Besom also assists groups from churches around the centre of London who have decided that they want to get out into the community and give their help to those in need. Over one hundred home groups have now done a project of this nature – usually painting, decorating, gardening or some other activity for someone in need,' explains James.

During his three days with us in Brazil, not only did James manage to spend good quality time with us both, and meet all the leaders in the ministry and our accountant, but he saw every stage of the ministry including an early morning start with the street team! We said goodbye clutching pages of precious charts and diagrams knowing that it was up to us to bring everything into reality.

Just in case this might help you, here is a brief outline of the new structure:

- There is a General Assembly made up of members of Happy Child Brazil, who meet once a year to agree on the next year's budget and plans. Every two years we meet to vote for the president, secretary, treasurer and new members.
- Joao and I are accountable to a board in Brazil made up of two pastors and two businessmen with whom we meet every two months or so to discuss problems, solutions and future plans.
- We give a monthly expenditure sheet with receipts on how monies are spent to Compassion International, the local government, people who support us through covenants and the European Community.
- We are also accountable as to how monies are spent to a board of five trustees in England, of which James Odgers is one.
- The ten leaders in the ministry meet once a month with us to talk about problems, solutions, activities, future plans and decision making. Although not active on a daily basis I am still involved with all major decisions.
- Happy Child produces a complete yearly budget, and every month does a budget-to-actual sheet so that we know whether we are spending more, less or exactly what we proposed.
- Happy Child produces a monthly cash flow summary.

Around the time that we were in the middle of this 'pit', I was watching a news report of a hurricane which had swept through a beach town in the States. The pictures showed the remains of houses without roofs, uprooted palm trees, overturned cars, broken telephone lines and debris all over the streets. As I watched, the thought came into my mind, 'This is what is happening to Happy Child: a hurricane is passing through us all and there is nothing we can do to stop it. There will be the consequences when it's past and no doubt it will take time to put everything in order again and settle into the new structure. However, this time things will be set with "deeper foundations" to resist the next hurricane should there be one!'

Looking back, the extraordinary thing was that the overall work with the children and their families was not affected. There was always food on the table, and the children kept coming in off the streets and their families kept on being helped and reunited. Six months later the girls' house started to flourish. With a new team and a lot of prayer and faith it is now full to its capacity with ex-street girls who are all at school and shining with the joy that only Jesus can give.

INTERCESSORS: OUR PARTNERS

A lady we have never met but who is one of our loyal and committed intercessors on the 'riverbank' at home, wrote to Joao and me around this time. Her words gave us tremendous encouragement: 'As your work expands I am sure the Lord is calling more and more people to intercede for you and your staff. If the leaders are strong the people grow in strength themselves, confident in their stride, bold in their faith and a relaxed happiness within themselves. I just happened to switch on the television before Christmas and heard these words sung 'inside sorrow there is a new plan'. May this new plan develop into the fullness that he has ordained.

'Oh how I ask the Lord to bless you, to enfold you in his love, which like his peace, is beyond understanding. I pray for protection for your children until they have the understanding of what your life's work for him is all about.'

One of our prayer groups in London, which meets and prays faithfully for our work every month, also sent us a fax when we were in the midst of the 'storm' with impressions and verses they had received from God during one of their meetings. It lifted us all up and made us feel that we were wrapped in his arms. This is some of what that fax read: 'Someone had a sense that the ministry was going through a storm. In the storm there were certain trees that stood up very strong and did not bend with the wind. We felt it represented people who had been with the ministry a long time and would stand firm through the storm. The sense was that the ministry was going through a kind of stripping down. All the leaves had been blown off the trees. Picture of axes, cutting away at a tree. Sense of the tree being cut right back, to the stump. Very painful, but necessary. Picture of a new shoot growing from the stump. Sense of resurrection (always from death). It will survive because it is God who has planted it. Sense of you at Happy Child Brazil going through the refiner's fire, a cutting away, a severe pruning. But in death and pain will come fresh new life, stronger this time.

'Someone else received this verse for you all: "What he opens, no one can shut; and what he shuts, no one can open. I know your deeds. See, I have placed before you an open door that no one can shut. I know that you have little strength, yet you have kept my word and have not denied my name" (Rev. 3:7–8). In other words, if the Lord has planted a thing, nothing can prevail against it. Even in times of death, it carries the seed of life. And, in his time, it will grow and flourish. In another passage, Ecclesiastes 3:1–8, 11, we find the words: "… to everything there is a season, a time for every purpose under heaven … He makes everything beautiful in its time." '

Our intercessors helped carry us through this difficult yet necessary time.

In a talk John Kilpatrick, who is the pastor of the Assembly of God church in Brownsville Pensacola which has over the past few years experienced a wonderful revival, spoke of how in the Bible God often compares himself to an eagle. Eagles are wonderful mothers. Deuteronomy 32:11–12 says, 'Like an eagle that stirs up its nest and hovers over its young, that spreads its wings to catch them and carries them on its pinions. The Lord alone led him, no foreign God was with him.'

Eagles love heights and they build their nests up high. First they lay the sticks and the briars, then they line the nest inside with rags and skins of animals, and finally with soft feathers. After a while, when the eaglets get to a certain size, the mother eagle starts to remove the feathers and the rags and the skins. The nest, you see, is too comfortable. John Kilpatrick explained, 'When God gets ready to change people, that's what he starts to do in order to move us on. Because he has greater things for us. He wants to take us further.' So the eaglets get uncomfortable and they start to feel insecure, because their comfort is being taken from them. Then the mother eagle, sensing their insecurity, opens up her massive wingspan and hovers over them. She lets them see her power. She's saying to them, "Don't worry little ones, I am still by your side." This is what God does with us. When we get to that point of despair, he flutters his wings to show us that he is right there with us.

'Then the eagle does something amazing. She stretches out her wing along the nest and the little ones climb onto her pinions. She steps off the side of the nest and soars into the sky. She locks her wings, picks the thermals and rides the air currents. The mother eagle gives her little eaglets a taste for the air. Then she takes them back to the nest, to the uncomfortable sticks and briars. The next day she repeats the same procedure until all at once her little eaglets start to feel secure in the air, and suddenly they have the courage to let go of their mother's pinions and soar the air thermals alone. Eventually they don't want to go back to the uncomfortable nest of prickly sticks and briars.'

An eagle can detect a storm when it is still a long way off. In the face of impossible odds, he locks his wings so that nothing can deter him from his upward climb and he rides the wind of God. He flies over the storm, twenty-five, thirty thousand feet up. The Hebrew word *ruach* describes the thermals of the desert. It was the same word King David used in Psalm 51 to describe the Holy Spirit – the breath of God: 'Take not your *ruach* from me.' The eagle fears nothing and even when we can no longer see him, he can see us. He can see for fifty miles.

'If the Christian walk is mere enthusiasm, we become nothing more than spiritual grasshoppers, going up and down but never learning how to soar.' Jamie Buckingham, *Where Eagles Soar.*[3]

In the Old Testament, God led the Israelites, his chosen

people, to Egypt. There they prospered and found favour with Pharaoh but God had greater plans for them. He wanted to lead them to a land of 'milk and honey'! So what happened next? When Pharaoh died his successor did not favour them. He made them his slaves, making bricks out of mud and straw. Finally they cried out to God and God 'fluttered his powerful wingspan' – he sent Moses.

In Exodus 13 and 14 we read of the miraculous ways God led the Israelites out of Egypt. Then came the grand finale – the crossing of the Red Sea.

> But the Israelites went through the sea on dry ground, with a wall of water on their right and on their left. That day the Lord saved Israel from the hands of the Egyptians, and Israel saw the Egyptians lying dead on the shore. And when the Israelites saw the great power the Lord displayed against the Egyptians, the people feared the Lord and put their trust in him and in Moses his servant. (Exod. 14:29–31)

Well, as you can imagine the first day after this miracle the Israelites were celebrating, dancing and praising God for their leader. The God of their fathers had broken four hundred years of slavery, and he gave them a new song. However, by the second day it was wearing off a bit, victories don't last forever. By the third day with no water they started to look to Moses. In Exodus 15:22–4 we read, 'Then Moses led Israel from the Red Sea and they went into the Desert of Shur. For three days they travelled in the desert without finding water. When they came to Marah, they could not drink its water because it was bitter. So the people grumbled against Moses saying, "What are we to drink?" ' I just find this whole thing a little bit curious. God, who lovingly led his people out of Egypt, providing miracle after miracle, suddenly leads them through the desert for three days without water to a bitter pool! Why? Well, as we just read the Israelites started to grumble and complain. Mind you they were still grumbling and complaining in Numbers 11, two books on! However, the next verse says that amidst all the complaining one man prayed, 'Then Moses cried out to the Lord, and the Lord showed him a piece of wood. He threw it into the water, and the water became sweet.'

You see, we have a choice: either we *moan* or we *pray*. If we moan and complain we will sink and it will solve nothing. We really have to check our attitudes and our tongues. Pastor John Kilpatrick says, 'We shouldn't curse that situation, but we should interpret it. We should never react to it, but we should respond. It is in those bitter places that we face God and he wants to give us a revelation.' God can change a bitter experience into a sweet one.

God wants us to look past the gift to the giver. Past the provision to the provider. God wanted to show the Israelites that he was their Doctor. And there are many who believe that the 'piece of wood' pointed forward to the cross. When God restores you after the revelation, when he brings you away from the 'refiner's fire', you will not be the same. You will come back to him on a higher plane of understanding.

Do you have a 'Red Sea' in your life? God wants you to call on his name. He is the God of our fathers, who changes history. And he is still working.

Barry Kissell, an Anglican clergyman at St Andrew's Chorleywood, Hertfordshire in England, for twenty-five years, has a testimony that makes my hair stand on end. His 'refiner's fire' is a little more dramatic than most. However, God prepared him for it. Today Barry professes to having a new perspective on life and on his relationship with God. Before his traumatic experience Barry had hosted numerous New Wine Conferences, had travelled to twenty-three nations, spoken in celebrations at twenty cathedrals, published books, operated a ministry through which he had ministered at over a thousand churches and had been interviewed on radio and television. At that time his children had all grown up and left home, and he lived with his wife Mary.

In July 1990 Barry attended a conference at Holy Trinity Brompton in London led by John Wimber and the Kansas City prophets. Suddenly Bob Jones, one of the prophets, whom Barry had never met before, said to him, 'I've got it now! The last two nights I have dreamt about you and this is what I saw ... The days are coming when God will take away everything you have built up and relied upon.' After the conference, Barry and Mary went for a walk in Hyde Park and sitting by the Serpentine, he wept because he just knew somehow that he was about to go on an uncharted journey with God.

In May 1994, while speaking at a church in Liverpool a woman prophet approached him and said, 'As you were speaking I saw that you were up to your neck in water. You were drowning, it was as if the enemy was pulling you down. Then I saw the Lord's hand reaching down and pulling you up ... But you must cry out to the Lord.' This woman had been a Christian for a relatively short period of time and had never read the Old Testament. Yet she quoted a passage from 2 Samuel 22:17: 'He reached down from on high and took hold of me. He drew me out of deep waters.' Earlier in the same chapter it says, 'The waves of death swirled around me. The torrents of destruction overwhelmed me. The cords of the grave coiled around me. The snares of death confronted me. In my distress I called to the Lord' (vv. 5–7).

Barry says, 'Around this time I was finding myself particularly challenged by the part of the gospel narrative when James and John come to Jesus and ask him a question. They prefix it by saying, "Will you do what we ask you to do?"

'And he says, "What do you want me to do?"

'One asks, "Would my brother and I be able to sit at your left and right hand when your Kingdom comes in power?"

'Jesus says, "It is not for me to do that." Then he asks them a question: "Can you drink the cup that I am going to drink and can you be baptised into the baptism that I am going to be baptised in?" In other words, "Can you drink the cup of suffering and be baptised into death?"

'They said, "Oh yes, we can!", again not really understanding what he was saying.

'And then he said to them, "You will." '

Barry continues, 'The Lord proceeded to show me two things about these two men. The first thing was that they wanted visibility. You couldn't have bigger or more visibility than to be at the second coming at the left hand and the right hand of the Son of God. They also wanted authority. They wanted exclusive relationships but above all they wanted their own kingdom within Jesus's Kingdom. This came to me as a very uncomfortable revelation because in many ways it was symbolic of my own life and my own motivation. And this is what the Lord showed me: I had built a kingdom within a

Kingdom. It is so subtle. Your ministry becomes your kingdom. Jesus said to me, "You have made yourself a somebody, but I am going to make you a nobody. I am preparing you for the harvest." '

In the context of the James and John narrative, Jesus says to them both, 'Look at me. When I came, I didn't come to be served, but I came to serve and to give my life as a ransom for many.' Barry explains, 'What he was saying to these two men was this: "There is a distance between where you are and your motivation and everything that you are seeking and where I want you to be. You are seeking visibility and authority and a kingdom within a Kingdom, but I am wanting you down here because I want you to bring in the harvest. To get you from up there to down here is a cup and a death." '

On the last day of a holiday in Cornwall with his wife Mary during August of 1996, Barry went outside and there was a rainbow which stretched from the river to the sea. He had never seen a complete rainbow before in his life. Barry pointed it out to Mary and said, 'We have committed ourselves to the Lord for this period and he has committed himself to us. That is the sign of the covenant. It is a complete sign, from one end of the bay to the other.' So they made plans to leave St Andrew's Church.

Two days later, the doorbell rang early in the morning and they found four very frightened young people outside. Their ages were twelve, thirteen, eighteen and twenty. During the night their father had murdered their mother.

'We welcomed them in, and wondered what we should do. Mary suggested that they stay with us for a little time,' continues Barry. 'They stayed with us for three weeks. After that Mary came to me and said, "Darling, I think the Lord said that they are to stay." I said, "Stay?

Stay where?" She said, "Stay here!" I said, "Well. Obviously we need to just check that out a bit." '

Eventually the mother's body was released after the trial and they had a thanksgiving service. They all gathered around the coffin and had a reading. 'As I was standing there,' says Barry emotionally, 'I heard the Lord say into my heart, "Today I give you this family to parent and care for." And I remember just standing there weeping and weeping.'

On 9 January 1997, Barry was surfing on a beach in New Zealand (his homeland). St Andrew's had kindly given them a gift holiday for three weeks, all expenses paid. It was supposed to be a 'holiday of a lifetime'. Suddenly Barry got a twenty-foot wave and he started to surf down through it. But this was a freak wave with a force that came from underneath. All at once he was tossed right up into the air and fell down into the surf. 'It was like being inside a washing machine. Then I felt and heard my neck bones crack. The last thing I remember saying was, *Jesus, help me!*

'Somehow I had been tossed right up the beach, probably about sixty or seventy yards. I remember as I lay there I had tremendous pain all over my body and I was paralysed in various ways. As I lay there I heard this voice which said clearly to me, "When you pass through the waters I will be with you, when you walk through the fire you will not be burned." ' Eventually, Barry was rushed to hospital and X-rayed immediately. The actor Christopher Reeve, who is in a wheelchair and needs assisted breathing, broke one bone – C1 – in his neck. Barry had broken four bones, including C1 and C2!

After a week in a striker bed that was turned every four hours like a barbecue there was no progress. The doctor eventually decided to operate. He explained to Barry that the worst scenario would be to wake up paralysed from the neck down. The operation was massive. Just to make things a little better for poor Barry, the anaesthetist then explained that he could not anaesthetise him! First he would have to put some rods down his nose and then he would have to cut his throat and put a rod in it and pump it full of whatever. Only then, all going well, could Barry be knocked out!

'I said to Mary, "I would love someone to come and anoint me and pray over me," ' continued Barry. 'I had just said these words when a young man walked into my room and said, "I am a pastor from a local church and I have heard what has happened to you. Would you like me to anoint you with oil?" I said, "Thank you very much." He said, "On the way up here I had this verse for you, 'When you pass through the waters, I will be with you, and when you pass through the rivers, they will not sweep over you. When you walk through the fire, you will not be burned; the flames will not set you ablaze' " (Isa. 43:2)!'

The operation took six hours. The first thought Barry had when it was over was, 'Am I paralysed?' He remembers patting all the way down his body and thinking, 'Oh Jesus, I am not paralysed. I am just not paralysed.'

During the time of recovery they put a 'halo' traction stretcher on him by boring four holes in his head. They attached it to a corset and Barry had to learn to walk again. 'The first half of each of the Gospels is to do with miracles and wonders. The second is to do with suffering. Jesus is in both halves,' relates Barry. 'He is in the miracles – I have seen him there – but he is also in the suffering. As I began to look back over my Christian experience, I realised that I entered it with a life which was much compromised in many ways. As you journey on the wide road, challenges begin to come because Jesus is always directing us towards the narrow way.

'I have seen that we are not excluded from difficulties but God comes to us in them and uses them to create his life in us,' explains Barry. 'He shows us in the difficulties that he is the resurrection and the life. I now realise that like many Christians, I had inherited an achievement-based acceptance by God. This came through speaking publicly, through writing books and through being a leader in a high-profile church. That sustained me and gave me significance. In the midst of it all I hoped that God accepted me. But as I was lying in my hospital bed achieving nothing, doing nothing, I realised that he accepts us as we are. That relationship sustains us and gives us significance, and out of that we may achieve, but we may not. God has given me another life. I was dead but I have come alive. I believe that is symbolic of the Church at this time. He is giving his Church another chance.'

Barry has written a book based on this extraordinary experience called *Riding the Storm*.

Sometimes God gives us trouble as a door of hope.

'Therefore I am now going to allure her;
I will lead her into the desert
and speak tenderly to her.
There I will give her back her vineyards,
and will make the Valley of Achor a door of hope.
There she will sing as in the days of her youth,
as in the day she came up out of Egypt.
In that day,' declares the Lord,
'you will call me "my husband";
you will no longer call me "my master".' (Hosea 2:14–16)

261

I don't know about you, but I don't want to spend my life just coasting along. I want there to be a deeper and deeper sense that, whatever I am going through in my life, I am going through it with him, so that I leave that master mentality and more and more I begin to see him as my husband. I want my relationship with him to go deeper. I want to be closer to him. Because I love him.

Kagawa of Japan wrote: 'In the blood-drops dripping along the sorrowful road to the Via Dolorosa will be written the story of man's regeneration tracing the blood-stained and staggering footprints "let me go forward"! This day also must my blood flow, following in that blood-stained pattern.'

THE TOP TEN KEY POINTS

- ❏ No Christian has ever plunged into a pit of affliction without finding God there in the midst of it.
- ❏ Before God uses you he makes you a nobody. As long as you are a 'somebody' God says, 'I can't use you!'
- ❏ When God gets ready to change people that's when he starts to make things uncomfortable for us. He wants to move us on, because he has greater things for us. He wants to take us further.
- ❏ If the Christian walk is mere enthusiasm, we become nothing more than spiritual grasshoppers, going up and down but never learning how to soar like the eagle.
- ❏ God led Israel from the miraculous parting of the Red Sea into the Desert of Shur. After three days without water he led them to a bitter pool! Why? Because he wanted to show them what was in their hearts. And he wanted to show them that he was their doctor.
- ❏ Don't curse the situation, interpret it. God can change a bitter experience into a sweet one.

❑ Do you have a 'Red Sea' in your life? God wants you to call on his name. He is the God of our fathers, who changes history. And he is still working today.

❑ Sometimes God gives us trouble as a door of hope.

❑ He wants us to look past the gift to the giver.

❑ When God restores you after the revelation, when he brings you away from the 'refiner's fire', you will not be the same. You will come back to him on a higher plane of understanding.

11
What has following my calling meant to me?

In this chapter I invited a variety of people on the front-line, with a variety of vocations, to share their experiences with you.

PAUL COWLEY co-ordinates the ministry in prisons and the Prison Alpha Initiative throughout the United Kingdom

When I first began to feel a pull towards the prison ministry I remember feeling confused and very inadequate for the purpose. At the time I was general manager of a very exclusive health club in central London, and the pull between the two worlds was increasing as my passion for the lost grew and as God expanded my heart to breaking point sometimes. I remember sitting in my office and saying to the Lord, 'How am I supposed to do two jobs at once?'

The work in the prisons was really taking off, and I was

spending every moment of my spare time in prisons. Men and women were finding the Lord in all types of prisons across the land. One afternoon I asked my PA to leave the office and close the door. I dropped to my knees and prayed for the Lord to sort this stuff out. He gave me a verse of Scripture, which was hard to understand at the time. What was I supposed to do?

I have said now, on many occasions, that you should be careful what you pray, because the Lord might just give it to you! A week later my boss called me to his office, he sort of looked at me in a confused way and said, 'Paul, are you happy doing this work? You have done a good job over the last year, you really have done all the things you were asked to do. The club is better now than when you started, but you don't seem happy.' If this was an answer to prayer, why was I feeling so scared?

I was about to get dismissed, how did I know? I just did. I was asked to resign. I trusted that the Lord knew best. I felt such peace. I was given three months' salary in lieu of notice. At the end of the three months (and the end of the money) I was asked to join the staff at Holy Trinity Brompton, in London, as a pastor with responsibility for taking the Alpha course into the prisons. I also put together a plan for the rehabilitation of ex-offenders.

The Lord has a way of telling you that you are in the place that he wants you to be in, but sometimes you have to step out in faith to realise you're in the right place.

One of the ways I have felt tested was on my first speaking engagement in my new role as prison pastor. We visited HM Prison Dartmoor, not the easiest of prisons to start with! I had just finished speaking to the Vulnerable Prisoners Unit (the VPU is mostly made up of sex offenders). During the ministry time I was asking the men if they would like to come forward to receive prayer. I remember thinking, *I can't work with sex offenders! I mean, I know what some of these men have done, and it makes me angry and sick to my stomach, it's not fair.* I don't hear the Lord that often, but I did this time. I felt him say to me, 'Paul, don't judge these men. If they want to come to me for forgiveness, that's fine by me. I didn't judge you when you came to me, did I?'

'No, Lord, you didn't.' I felt humbled. 'And Paul, you also didn't tell me everything at first, did you?' 'No, Lord, I didn't.' They started to come forward. Then I noticed the man who stood in front of me: what a mess! His hair was all matted, he had a skin complaint and he stank, and those were some of his good points! He looked me square in the eye and said, 'I would like to know if all that stuff you have been talking about, stuff like God loving everyone, God caring for all of his children, like would he love someone like me?' What was I to say? We prayed. He gave his life to Christ and he started to cry, so did I.

When we finished praying he opened his eyes, took a step forward and gave me the biggest hug I have ever had. While he was hugging me I remember thinking, *Lord, do I have to do this?* Stepping back and again looking me square in the eye he said; 'We're brothers now, aren't we?'

'Yes,' I said.

'Jesus has cleaned me up, hasn't he?'

'Yes,' I nodded.

'Thank you, Lord,' he said.

I knew then, as the world seemed to stop, that for a moment there was him, me and Jesus standing together. I knew there and then that my life would never be the same again. It was at this point that I knew I was meant to be involved in prison ministry as I realised the verse of Scripture the Lord had given me was unfolding before my eyes: 'He tends his flock like a shepherd: He gathers the lambs in his arms and carries them close to his heart; he gently leads those that have young' (Isa. 40:11).

COUNCILLOR SUSAN PHILIPS Frontline living in the political scene, Southern Ireland

8 April 1999 – Later today there is the General Council of Ireland's County Councils. It will be held in Waterford City and will be attended by An Taoiseach, Mr Bertie Ahern. Nothing unusual. Only today I have to face a thousand people with my reputation in tatters, a part of my heart grieving, and my pocket certainly hurting. If you choose to use your role in life in order to speak up for biblical truths, or just speak up as the Spirit of God appears to prompt you, there will be some backlash. The question, therefore, we have to ask ourselves is quite simple: is God able to reverse setbacks, is he able to really take our burdens and swap them for his, and, when it is physical danger that we face, is he prepared to direct his holy angels concerning us? If the answer to all three is 'Yes', then we can survive and continue. This week has been one of the worst.

As a politician, and an Independent one, you can pick up the phone to the media over almost any subject. Right enough the press are all pretty liberal, but if you avoid presenting yourself as a right-wing fundamentalist crank, and if you are there for the long haul, there will be plenty of times to speak on subjects ranging from good planning to new age philosophy, from county landfills to issues about so-called gay rights and abortion. My voice is heard frequently and no one is under any illusions as to where I stand with regard to biblical truths. You just keep thumping them out. And of course the enemy keeps throwing his darts. Sometimes they seem particularly blunted and you get lulled into a feeling of well-being. And of course you have to earn the right to speak politically, since for every minute on the airwaves you have to deal with at least ten hard cases which go with the job of public representation. Sometimes weeks can go by when nothing particular stirs, and then like last week we had a big shot faith-healer (connect with your higher consciousness, etc.!) on RTE 1 and a challenge was needed! Shortly afterwards, a gay rights magazine aimed at the young was allowed to be placed in our libraries and public places. That needed a good challenge too and, rather than just condemn, you have to stress sensitively that there is a better way for young people, and that is a man/woman situation within the context of marriage. A few telephone interviews with Sunday papers followed: same ground to go over, compassion, but a warning that the gay lifestyle can lead to loneliness, health risks and often despair. I felt rather clever.

And then the bombshell. That night my beautiful brood mare delivered a fine healthy filly, only she died shortly after birth. No explanations, and it happened between eleven and dawn. Just a solid stiff crumpled heap in the corner of the stable, watched over silently by the distraught mother. You kind of felt an evil had been visited upon us, confirmed by a dreadful dream which had shot me out of bed and into the stable to check. And then one Sunday paper: 'Councillor Philips says gay men in Wicklow are lonely, diseased and live lives of abject distress.' Actually that kind of blatant misquote wouldn't have mattered terribly since the paper was a rag, but the woman who does *What the Papers Say* thought it sufficiently good copy to include it in her fifteen-minute national RTE 1 programme. The nation now knows that this so-called Christian loving exponent of truth is in fact a second

Himmler dressed up. The next day I met a huge tour bus coming around a steep corner on a tiny hill road. Car severely damaged.

Frontline living carries risks. But rather than an option, it is a political duty to speak up since most of the world would like to but can't. Intercession is frontline stuff too and carries penalties, because our struggle isn't against people, but against the powers and principalities. And whether you are rescuing children and telling them about Jesus, or simply proclaiming some common-sense biblical truths as part of a broadcast, you are putting your finger into the eye of a malevolent force. Fortunately God is stronger.

Encouragement? Always to hand. It is a fact that, even when a vote has to be taken on subjects like physic health centres and you tell your Board exactly what that means, God always, always provides a backup. I have faced discussions thinking I'm alone, to find support from such unlikely people as far-left trade unionists. So we keep going, we keep making human mistakes, but one mistake must never be made. The choice to keep silent.

PHIL WALL Mission Team Leader, The Salvation Army

I think that there are three primary challenges that I have faced in seeking to live out my calling. The first is the myth of immortality. Up until two or three years ago (I am now thirty-five), I believed I was immortal. I believed I could work as many hours as I wanted for as many weeks as I wanted without having any adverse physical effect on my mind, body or spirit. I also believed that nothing anyone said or any discouragement or disappointment that came along could in any way impact my life. Then a couple of years ago I discovered mortality. I discovered that I could get tired, I could get sick because of that tiredness, and I could be hurt by things that people said and incidents that occurred. Coming to terms with this and changing my working style (which in truth I am still working on) has been one of my great challenges.

The second great challenge is as a father and husband to wrestle the priorities of work and family life. Like many parents you tend to walk around with a permanent guilt trip, realising that you are not doing what you should do, and fearing that one day you may not be there when they need you the most. I confess that I have failed miserably at times to get this balance right and find it a constant tension in my week by week lifestyle.

The third great challenge I have found is in the area of authenticity and integrity. I find it much easier to preach and write things I believe than I do to live them. To have a common resonance between my rhetoric and the reality of my lifestyle has been an immense challenge to me. I believe passionately that Christianity is an all or nothing thing that demands total obedience and surrender to the will and purpose of the living God. I believe our lives should be counter-cultural signposts for the unbelieving world in which we find ourselves. I believe Christians should be passionate and zealous for the gospel, being ever ready to share their faith, pray with the sick and give bucket-loads of compassion to those that cry out for it. Tragically the reality of my life has often been very different. I have found it easy to talk the talk but much more difficult to walk the walk.

In facing these issues, the following three things have helped me to keep on track. The first is a commitment to vision. The Word of God states clearly that without vision people perish and probably more Christian leaders have left the work or have been discouraged to impotence because of a lack of clear vision of what it is God would have them do than anything else. I discovered my life's work two or three years ago and in my times of discouragement, spiritual attack and failure I have come back to that vision time and time again.

The second thing that has helped me, in addition to what it is God has called me to achieve, is having a set of values which have helped determine how I will achieve those objectives. As I have increased in my levels of responsibility, and more and more options open up in front of me, these have been incredibly important. The challenge to sell out to pride, self-centredness and just aping the world's model of leadership has been significant. Having values upon which I try to live my life, has been incredibly important.

The third and final dynamic within this has been to have a brother who has walked with me in helping me to remain true to these ideals. I meet with my pastor most Thursday mornings and over these last ten years he has been my constant friend, comforter, challenge and co-warrior in the battles of the Kingdom. He has wept with me, prayed with me and called me to account many times. He knows the vision I want to live for, the values I want to live by and the kind of husband, father, friend and leader I want to be. Proverbs 27:17 says, 'As iron sharpens iron, so one man sharpens another', and this has certainly been true within my life. I have considered giving up many times and it is my friendship with my pastor that has called me on each time.

Somebody once said that followers look for easy answers and easy ways, whereas leaders know there aren't any. That has certainly been true in my experience and in wrestling with my weakness and failure those things that I have just mentioned have helped me stay within the fray.

ANNIE SINCLAIR Missionary working with homeless teenagers in Harare, Zimbabwe

I came to Zimbabwe in 1995 having finished a degree in art and longing to use my skills somehow to work amongst young people on the streets. God had put this desire in my heart a few years earlier and I had been praying for some time about how it would come to reality. Another English friend, Caroline and I got to know many of the boys living on the streets of Harare. Most had been in and out of jail and detention centres, and were involved in lives of crime, prostitution, drug and alcohol abuse. Having been on the streets from a young age, most of these boys were hardened to street life and did not seem to have much hope of ever leaving. With the help of some local Zimbabwean people, in particular the generosity of a local Presbyterian pastor, we were able to start a small art workshop. Here the boys can come to learn skills in art and craft which can enable them to leave the streets and earn a honest living. The project is called 'Madzimbawe' which means 'House of Stone' (based on 1 Peter 2:4).

The centre of the work is to communicate to these despised and rejected young people that the God who made them loves them, and to provide an opportunity for them to turn from their old ways and follow Jesus. It has been a difficult job from the start, we are a small group of volunteers. It can be a lonely and thankless task, yet there are also encouragements as we see God at work. There is a constant struggle going on as we try to pull over these boys from the devil's territory, where he is destroying their lives. I had never been so aware of the devil before I began this work.

To begin a project with excitement and enthusiasm is a very special time. However, the ongoing responsibility of seeing a vision through is much harder. Sometimes other people are unsupportive or discouraging; sometimes results are very difficult to see or analyse. There can be great disappointments when boys turn back to street life after so much energy and time has been spent on them. Even sometimes – and this is the most painful thing – the very people you have come to help and serve, turn around with hostility and ingratitude. In the midst of all this we can only persevere and continue to show love, by holding onto God's promises. Particularly Galatians 6:9: 'Let us not become weary in doing good, for at the proper time we will reap a harvest if we do not give up.' I have realised that my task as a Christian is simply to sow the seed in obedience and wait. It is God, not me, who will bring the harvest. I have also found it invaluable to write down and also to share with others all the things I see God doing. Even the smallest sign of change in a person's life, which reminds me to be expectant and joyful.

Spending time with Christian friends outside of the project has also been crucial to survival. It is so easy to become introverted and bogged down in the work. Sometimes an outside perspective stops me from getting things out of proportion. I have several times found myself near to breaking point. This kind of work is very draining because people look upon you as a source of support; they are forever faking and do not really appreciate that I also have limits. I now know it is essential to make time for rest, recuperation and fun. Though God calls us to be a living sacrifice I don't believe he wants me to be a half-dead, burnt-out one!

The most satisfying aspect of this work is to know I am where God wants me to be and to be part of the frontline. It is amazing to see a great hunger for God's Word amongst the street boys and to see the numbers at our weekly Bible studies grow bigger and bigger. Seeing God answer prayer, seeing him work in people's lives, that is exciting. I would not want to be anywhere else!

DAVID CHARLEY Eighteen-year-old student in his gap year

I decided to take a year out, between secondary education and university, to serve God in some way. I thought that I would be sent out somewhere soon after my summer exams, so God could use the full year to work through me, and in me. I came to realise that everything has to be in God's timing, and it was after six months of searching for what God wanted me to do, that I was called to work with the street children in Brazil.

I found myself, straight out of school, with very limited life experience, in a country where I knew no one, and didn't speak the language. Not only that, but daily I was witnessing poverty and injustice that I couldn't have ever imagined. This was the first time in my life that I really felt I had to depend on God totally for all that I needed. It was a humbling time, but a transforming time. Relying on God for everything deepened my relationship with him so much, and receiving his blessings was wonderful. God became so real to me, in a way I never knew he could.

The initial obstacle in my calling was the sense of uselessness, wondering what could I do to help these children. Yet, in the first week out there, God showed me that it was his life in me that would reach the children. It was holding onto this, the promises of the love of God, that had to be my focus always. In all the difficult times, when there seemed to be no hope, it was God's love for these children that kept me going, and helped me not to despair of it all. Once I had my focus, there was the problem that I didn't speak a word of Portuguese. I was never very good at languages at school, and I needed to be able to talk with the kids and deepen my relationships with them. One time, when I was praying, God promised to bless me with the language, and after that I started to pick it up incredibly quickly.

Working on the streets was a joy, but spiritually it was right on the frontline. Everything we did was centred around prayer, and it had to be. God also blessed me with the gift of praying in tongues. This was a true blessing, because many times no words could express how I felt. Prayers for the protection of my life, and that of others, became a daily routine. This I found to be very exhausting at times, and it was important to know when to stop, and rest. It is very easy to become so involved in what we are doing that we forget about our relationship with God.

The most fulfilling part of the work was seeing the difference God can make in people's lives. God's love is the only thing that can really reach out and touch people so deeply. The transforming of previously hopeless situations into celebrations of absolute joy will always remain in my heart. Being on the frontline is by no means easy at the best of times, but to be working for our God, and reaching people in his name is a life-changing experience. God can work miracles through anyone, if we will let him. God bless you, trust in God's guidance, and hold on to his love always.

JESSICA DAVIES Missionary with Worlds End Community Church, London, working on a housing estate

I work full-time with a small church on a housing estate in central London. Previously, I was in Brazil with Happy Child for two years. During that time I was aware of children in England facing similar issues to those people face in the *favelas* of Brazil: drug addiction, abuse, poverty, neglect and despair are not exclusive to Third World countries.

As a church, we meet to worship and that is our main purpose, but we are also here throughout the week running various activities and training programmes for people on the housing estate. These include after school homework clubs, computer training for children and adults, and English lessons for foreigners. Wherever possible we work together with local organisations such as schools, other church denominations and the social services. Everything we do started on a small scale out of an awareness of the needs of the local people. Unemployment is commonplace, so education and training are key. So is building trust and good relationships in the community.

Before I got involved, I prayed a lot about being accepted here. My background and circumstances were so different from the majority of the people on a council estate. I had lived much of my life a few hundred yards away but in a very different world. I can honestly say it has never been an issue; just as God sees us as *who*, and not *what* we are, so he calls us, and that is why, I believe, we are received. I am sure that prayer is the key to removing those barriers (fears) that separate us.

I find it a challenge to keep my eyes on the Lord in this culture: it screams independence at us from every angle.

In many ways, I was so much more aware of my need for God when I was in Brazil where the culture and language were unfamiliar, physical danger was more apparent and living in community is a constant reminder of needing the grace of God in our lives! Here, in London, I find it easy to slip into independence and relying on my own strength. But I am learning to choose to live in that place of dependence, to choose to be disciplined in my walk with God. I have always loved the adventure of travelling but I am discovering that the real adventure is being obedient to God; it is not about geography but about his purposes. That is really my hope for these children, that they discover God's purpose for their lives. For that to come about, we need to respond to God's call on ours.

ANDY AND FAYE MAYO Yugoslavia, May 1999 – on the frontline during the war

Blue Danube and a devastated frontline town
As I write this evening, the sun is dipping towards the Danube. Frogs call from their hiding places by the water and pheasants brush through the long, lush spring grass. Minutes ago, I drove through the shelled remains of a frontline town. Ghostly skeletons of bomb-gutted buildings offered only the slightest glimpse of the desperate misery that was suffered. A minefield marked by a comical jolly-roger-type skull and cross bones. And then, I was driving past the site where 198 bodies were pulled from a mass-grave. The only monument to their deaths is a twisted water tower standing guard and blown apart.

But this is home!
Despite the chaos here in former-Yugoslavia, this is where we call 'home'. We first came here to help the refugees

that were fleeing to survive the fighting in the early nineties. At that time – when Andy was teaching Design and Faye was creating and selling her sculptures – we came to Yugoslavia using our breaks from work to help to bring in 'Oak Hall' transports of aid.

'I am not sorry for all the things I have lost …'

With each aid packet and throughout every journey, we would speak of the suffering Jesus Christ who has come to carry the sinfulness of this rebelling world on his own shoulders. Some refugees experienced life-changing encounters with Jesus Christ – finding peace and experiencing hope and forgiveness in the midst of the hopelessness. There was joy in the eyes of the refugee who said, 'I am not sorry for all the things I have lost because now I have found true life in Jesus Christ that cannot be replaced by anything else!'

Moving our life to Yugoslavia – God directed our steps!

Then, over a period of a year, God used many different people, Scriptures, times of prayer and various circumstances to bring us to the point of being convinced that we should move our lives to Yugoslavia.

Faye will never forget one quiet time when she was reading on through Hebrews. That evening, the question of moving to Yugoslavia filled her mind and as she prayed and read, these words struck her with such force: 'By faith Abraham, when called to go to a place he would later receive as his inheritance, obeyed and went, even though he did not know where he was going. By faith he made his home in the promised land like a stranger in a foreign country' (11:8–9). What a hero! What a trust in God! He moved to the frontlines and out of his place of luxury in obedience to the Almighty God!

And so three years ago, invited by and working with
local believers we moved to Yugoslavia. Here, we had the
specific task of beginning a Bible Study Centre for disci-
pling new Yugoslav Christians and helping them to
prepare for a lifetime of mission.

Sixty-seven ambassadors move out to the frontlines!
Zelimir is one of these new believers. His name means
'man who wants peace'. After a violent involvement in the
civil war, Zelimir had finally and personally met with the
Prince of Peace and experienced his life-giving and hope-
bringing touch. He, with sixty-six other men and women,
has completed a year's preparation with us and our team
at the Bible Study Centre. Now he finds himself placed by
God on physical and spiritual frontlines and is taking every
opportunity to point to the Jesus who brings peace.

Good news in a bomb shelter!
Just a few days ago, teams from our Bible Study Centre
were in the bomb shelters giving people copies of John's
Gospel as the bombs fell around outside! What a radical
action on the frontline! What they were doing was
far more important than the politicians, pilots, spin
doctors ... they are ambassadors for the Prince of Peace!

Air-raid sirens. And what next?
As I finish writing here by the Danube, suddenly air-
raid sirens pierce the calm of the evening warning of an
approaching attack. What is the future going to hold?
Where is all of this leading?

Together, we are simply continuing to pray, 'Lord, teach
us to be like Abraham continually stepping out in faith
on the frontlines for you!'

DAVID AIKMAN Journalist, USA

I have spent almost all of my professional and adult life as a journalist, and the great bulk of that time was as a reporter for one of the world's leading weekly news magazines. Yet I never originally wanted to be a reporter. I actually had ambitions to be a diplomat. It wasn't until door after door had miraculously opened up within journalism – and I discovered later that I enjoyed being a journalist far more than I would have enjoyed being a diplomat – that it dawned on me that the Lord had engineered all this. He had not only wanted me to be a journalist, he had really called me to be one.

There were times when that calling was challenged head-on by secular colleagues who resented the fact that any colleague really believed in truth, or thought that truth could be knowable in a personal way through faith in Jesus Christ. At other moments, the natural desire to be sociable and to be accepted by my peers, clashed with a discomfort I never got over of being around people who were – as journalists sometimes can be – very coarse in speech or aggressively cynical about life in general. It was often a struggle. How to be pure in heart without appearing prudish? How to be warm towards colleagues whose lifestyle I did not really respect? I'm not sure I ever got it entirely right.

But against all this there were the wonderful moments when it was as if I were being guided and borne along by the Holy Spirit himself like a following wind. Moments of professional opportunity and favour would miraculously open up, often after periods of dryness and self-doubt. Other Christians would unexpectedly offer encouragement and a salve for the soul, or there would be an unexpected opportunity to share the gospel openly with someone.

281

Since I left working full-time for the news magazine I have found a new calling within a calling, so to speak: the foundation of a global fellowship of Christians in journalism that we call Gegrapha (Greek for 'I have written', as in John 19:22). It has been wonderful to see how journalists who are Christians encourage each other so deeply both in their faith and in their professional lives. And if journalists can encourage each other, perhaps they can also encourage, just a little, our world. The news may not always be good, but the truth always is.

(David Aikman is a freelance print and television journalist who works from Washington D.C. The organization Gegrapha can be located on the Internet at www.gegrapha.org. Aikman's e-mail is aikmand@aol.com)

SUE RINALDI Singer/Musician

> **restless pilgrim**
> Give me the eyes of a prophet,
> Help me to see the unseen,
> I long to hear the music of heaven
> As the angels play in my ears.
> Sometimes I'm war-torn and weary,
> Sometimes I'm willing and strong,
> But at this moment I'm standing before you
> As your restless pilgrim.
>
> So I'll fix my eyes on you ... I'll tread this
>   path with you ...
> I'll be a warrior of love for you ...[1]

I love watching the adverts on the TV – so often they are

the popular prophets into our generation. 'Nike', for example, have recently changed their slogan from 'Just do it' to 'I can'. I believe they are picking up the temperature of the people – that it is possible to *make a difference.*

I have always felt that I wanted my life to count for something or someone. This desire was there long before I even decided to follow Jesus and the Christian faith. I guess the longing to have a destiny is inside each one of us. I do feel that I am on a journey and there have been times when I could have easily stopped and said, 'I have had enough … I've had my share of thrills and I have had my share of pain … let me now retreat to a comfort zone.'

But I simply cannot do that. Especially when there is so much left undone, whether it be in the realm of personal dreams and ambitions or the overwhelming desire for justice in a world that often displays such intolerance and prejudice.

Music has been described as 'the language of today' and I am privileged to have the opportunity to travel around the world communicating through words and music. Music has the potential to unlock the soul and it is always my desire that people will be inspired and provoked to gaze into the eyes of Jesus and discover hope, purpose and love.

I am always deeply challenged to be real. Sounds so simple but it is one of the most difficult lessons of all time. We can all wear masks and there is such pretence in our society; but the challenge is to be yourself and respect others enough to allow them to be themselves.

At times I have felt discriminated against because of my gender and I have been aware of being considered unfulfilled and 'half a person' because of my single status. I know things are changing and that society is taking significant steps away from marginalising certain people groups – but it still happens and the road has been tough. But I know God has called me to walk this path and I have received comments along the way from other single women who have taken encouragement from my journey. We all need role models – I have mine. Thankfully we are beginning to see equality modelled – where people are operating in a particular role not because of gender and status, but because they exhibit the necessary skills, potential and gifts.

I hope to continue and develop my music, writing, speaking and media opportunities but my overwhelming desire is to be part of a 'red hot and holy' generation who are endeavouring to follow the example of Jesus and make a difference in this world.

ANTHEA MUSEGULA (née PARSONS) Missionary in Uganda and author of *Beyond the Horizon*

Travelling to remote villages to plant churches or work with newly established ones in evangelism and teaching certainly has its challenges. Getting to each place can be quite a feat of faith – crossing game parks, driving on rough tracks and even cycling or walking the last part of the journey when necessary. Life in the remote villages is very different from life in the towns! A comfortable night's sleep, regular nutritious meals, water on tap, electricity at the flick of a switch, and privacy become rare luxuries. Where disease and sickness is rampant, I have to combine faith in God and common sense to preserve good health. This type of lifestyle, together with the tropical heat, can drain my physical body, especially if prolonged for a number of months, and the energy factor sometimes affects the amount of work achieved. The right balance of rest and work is needed.

Where a fierce battle rages for the gospel to prevail, God's people live in intense prayer to enable them to stand. Souls come into the Kingdom of God in great numbers, the sick are healed and demons are cast out. The spiritual oppositions can be very obvious, working through people or events and attacking the mind and emotions of the labourers. I have discovered that the secret of overcoming is to think and act in line with what God says rather than looking at the circumstances or responding to my feelings. Unity in relationships must be guarded in such pressure situations. Another key is to pray in tongues constantly and be in touch with God throughout the day and at intervals in the night. Jesus, in his earthly ministry, sometimes spent the whole night in prayer. With all the power and authority available to him, he still needed constant communion with his heavenly Father. Before results can be seen, sacrifice of various kinds is necessary.

Reaching people costs money. One white man in an African village speaking with no microphone can draw a crowd of forty or fifty people. A team of musicians with musical equipment powered by a generator, and the gospel message going through the PA system can draw a crowd of 400 or more and the whole village can hear the message in their homes. When we go out in the name of Jesus, villages are transformed by the power of God as people's lives are changed and sinners stop their evil practices. The Apostle Paul says that it is Christ's love which compels us. No matter what the cost, God's call is stronger. The spiritual hunger of the people is like a magnetic pull to those difficult places. Hurdles are overcome and the impossible is achieved again and again.

HOLLY PIERCY Sixteen-year-old student

This year I felt that God was calling me to do something other than sit around at home pretending to be a really good Christian. My life has always been easy and protected: the same church, the same Christian friends, the same weekend breaks. I wanted something different and what's more, I felt that God wanted me to do something more important.

I had a tough time for a few years due to medication for mild epilepsy. Things weren't easy, and my faith in God nearly disappeared completely. But, thanks to a lot of prayer and a lot of care, I grew up and out of my epilepsy. During this time my relationship with God grew, and I began to realise that he cared for me and wanted to use me to share his Word.

I had a few obstacles in my way, one of which was my age. At sixteen there didn't seem much open to me – I couldn't just drop school and go into frontline mission for a few years. I spoke to a close friend of mine, Clare Hester, who was going out to Brazil to work with Happy Child. She suggested that I contact a Christian mission organisation called CRUSOE. I wrote to them to find out if I qualified to go. Four months later I have been invited on a team to Chile in August, with nine other 16–22 year olds, to work with street children and churches out there. God made it easy for me to get on a team; he opened up the paths for my desire to share my faith with others.

Being a Christian at school has never been easy – there are only about six of us in a school of 350. Everyone knew I was a Christian and simply let me get on with it, as long as I didn't interfere with their personal lives or try to get spiritual with them! However, through my fundraising for this mission to Chile my channels of conversation have opened up with the people who seemed least likely to care about me or my faith. I received an overwhelming amount of enthusiasm and excitement from my non-Christian friends; I found myself talking to the people at school every day about the reality and excitement of God's work. Frontline mission doesn't just open up God to foreign people that you don't know: it allows you to share your faith with the people around you. The fundraising involves your friends, relatives, church and school with mission and the Christian faith. It is a way to challenge people whom you wouldn't have told about God otherwise – the people closest to home!

For a while I felt that I wasn't the type of person God would be looking for. I wasn't strong enough in my faith to do mission. God didn't think that though. He has used the project to strengthen our relationship and to help me tell my school friends about my faith. I am so excited about God and my mission. The lump sum that I have to fundraise is a challenge that I want to go into head first! The most satisfying thing is knowing that you could change someone's life, that God will use you to tell people about him and encourage people who are struggling to keep up their faith.

JOAO LEITE Former top Brazilian goalkeeper, now a State Deputy in the State Government, Brazil

Sport – I was already playing professional football for the 'Clube Atletico Mineiro' (one of the top clubs in Brazil) as goalkeeper when I asked Jesus into my life. Up until that point I had lived with a deep feeling that something specific was missing in my life.

I also saw my friends and colleagues around me getting rich, famous and well known and yet remaining unsatisfied and without peace. My sisters tried to tell me about Jesus. On one occasion I broke a finger and the physical pain seemed to give way to another type of pain that I was feeling on the inside, and I asked my sister Rita to take me to church. We went to the Baptist Church in Belo Horizonte and I heard the message about repentance. I gave my life to Jesus and that same night decided to become one of his faithful followers.

I had lived twenty-one years without anyone telling me that Jesus had died for me. And I soon realised that in the world of my work I was surrounded by athletes in a similar situation who could die without ever knowing Jesus.

Driven by this concern, in 1981 I joined with fellow Christian Abraao Soares – the famous Brazilian basketball player of that time, who was also involved with Youth for Christ – to start a ministry with the aim of sharing the love of Jesus Christ in the midst of the sporting world, later known as 'Christians in Sport'. A small group of athletes well known in my country started meeting. The general public started to notice our presence when we distributed small Bibles to the opposing teams before our matches started. In the beginning there was a reaction from various other clubs, who suggested our activities were not professional.

Today it is another story. Managers of football clubs throughout the country recognise that members of Christians in Sport set a high example for their contemporaries. This ministry has grown and we are in nearly all the big Brazilian clubs. There are nearly 10,000 Christians in Sport throughout the world! In the World Cup there were six Christians in the Brazilian team: Taffarel, Jorginho, Mazinho, Muller, Zinho and Paulo Sergio.

Politics – At the end of my sporting career, while seeking God for a new direction in my professional life, I was invited for the second time by the Mayor of Belo Horizonte, Eduardo Azeredo (he was Governor for the state of Minas Gerais from 1994–8) to stand as a candidate for the Belo Horizonte Council.

Supported by my brothers and sisters in Christ, I received one of the highest totals of votes in the 1992 elections, and was immediately invited to assume the position of Municipal Secretary of Sports. In 1994, I ran as candidate for a State Deputy and received enough votes to assume the position of President of the Commission of Human Rights of the Legislative Assembly from 1995–6. In 1998 when I again stood in the elections, God blessed me with the largest amount of votes ever recorded in the history of legislation in the state: 78,977 votes!

The outcome of this overwhelming result enabled me to take up the position of President of the Commission for Human Rights, on a permanent basis. I am representing those in society who are excluded and marginalised, with the violent and with criminals. However, in the midst of this 'sea of great need' there is a light. It is the love of Jesus Christ – God is giving me the opportunity to take to these people the justice and the brotherly love within the pattern and principles revealed in the Bible.

VIC JACKOPSON 'Hope Now' in the Ukraine

For six years, since Ukrainian independence from Russia, I had worked under Hope Now ministering to the physical and spiritual needs of these amazingly resilient people. It was natural for me as an ex-prisoner to find a niche in the top security Prison 62. The men accepted me as their 'apostle' and many had already become Christians. So much so that we had already outgrown the first little chapel and were now bulging at the seams of the new, much larger facility. The foundation stone had already been laid for the new purpose-built church to accommodate up to 350 men at a time.

Things could not have been going better. Two teams had been trained in the U.K. to conduct summer camps at Mikailovka Orphanage and the Cherkassy Children Rescue Shelter. Both ministries were close to my own heart because I had grown up in an orphanage and knew what it was like to be a homeless street kid. We had built a church at Korsum; established health programmes for the children with cleft palates and leukaemia; opened a new ministry at the Preluki Detention Centre; delivered many containers of humanitarian aid; and were sponsoring a variety of educational initiatives such as the Music School, Language School and student exchange programmes. Twenty exciting, growing, useful evangelistic endeavours.

Why then was I feeling so low? Unable to sleep for several weeks I had gone to the doctor to ask for some sleeping pills. To my surprise I came away with a prescription for the anti depressant drug Prozac and orders to rest instead of leading the two camps. What devastation! What confusion! What anger! Worst of all – what guilt. Surely, this could not be happening. Why should I be depressed?

When friends had questioned my workload I had always given the stock answer, 'I would rather burn out than rust out.' Now my glibness came back to haunt me. Burn out was no fun. Juggling a heavy speaking schedule with the organization of Hope Now and its overseas projects had begun to take its toll on my health. Why had I not seen it coming?

Was it because I enjoyed my work more than any leisure activity? Was it because I hogged the work to myself and could not trust others enough to delegate responsibility? Was it the false economy (touched with a dash of pride and dogged arrogance) which refused to allow Hope Now to spend on administration what could be better utilised on the field? Was it God's judgement on me for working seven days a week? Yes! All of these and maybe more.

I had become a man driven. Driven by the sheer plethora of needs. Driven to preach the gospel. Driven to achieve. Driven by what was good but missing God's beat.

Now I take my day off each week and reduce my hours to between 8 and 10 hours a day (on most days!). I have more time for leisure – even an occasional round of golf. More time to read. More time with God. I am off the Prozac and keeping my blood pressure under control by medication, exercise and weight loss. Most importantly, others have been brought on to the staff of Hope Now to share the workload: two in South Africa, four in Ukraine, four in the U.K. and two in the U.S.A. Now we are a team. Mike Perreau has become C.E.O. and released me from all organisational responsibility so that I can focus upon evangelism, teaching, writing and equipping the next generation of upcoming evangelists.

I still live on the cutting edge but hurt less and share more.

ISABELLE ROSIN The Pavement Project, London

God has a plan for you 'plans to prosper you and not to harm you …'(Jer. 29:11). How many times had I heard that and thought I had understood it? In the midst of my BBC Television days, was I not seeking God's plan?

But one day, as I woke up, the truth just hit me. For many months, I had been reflecting as to why God was keeping me in such a difficult, Godless environment, where each breath was thickly motivated by self, power or money. As I lay there in my bed I realised that, in fact, I had never asked God if I was to work for the BBC. Yes, God was using me there, but my career choice had been made with no reference to his plan for my life. Listening to his will for my life, seeking his wisdom and wanting to hear his voice has been the most unbelievable experience in the supernatural: I have discovered that Jesus, through the Holy Spirit, wants to guide me in a very personal way.

Holding on to the promise in Jeremiah 29, and prompted by the Spirit, I decided to resign from my 'successful' career. As if the insecurity of jumping into the unknown was not enough, a number of obstacles soon reared their ugly head. A colleague made it clear that if I resigned, he would make sure I would never work again at the BBC. Fortunately, I was wisely reminded by my vicar who the real One in authority was!

Also, within days of deciding to seek God's will for my career, I began to have clear visions regarding the man who had proposed to me just three weeks earlier. These visions were confirmed and led to our separating, but I continued to be under intense attack. Instead of resigning I clung to my job for safety. I felt I was being destroyed. At my lowest point, God revealed how he was protecting me and why. His Holy Spirit encircled me and encouraged me to seek his righteousness first so that the accompanying promise of future blessings could then be fulfilled. With that new insight my faith recovered, as did my physical strength, helped along by a non-Christian friend who took me out and fed me every single day for the next two weeks!

Seeking God's will has brought me to work with street children in the most amazing way. Initially it was in Brazil with the Happy Child Mission. To see such destroyed children being restored and filled with the Holy Spirit was the most beautiful and humbling experience. To help children turn from hate to love, worship God, talk in tongues and start playing children's games again was like coming home. God knows the desires of our hearts. So much so that he took me back to my early teenage dreams – to work with street children ... in Brazil!

And the leading did not stop there. Whilst at Happy Child, God showed me that I was not to seek a job on my return to England. Within days of being back home, my telephone rang. I was invited to help set up a new project called the Pavement Project, born out of Scripture Gift Mission. It is a huge vision, the type I now expected from God! The aim is to make Christian games and other resources for street children all over the world, to help heal the deep psychological and spiritual wounds these children have suffered.

Difficulties did not just stop once I was following God's guidance, but the burden became considerably easier as I became surrounded by Spirit-filled Christians. God has brought me to a place of real fulfilment and it is, I hope, only the beginning. I would have hated living my whole life without ever experiencing God's exciting plans for me. ' "For I know the plans I have for you," declares the Lord, "plans to prosper you and not to harm you, plans to give you hope and a future." '

BEKKI MORRIS Missionary in Southern Russia

I have been working with IFES in southern Russia for eight months now and since my arrival in the city where I work I have known with great certainty that I am exactly where God wants me to be, doing what he wants me to do.

I first realised that God was calling me to work in Russia in the summer of 1995 but it wasn't until February 1998 that the call came to go '*now*'. I had looked forward to this time for so long but when it came to the crunch I didn't feel the excitement that I had anticipated but pure fear, despite the fact that I speak Russian, have been to Russia several times before and have many Russian friends. God encouraged me with words from 2 Chronicles 16:9: 'For the eyes of the Lord range throughout the earth to strengthen those whose hearts are fully committed to him.'

As I grasped the meaning of that verse I chose to obey God's command and go to Russia as soon as possible. Only then did I feel excited! The next few months as I prepared to go were a rollercoaster of emotions and there were many times when I wanted to 'do a Jonah' and run in the opposite direction of God's calling. The most difficult thing during these months was the knowledge that for the first time in my life I was doing something that my parents really didn't want me to do and could see the pain I was causing them. I wanted to be able to say, 'All right, I'll stay here', but I knew that I couldn't.

The reason I wasn't able to stay in England was my conviction that God had spoken directly to me and that not to go to Russia would be outright disobedience. If this were God's will, then he would take care of my family, my career, my personal safety, and everything else. My constant prayer for my parents was and is that, as I step out in faith, their faith will be strengthened and they will walk more closely with God. Even before I left home in September 1998 I could see God answering this prayer.

Since arriving in Russia the most difficult period I have had to deal with was when I returned to my city after the Christmas break and in the first week back heard that my grandfather (Poppa) had cancer. Within two weeks the doctors told us that the tumour was inoperable and that Poppa may not live more than a few days longer. God worked miracles with visas and a week later I was home. In the end Poppa lived for another month – so long that I had to say goodbye and return to Russia a week before his death, having spent almost three weeks at home with my family.

The last two months, overshadowed by Poppa's illness, have been awful and many times I have wondered whether I am really up to coping with this life that God has called me to. The answer is that I am not. The only reason I have been so calm and even joyful since I returned to Russia, in fact the only reason I was able to come back, is because God has met all my needs according to his glorious riches in Christ Jesus (Phil. 4:19). In fact he has given me much much more than I need or would even dare ask for; 'I can do everything through him who gives me strength' (Phil. 4:13).

SHEILA BRIDGES Mother and author

I'm someone who for a long time felt confused about my vocation in life. I am a wife, a mother, a writer, a church leader and preacher, a homemaker and a dog walker. I spent my time shuttling between these 'vocations', never quite sure which one should get top billing.

It was only when I lost almost all these 'callings' in life

that I discovered my one true vocation. This happened when my husband's job caused us to move away from a church where I had been very busy and fulfilled. I'd run the Toddler Group, the Sunday School and preached and led services (not all at the same time, naturally). It was difficult to give it all up but also a relief. I was exhausted, 'running on empty' spiritually speaking.

'You need to learn about "being and not doing",' my new vicar said to me when I arrived in a fragile state. He was right but simply 'being' God's child isn't easy. For the next year I learned that God loves me for who I am and not for what I do. I couldn't write and I rarely preached. I learned that if God has a special task for me he will let me know, otherwise I am to get on with the daily everyday things: mothering, cooking, loving and listening.

Suddenly the world turned upside down again: we were to move again, back to Rugby! If I'd been confused before, I was even more confused now. I muttered to God a lot about 'blind alleys' and 'U-turns'. Before our move back, I was asked to preach my first, and last, adult sermon in the little village church. The subject was 'Calling' and in the course of preparing that sermon I found the answer to my own muddled sense of vocation. The problem about calling wasn't the fact that I spent most of my life juggling various roles and shuttling between one occupation and another. It was the fact that none of my occupations were my primary calling. My primary calling – everyone's primary calling – is to *Someone* (God) not to *Something* (career, motherhood) or *Somewhere* (Rugby, small village in Lancashire, England).

God had taken me north and made me drop everything to learn this simple fact: 'I am called to Someone'. And that 'Someone' loves me. He is not a tyrant moving me up and down the country at a rate of knots for no reason. He has not overlooked me or rejected me. He has planned good for me.

The fact of God's love changes everything. He took me aside from all the busyness of life because he wanted me to be more preoccupied with him, less concerned with tasks, more thrilled by the fact that he loves me than by the approval of others. He may have some great task for me now or he may not. What matters is that, whatever my secondary callings (career, writing, ministry), I can only follow them without drying up by never taking my eyes off the One who loves me and who wants everything I do and everything I am to be a way of returning that love to him.

A BUSINESSMAN IN LONDON

I work for an international investment bank in London, investing in private companies. I am married and have three small children.

I became a Christian five years ago. Shortly afterwards, I moved job. I decided from the outset to be open about being a committed Christian. I have grown to realise that my work is my mission field, my frontline. The bank that I work for is expanding and, whenever someone joins my team, I try to find an opportunity to tell them about my faith in a natural way. Whilst they often disagree, they have almost always been interested. I am lucky – I have never been ridiculed. Two close colleagues have subsequently become Christians, which was fantastic. I have been helped enormously by praying every week for over two years with three members of my church who also work in the City. We all struggle with the same issues. We support each other and we are becoming increasingly accountable to each other. We remind each other that we are in the City to serve God. We have become very good friends.

It is very easy to become intoxicated by the excitement of the City. The focus is on profits, doing deals and beating the competition. Patience, kindness, mercy and gentleness are rarely displayed. As long as you operate within the law and regulations, almost anything goes. Sometimes I forget to think about whether what I am doing is right and just. I can be selfish. I worry about how much my bonus will be, whether I will be promoted and whether I am highly thought of. I certainly struggle to love the people whom I am competing against or negotiating against.

As well as trying to do God's will in the City, I believe that he wants me to contribute in other ways. He has put Happy Child on my heart and on my wife's. It began three years ago when I heard Sarah speak about the children living on the streets. I felt upset and wanted to find out if I could help in some way. We have subsequently been supporting Happy Child by praying, giving and helping with administration. God has truly put the desire to help on our hearts.

We have been kept up-to-date by newsletters and by seeing people when they return to England. After three years my wife and I visited Happy Child in Brazil and we saw the children and the volunteers whom we had been praying for and giving to. We now realise how much we are a part of the team and how important it is for the volunteers to know that we are rooting for them. We have been truly blessed that God has involved us in his work. He could have done it without us. Seeing him in action has strengthened my faith and my understanding of God. It has also helped me in my own frontline, in the City of London.

CAROLINE TAYLOR Missionary, Happy Child Brazil

When I was young my mother sent me to a Catholic convent where I grew up with the teachings of Jesus. Pictures of dying and needy people round the world covered the school walls. We regularly prayed and raised money for developing countries and from an early age I felt a yearning to get involved with the poor.

Before leaving London to start my new life I spent seven years working with refugees from all over the world. My job involved supporting those who had come out of war zones and places of political persecution to reintegrate into British society. Suffering people came right to my doorstep. However, in August 1998 the Lord called me very clearly into full-time mission in Brazil.

Recently I have been reading about the life of Abraham, one of God's greatest missionaries. Like me he lived in a prosperous city, had a very comfortable life and lots of friends. Suddenly God asked him to leave everything behind and go to another land. In Genesis 12:1 God commands Abraham, 'Leave your country, your people, and your father's household and go to the land I will show you.' Abraham was seventy-five years old when God asked him to do this. He must have wondered what was going on!!! What was his response? In Genesis 12:4 we read: 'So Abram left, as the Lord had told him.' With outstanding obedience and commitment Abraham left the settled world of the post-Babel nation and began a pilgrimage with God to a better world.

There will be times in our lives when God comes in and unsettles us, when he asks us to do things for him and go to places for him that we wouldn't normally dream of. That's what happened to me. Nevertheless, this is not the end of the story because God promises that when we step out in obedience to him and make ourselves fully available for service in his Kingdom he *will* bring blessings into our lives. When God called Abraham he promised him seven things. He said: 'I will make you a great nation'; 'I will bless you'; 'I will make your name great'; 'you will be a blessing to others'; 'I will bless those who bless you'; 'whoever curses you I will curse'; 'and all people on earth will be blessed by you'. How could Abraham stay behind with all these different kinds of blessings lined up for him? Therefore, if I too am to catch the blessings, then I too must be obedient to God's call on my life just as Abraham was.

In the Bible seven symbolises perfection. Abraham was seventy-five when God called him. It wasn't too late. God's timing was perfect. After seven years I left my job for full-time mission. After seven years of supporting Happy Child in London God called me to Brazil. It wasn't too late. God's timing was perfect. Today I am still adapting to life in a new country with all the changes this entails – the daily process of settling into a new culture, a new community, and a new church all bring their own challenges. However, the promises in God's Word sustain me daily and, as I experience his blessings every day in some form or another, I urge and encourage all those of you who read this book to step out and catch the blessing.

WHAT MY CALLING MEANS TO ME

This is an opportunity for you to apply some of the teaching in this book to your life. Use the space provided here to write down where you feel God is calling you to serve. What is your 'frontline'? What are the challenges you must face? How can you better equip yourself to fulfil your role?

Notes

Chapter 1

1   Joyce Huggett, *Listening to God* (Hodder & Stoughton, 1986).
2   Loren Cunningham, *Is That Really You, God* (Youth With A Mission Publications, 1996).
3   Jean Vanier, *Community and Growth* (Darton Longman and Todd).
4   Charles Swindoll, *Improving Your Serve* (Hodder & Stoughton, 1997).

Chapter 4

1   Loren Cunningham, *Daring to Live on the Edge* (Youth With A Mission Publications, 1996).
2   Jean Vanier, *Community and Growth*.
3   David Aikman, *Great Souls* (Word Books, 1998).

Chapter 5

1   Loren Cunningham, *Daring to Live on the Edge*.

Chapter 6

1 Dean Sherman, *Spiritual Warfare for Every Christian* (Youth With A Mission Publications, 1996).
2 Nicky Gumbel, *Questions of Life* (Kingsway).
3 Larry Lea, *Weapons of Your Warfare* (Word Books).

Chapter 7

1 Elizabeth-Ann Horsford, *Complete as One* (Hodder & Stoughton, 1987).
2 Derek Prince, *God is a Matchmaker* (Kingsway, 1986).

Chapter 8

1 Brother Andrew, *God's Smuggler* (Hodder & Stoughton, 1974).
2 Loren Cunningham, *Daring to Live on the Edge*.

Chapter 9

1 John Bevere, *The Bait of Satan* (Word Books, 1994).
2 Selwyn Hughes, *Your Personal Encourager* (CWR Publishing).
3 Gene Edwards, *A Tale of Three Kings* (Tyndale House Publishers, 1992).
4 Jean Vanier, *Community and Growth*.
5 NIV Life Application Bible (Kingsway, 1997).

Chapter 10

1 Roger Ellsworth, *Faithful under Fire* (Evangelical Press).
2 Hannah Hunnard, *Hinds' Feet on High Places* (Barbour Books, 1996).
3 Jamie Buckingham, *Where Eagles Soar*.

Chapter 11
1 'Restless Pilgrim' features on the album *Promise Land*
   by Sue Rinaldi (Survivor Records).

Addresses for correspondence, information and donations:

BRAZIL (Reg. charity no. 84820):
Programa Crianca Feliz
Caixa Postal 370
Belo Horizonte
MG 30–123–970
BRAZIL
e-mail: c.feliz@horiz.com.br

UNITED STATES (Reg. charity no. EIN 75–2489963):
13210 Glad Acres Drive
Dallas
Texas 75234
USA
Bank details: HAPPY CHILD MISSION, a/c no.
1291883198
Nations Bank of Texas NA, 3601 N Josey Lane,
Carrollton, Texas 75007, USA

UNITED KINGDOM (Reg. charity no. 1042236):
Old Tunmore Farm
The Street
West Horsley
Surrey
KT24 6BB
Bank details: HAPPY CHILD MISSION, a/c no.
91790358
Midland Bank plc, P.O. Box 160, Guildford, Surrey, GU1
3YE

Also by Sarah de Carvalho

The International Bestseller
The Street Children of Brazil
One Woman's Remarkable Story

Her glittering career in film promotion and TV production took her to California, Sydney and London. But her international lifestyle and fast-lane salary gave her no time to enjoy herself.

Through a series of remarkable events, Sarah left her career and joined a missionary organisation in Brazil. There she met children from the age of seven living on the streets, taking drugs, stealing to survive and open to prostitution and gang warfare.

This is the remarkable true story of a life transformed. It tells of the incredible work that Sarah de Carvalho and her husband have founded in the Happy Child Mission. It is a story of immense faith, suffering and love. The children whose stories are revealed in this exceptional book will change the heart of every reader.

Hodder & Stoughton
ISBN 0 340 64164 9